being Ted Cullinan

edited by Alan Berman and Ian Latham

Axonometric drawing (detail) of Edward Cullinan Architects' 1979 project for Bradwell Common 2 in Milton Keynes

Being Ted Cullinan

What made Ted

What Ted made

What Ted taught

Edward Cullinan (1931-2019) was one of the most respected and charismatic architects of his era, inspiring generations through his teaching and buildings.
But what made him, what did he build and what did he say?
We asked Cullinan's colleagues, collaborators, friends and critics for their perspectives on what it meant to be Ted and what will be his legacy

Introduction
Alan Berman

Ted Cullinan was an iconoclast: so much of what he practiced and taught was contrary to mainstream British architecture that it took many failed nominations before he was awarded the Royal Gold Medal in 2008. While the 'star' architects of his generation took to the world stage in designer suits, showcasing their extraordinary skills, Ted would be down on his Peak District farm in black tee-shirt and jeans, ankle-deep in mud. With colleagues and friends he was cutting, hammering, experimenting and exploring the qualities of materials, always learning about making buildings. Or he might be marching to Trafalgar Square, demonstrating against injustice or for some humanitarian cause. Ted Cullinan's way of being an architect was very particular, very grounded and deeply human.

In his practice and teaching Cullinan always followed his conviction that architects need a deep understanding of materials and construction to inform their creative imaginations so that, above all, they could serve people and communities. He aimed to work for better futures for everyone by making architecture 'with people and for people' – a credo which underpinned almost everything he did in his life and work.

Cullinan's values were rooted in his upbringing by Christian socialist parents and his schooling at Ampleforth, where he and his two younger brothers, Timothy and Anthony, were taught the caring values and discipline of the Benedictine order. Like their sister Susan, each pursued lives

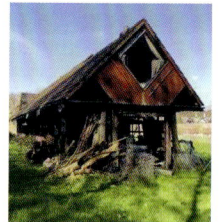

in which service and hope were much present, but they were also all unafraid to challenge established ideas. Anthony became a monk – Father Tom – and went on to set up his own Benedictine community of Ince Benet near Liverpool. There, Ted designed the communal house, to be self-built using recycled materials, and it speaks volumes that both Anthony and Ted were content to remain in the homes they built for themselves early in their lives

Ted Cullinan's architectural office was established from the outset as a profit-sharing cooperative which valued everyone for who they were and for their ideas. The extent of his commitment to cooperative working was set out in an unusual practice manifesto which stated: 'Fees are shared in agreed proportions as and when they are received; any surplus is shared out or used otherwise by agreement. Making the practice have no book value ensures that it is no one's possession nor anyone its servant'. That an ambitious young architect should conceive a practice with this extent of sharing, and with the intention that his working life would result in zero asset value, is in marked contrast to those for whom architectural practice is a business venture. Cullinan understood that, as with makers, craftspeople and artists, the real assets of the architect are creative imagination, curiosity and skills, and an ability to look at things differently.

Notwithstanding Ted's commitment to collective endeavour, when working in the studio he would often deploy his considerable persuasive skills to steer designs in the direction he wanted. His talent was not only to originate but to absorb, adapt and remake ideas and mould them into his own particular architecture. It has been said that Ted's cooperative consisted of cooperating with Ted – a reality evident in the observation by former colleague Hannah Durham, who when first visiting the office found Ted 'centre stage... like a spaceship commander, at his desk with drawing tools and his team around him... with a passion and focus for *his* architecture'.

Cullinan's architecture was based on clear, pragmatic principles that were developed early and held throughout his career. A key tenet was

that a building's design should meet the needs and aspirations not only of its commissioning client but of its present and future users. His declaration that 'architecture… is the subject whose objects touch us all, most of all, most of the time… I am totally committed to making architecture with people and for people', aligned him firmly with the social idealism of William Morris and its moral crusade that design should be directed to create a better world for all.

Cullinan was not interested in the kind of architectural form-making which preoccupied many of his contemporaries, nor was he inclined to articulate any particular theory, but he did have a deep understanding of architectural history. He was in accord with philosopher John Dewey's view that buildings 'celebrate with particular intensity the moments in which the past reinforces the present… which also suggests the future'. Cullinan's acute analysis of historic buildings informed many of his own designs in which he reinterpreted established forms and technologies in a contemporary manner. He would also cite historic examples to help explain his own ideas to colleagues and clients, not to legitimise them but rather to communicate the way a design might serve its occupants' needs.

The contemporary urge to fashion novel and abstract forms and reject traditional types represented for Cullinan a corruption of the truly modern ideals that, for him, were exemplified by the hands-on workshop production of the Bauhaus, with its 'truth to materials' ethos. He learned much from a detailed study of the design inventions of the Modern Movement, and he particularly admired the potency of form, space and light, the importance of the plan and the organisational significance of the 'promenade architecturale' in the work of Le Corbusier. He

also admired Frank Lloyd Wright and Louis Kahn for their command of materials, and how they were unashamed to embrace vernacular traditions. But he felt that pre-modern architectural history was of equal importance, and it is a mark of Cullinan's open-minded interests that, unusually among his generation, he recognised the value of much nineteenth-century British architecture. In particular he learned a great deal by analysing buildings by Richard Norman Shaw, Philip Webb and other 'arts and crafts' architects. Their influence is apparent in the practice's then unfashionable use of coloured brickwork at Winchester School and the Uplands Conference centre which today would hardly elicit comment. More potently, he was among the first post-war British architects to appreciate and take lessons from the straightforward construction and appropriate use of local materials in vernacular architecture – an interest which at the time was considered esoteric and somewhat disparagingly labelled as 'romantic'.

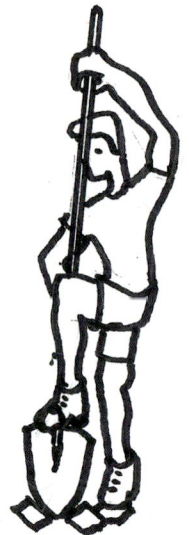

An imperative of that tradition – that buildings are built simply and of local materials – requires an understanding of the ways in which people experience and react to their environment. Ever pragmatic, Cullinan was mindful, for example, of the fact that most people don't perceive buildings in the way architects do, but rather in terms of

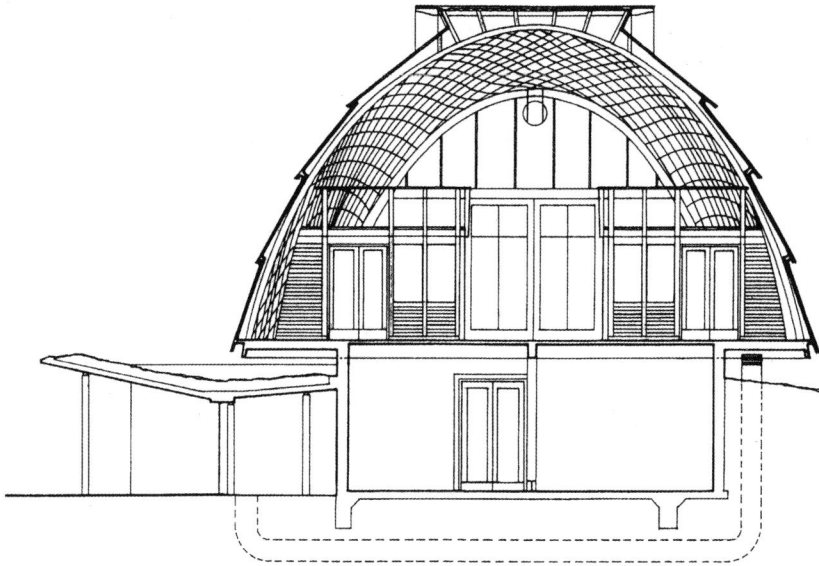

Above
The legible 'honesty' of Cullinan's approach to construction and detail is demonstrably featured on the corner of his own, self-built house at Camden Mews (above left). These same values were carried through to later projects, such as the Weald & Downland museum, where a timber structure also sits on a masonry base.

Opposite John Ruskin sent his students from Balliol College out from their lecture halls and garretts to remake the main road through the village of North Hinksey near Oxford in 1874, documented here by Henry Taunt. Cullinan, like John Ruskin and William Morris, valued manual labour and social improvement as highly as academic pursuits.

that imbued Cullinan's whole approach to making buildings.

These ideas are manifest in Cullinan's approach to detailing. Details were as simple as could be, and flush joints, hidden fixings and sophisticated gaskets were avoided wherever possible. Materials would be lapped over each other with fixings such as bolts or pegs left visible. Joints would be easy to make and celebrated as an essential part of the architecture.

The appreciation and enjoyment of Cullinan's buildings is heightened by the way in which material quality is exploited – the contrast between the brittle smoothness of glass and the solid roughness of timber, between the warmth of oak boards and the cold feel of stone, between the stick-like quality of a frame and the planar nature of panels or masonry. But his choice of traditional, tactile materials led some critics to dismiss him as an outdated romantic. One complained that the dry stone walls at Fountains Abbey visitor centre were 'so obviously hand-crafted that just looking at them is exhausting', but to my mind it was an entirely appropriate practical and symbolic response to the context.

Cullinan's hands-on understanding of materials, combined with an inherent grasp of structural principles, enabled him to develop construction techniques that were simple, economic and buildable. But this didn't preclude interesting and unusual structures, even when using off-the-peg or as-found materials, as is particularly evident in the Olivetti buildings, St Mary's Church at Barnes, Westminster Lodge at Hooke Park, and the Weald & Downland Museum Gridshell.

This celebration of the expedient, the ordinary and the readily available reflects Cullinan's

what they touch and see from eye level. At a time when deep-plan, artificially-lit spaces were being espoused as efficient and progressive, Cullinan recognised that good daylighting was crucial to peoples' well-being and their enjoyment of a building; his sketches reveal a constant exploration of ways to admit light and facilitate views out by means of the section. The split-roof became a key organisational component in many of Cullinan's designs, and often it would be allied to a clear plan which allowed intuitive navigation and reduced the likelihood of people feeling disorientated or inhibited. Circulation spaces were conceived not just as ways of getting from A to B but as opportunities to create useful and enjoyable places to sit, meet, take in a carefully framed view – and they were always full of light.

Ruskin's call to connect with people through hand-made things – cited by Richard Sennett in his wonderful book 'The Craftsman' (2008), which examines the social value of craft – is essentially the same credo that led Cullinan to make buildings the way he did. He regarded materials, texture, colour and detail not so much from a formal point of view, but rather how they would be 'read'. The reading of a building, the wish to demystify architecture and make it comprehensible, was important – 'honest' in Ruskinian terms – an artless straightforwardness determination to make art from the artless. The sophistication needed to create the luxuriously smooth, hygienic surfaces of minimalism and the precise, machined components of high-tech involve a reductionism and obsession that were not his. Buildings involve all the senses, yet with virtually everything now designed on screen, the all-pervading power of the visual sense ironically produces a certain blindness which can occlude the other senses and deny the essential physicality of buildings. Hence the importance Cullinan attached to texture, colour, sound and comfort, and it is these physical qualities that give the practice's buildings their human character – as Aldo van Eyck put it, architecture can 'assist man's homecoming'.

Yet while enjoyable simplicity and practical logic characterise so much of Cullinan's work, some later projects were prone to over elaboration, a trait often evident in the work of mature architects at the top of their game. Their ease of invention seems to encourage a playful exaggeration, and in Cullinan's oeuvre there's a sense of this in the Charles Cryer Theatre in Carshalton, St John's College Library at Cambridge and the Cheltenham & Gloucester College.

From the early days Ted delighted in the outdoors, and his family and studio team alike shared in many of his hair-raising escapades and construction challenges. He relished physical activity and drew enormous satisfaction from reworking the run-down farm buildings at Gib Tor which he and Roz bought in the 1970s on a bleak Staffordshire moor. While this experience added to that of the earlier self-builds in California, Hampshire and Camden, the farm also facilitated the creation of the shared working community to which Ted had long aspired. Sharing manual work, cooking around camp fires, sledding in the

snow and outings to look at buildings in the vicinity all helped to forge the collaborative culture which created such an unusual and warm office environment back in the London studio.

Cullinan's generous nature and evident moral convictions naturally attracted many young architects, full of 1960s radical enthusiasms, for here was an architect whose manifesto proclaimed architecture to be a social act and who fought against the injustices of America's war in Vietnam and South Africa's apartheid system. It is not surprising that the establishment did not feel he was one of them, or that the number of commissions from commercial developers was few. Rather, and initially in an era of increasing state patronage, the majority were buildings for public use with social purpose: visitor centres, libraries, education, health centres and social housing.

Cullinan's enjoyment of the Derbyshire Dales reflects an appreciation of landscape that is manifest in much of his work, and his stories about how designs were developed would invariably start with a description of the physical features of the site. His reading of the topography was often crucial in establishing the initial strategic layouts, whether of the early Horder and Marvin houses, or later, larger projects such as Minster Lovell and the RMC headquarters. At Fountains Abbey, where as Simon Henley suggests Cullinan 'made a friend of the site', his careful analysis of the landscape and its development led to the visitor centre being located on a site quite different to that first envisioned by the client.

Explaining ideas is essential for architects, and Cullinan's communication skills were legendary. The carefully calibrated unfolding of ideas and clear justifications of every aspect of a design, delivered slowly with long pauses, seemingly

Above Dry stone walls, here at Fountains Abbey visitor centre, represented what Cullinan described as 'a notion of purity and honesty... honourably and morally good, natural, linked with a purer past and a possible future, even fatuously as a lost art vaguely connected with ley lines and the wisdom of the ancients'. The lead upstand on the eaves was borrowed from a detail Cullinan had noticed in Moscow when he was involved in the British Embassy competition.

off-hand but masterfully timed, displayed the skill of an actor and captivated his audience. As many have commented, Cullinan's talks were mesmerising, and wherever in the world he lectured, invariably the venue would be packed.

Storytelling was an essential part of Cullinan's art and his stories would be illustrated by rapidly drawn yet highly accomplished sketches. These allowed him to express ideas, making them easily grasped not only by colleagues during the design process but also by clients and public audiences. Stories were not only for communication, however, and they were often an integral part of a design's conception. Cullinan made sketches showing what it might be like as people approached a building, walked through and looked out, and how they might enjoy the spaces: people swinging from balconies, walking their dogs, reading in bed or lifting weights – a warm-hearted nod to Le Corbusier.

As the essays that follow make clear, Cullinan's convictions and creativity, his way of practicing,

his drawing and making skills and inspiring teaching, and his ability to empathise with anybody, constitute an unusually rare and holistic way of being an architect. His perceptiveness and ability to learn lessons from seeing beyond what most people see is encapsulated in his analysis of the simplest example of vernacular construction – the dry stone wall. Made without artfulness, dry stone walls require an understanding of stone, manual skill and collaborative work. They are functional and sustainable: stones are cleared from land to make it productive and then reused to build walls to enclose the land; and the walls are repairable and the stone is reusable. Likewise, in a woodland context, Cullinan grasped the potential to use the pliable but strong forest thinnings to make roof structures. The delight and understanding of these simple ways of building speaks of the man and his attitudes.

Ted Cullinan's building of dry stone walls and his planting of thousands of trees represented acts of hope for the future. So too was his devotion of much time, energy and patience in teaching young architects to use their creativity to build a better world. He was unstinting in his encouragement and support of those in the office, and he remained loyal to those who left to set up their own practices. This is why Cullinan's beliefs, his thinking practice and teaching continue to command so much respect. His values remain more relevant than ever in today's world and should not be forgotten. Hope and a belief in the powers of curiosity, the imagination, creative invention and shared endeavour were in his blood, and kept him optimistic, active and engaged until the last days of his long, productive life. Ted left us all a typically optimistic valedictory hand-written message, printed on the order of his funeral service: 'Cheerio my friends… and remember to keep on imagining'.

Cullinan's reconstruction of the derelict Belle Tout lighthouse for his parents provided his first opportunity to try out the ideas, principles and ways of working that set the foundations for much of his life and work

Force of Nature
Ian Latham

'He was excellent company; a man of outstanding kindness, who was always impressed by the good qualities of those with whom he dealt; he was an inveterate supporter of the underdog, and his skill as a raconteur was supplemented by his inexhaustible fund of stories.' The British Medical Journal's obituary for Edward Revill Cullinan (1901-65) – chief physician at London's St Bartholomew's Hospital, climber, restorer of canal boats, glass collector, and member of the Magic Circle – could easily characterise his eldest son, architect Edward Cullinan (1931-2019).

In 1953, Ted's parents happened to drive past the derelict Belle Tout lighthouse at Beachy Head in East Sussex. His mother, Dorothea Joy Horder, keen to divert her husband from his ambition to run a farm in his retirement, said 'I would live in that'. Its owner, Eastbourne council, was faced with a £5,000 demolition cost, so offered them a lease on a peppercorn rent if they made it habitable. The project was entrusted to Ted when he was in his mid-20s and studying at Cambridge and the Architectural Association (AA) in London, but the experience of designing and building his first substantial live project was the most profoundly formative part of his education.

Joy, an artist who had studied at the Slade, was the daughter of royal physician Sir Thomas Horder, and brother of publisher and composer Mervyn Horder. She and her husband lived next to London's Regent's Park on Park Village East with their four children, a nanny, a cook and Aalto furniture in the nursery. Ted, the eldest, had been born in 1931, the same year as Le Corbusier's Villa Savoye, Dudok's Hilversum Town Hall and Van Alen's Chrysler Building, he would proudly declare. He went to school at Ampleforth where he was crammed in Latin for Cambridge entry and learned to draw. Uncle Mervyn would take Ted, and sometimes also the artist John Piper, on tours in his Rolls Royce to visit cathedrals, setting him on the path to architecture rather than medicine from a young age. Mervyn's cousin was the prolific architect Percy Richard Morley Horder (1870-1944), and Cambridge had been recommended by Ted's brother's godfather Anthony Chitty, a colleague

Belle Tout (1955-56)

Built in 1832 at Beachy Head, East Sussex, Belle Tout lighthouse was set back from the cliff edge so that its light indicated to sailors that they were a safe distance from the rocky shore. However, erosion gradually exposed the beacon to closer inshore and it was often shrouded by sea mists, so the lighthouse was decommissioned in 1902 and a new sea-level structure built. Trinity House sold Belle Tout to private owners, but while they were evacuated in the second world war, the lighthouse suffered collateral damage during firing practice by Canadian troops. Eastbourne council acquired Belle Tout in 1948, and in 1953, with much of the structure derelict and the lantern gone, leased it to Ted Cullinan's parents rather than face a costly demolition.

The decision was taken to repair what was reparable and demolish and replace what wasn't, which was primarily the upper level of the house, with a modern intervention. Cullinan's design was strident and uncompromising – 'change', he would later argue, 'is traditional'.

Cullinan's first lessons were in demolition. With friends he threaded steel ropes through the windows and attached them to a winch to bring the walls down. Cullinan was the first to admit that he could be cavalier when it came to health and safety – a symptom perhaps of his intolerance of what he saw as inflexible or needless regulations – although he later conceded that the demolition dust of Belle Tout may have contributed to his later health issues.

of Berthold Lubetkin in the pioneering modernist architectural practice Tecton. A critical essay on Victorian theatres and a fluent drawing of an eighteenth-century fireplace secured Ted an Anderson & Webb Scholarship to study architecture at Queen's College. 'On day one', and somewhat at odds with the Cambridge school's pervasive arts and crafts ethos, he was instructed to read Le Corbusier's Vers une Architecture by his tutor David Roberts (whose later advice that Ted should abandon his daily commitment to rowing fell on deaf ears). He professed to having learned more about architecture at the AA, however, where he was taught by distinguished practitioner-teachers John Killick, Arthur Korn, Leonard Manasseh and Peter Smithson.

Alongside his formal education Cullinan would cajole friends from Cambridge and the AA into spending their weekends helping the contractor Llewellyn to rebuild Belle Tout. Such hands-on experience wasn't the norm for architecture students, but for a generation grounded by National Service it would have seemed second nature. This sense of working and making together became fundamental to the Cullinan ethos – placing manual pursuits on a par with mental labours – and it came to be instilled in generations of colleagues and followers.

In other respects too this first project came to define Cullinan's direction of travel. Impatient with conventional modes of architectural practice, he sought to reset the ways in which an architect could operate and what kind of architecture that might produce. This was born not out of dogma, however, but simply how Cullinan found he could best achieve results – the act of making a building needs people with a range of skills, people work better in collaborative teams; materials are easier to obtain locally, and to assemble by hand with straightforward fixings; and so an architect should design simply, as if they were going to build it themselves. While there's an elegant simplicity to this notion, Cullinan's direct ways nonetheless belie a rigorous analysis of intentions and possibilities that were tested with colleagues and consultants and practiced by making prototypes.

13

By gathering together like-minded individuals the Cullinan practice evolved as a means to make Ted's architecture. While this was a didactic process, it also entailed learning from what worked and what didn't, a methodology that became a hallmark of the practice. And although Ted would regard particular projects as benchmarks, there was always a shared determination, impatience even, to constantly move forward and make each scheme better than the last.

Cooperative teamworking, hands-on making, the integration of life and work, the employment of low-cost and reused materials, responding to architectural precedent, and repurposing an existing structure were all part of the Belle Tout experience that became central to Cullinan's approach. Further along its journey the practice consolidated these concerns, pioneering much of what later became mainstream in terms of people-centred design, with airy, daylit spaces that were low in energy use and environmental impact.

Belle Tout, poised precariously on an eroding cliff edge, battered by elements but determinedly aspiring to a distant horizon, is an appropriate metaphor. For Cullinan, at the outset of his career, the project provided a fortuitous context with which he could engage his zest for life. The acts of demolition and hauling massive stone blocks across the site flowed directly from Cullinan's affinity for physical activity, whether rowing, judo or skiing on snow and water. Ted could be ferociously competitive, both intellectually and physically, and he would push not just himself but friends well beyond their comfort zones. However, this physicality was also manifest in the warmth of the embrace that Ted and Roz Cullinan threw around family and friends alike. Gatherings that were first played out at Belle Tout would continue at Camden Mews and Gib Tor as well as in the practice's offices and in its outings. Such occasions nurtured Cullinan's craving for an audience, and he went on to hone his facility for storytelling not just to engage listeners but to communicate architectural ideas as he saw them, disarming doubters with an easygoing yet compelling manner that belied the underlying complexity of thought.

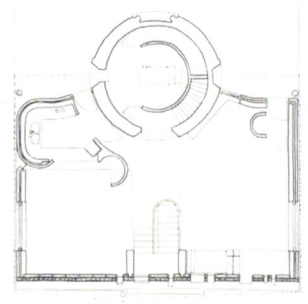

Belle Tout (1955-56)

The demolished upper storey of the lighthouse was replaced by a new concrete floor and roof slab on columns, infilled with brick and stone. The design shows Cullinan beginning to imbue his work with architectural influences, but in an explicit manner as might be expected in a student project. The landward entrance facade is canted inwards, its stone face peppered with 12 windows in the manner of those at Le Corbusier's Ronchamp chapel, which Cullinan had visited soon after its completion in 1955. A single piloti, mounted on a plinth that sits delicately on the projecting entrance porch, is placed to draw attention to the Corbusian wall and the sweeping curve. The new door below is a composition of diagonally shuttered concrete and wired glass panels and metal rail in the manner of De Stijl. Such literal references reflect a youthful naivety, 'a mistake that wasn't repeated', Cullinan later said. More indicative of his immediate direction is to be seen in how the external wall is modulated in response to the interior spaces rather than composed as a formal elevation. The curving walls partially embrace functional areas within the open, free-flowing main floor, defining 'rooms' while responding to the 'drum' of the tower.

Left New first-floor plan; Cullinan would regularly gather family and friends at Belle Tout, here including Julyan and Tess Wickham, and John Money-Kyrle.

Cullinan identified as an 'Expressionist', allying himself to the modernist cultural movement that valued emotional experience over physical reality. A staunch defender of artistic freedom, it is telling that, when later reflecting on the experience of Belle Tout, he expressed some pleasure at having had the opportunity to make a radical intervention that would nowadays be much constrained by protective regulations.

In 1956, with work at Belle Tout essentially complete, Cullinan won a King George VI memorial fellowship to spend two semesters at the University of California at Berkeley, mistakenly assuming it was near Hollywood. Rather than rubbing shoulders with James Dean and Marlon Brando, however, he became enamoured with the buildings of Bernard Maybeck, Greene & Greene, Rudolph Schindler and Richard Neutra. His transatlantic cabin companion, also on a fellowship, was John Garrett, a Labour party member since 1951 and later Member of Parliament (and, like Mervyn, an early client), and a neighbour at Berkeley was Allen Ginsberg, soon to gain notoriety for his poem Howl. Cullinan spent much of his time painting and reading but California's Beat-generation culture struck a chord, fostering values that came to provide a framework for the intuitive lessons of Belle Tout.

Cullinan had been 'an anarchist, an innocent lefty with hippy views', drawn to Pyotr Kropotkin's ideal society in which people would 'take what they need and give what they can'. Rejecting both capitalism and state Marxism, Kropotkin's libertarian socialism chimes with Cullinan's disdain for dogma and suspicion of authority. It also contextualises his affinity for America's constitutionally enshrined freedoms and with the utopian socialism of William Morris. While he wasn't a regular participant of protest marches, Cullinan lent robust support to campaigns such as nuclear disarmament and anti-apartheid. Aside from helping Mark Fisher and Richard Rogers to draft the Labour party's architecture policy in the late 1980s, however, his political engagement was tacit, but his commitment to deploying his architecture to support social progress, fairness and equality was unstinting.

While recognising his privileges Cullinan said he never felt like part of the establishment. Such sentiments were exacerbated by a near-miss in 1983 in the hard-fought competition to extend the Royal Opera House, a commission that would have sent out shock waves and propelled the practice into the mainstream – it must have felt like bitter rejection. A year later, however, Cullinan was characterised by Prince Charles, in his controversial 'Hampton Court' speech that otherwise castigated modern architects, as 'a man after my own heart, as he believes strongly that the architect must produce something that is visually beautiful as well as socially useful'.

There was dogged resistance within the prevailing high-tech faction of British architecture to the nomination of Cullinan for the Royal Gold Medal for Architecture, at least until 2008 when his former colleague Sunand Prasad was RIBA president and able to assemble a sympathetic selection panel. In the meantime however the studio had been winning projects in the hallowed ground of Cambridge University, and in 1991 Cullinan was elected as a Royal Academician. He must have been considered for a knighthood, which he would probably have accepted. Finding himself increasingly drawn into spheres of influence that he had spent much of his life challenging, there was certainly some irony in Cullinan's position. By then, even if he was finally in a position to push for change from within, it was clear that his most enduring legacy would be in the example of his life, work and teaching.

By the end of the century, 40 years after its restoration and following several changes of use and ownership, Belle Tout was increasingly threatened by the receding cliff edge. A positively Cullinanesque solution was engineered, raising the 850 tonne structure on hydraulic jacks and sliding it 17 metres inland, while also enabling the insertion of a new lower floor. Audacious and imaginative, it must have thrilled Ted, and not least because his nephew Dominic Cullinan was architect for the project. It was a fitting coda to Ted's long relationship with Belle Tout, the place he first learned to harness life and work to make honest, transformative and beautiful buildings.

> Ted Cullinan's architecture was inseparable from his commitment to social progress, energised by modernism's aesthetic discoveries and underpinned by a profound engagement with people, history and nature. His mission, through this radical ethos, was to transform the mainstream, where he saw conservative values and traditional urban manners prevailing, but his more vocal critics saw themselves as the radicals

Cullinan's Aesthetic Universe
Sunand Prasad

Ted Cullinan was among the best loved British architects of his times. His generosity to his colleagues and collaborators is legendary. So is his unfailing commitment over almost 50 years to teaching architecture, which he would describe as 'spreading passion'. And yet, there is often a 'but' in the critical response to his architecture. Canvassing views in connection with his nomination for the Royal Gold Medal, I found a consistent seam of doubt, running also through those who ostensibly shared much of his philosophy – a thinner seam, but real enough. No architect or artist has a perfect record of course. Cullinan in private was his own sternest critic. He would tell of Richard Norman Shaw's pain at being asked which was his best building, and replying that none was yet good enough. That story is perhaps apocryphal but when asked the same question, Cullinan would say 'the one we are working on'.

As a disciple, I have found the sometimes quite aggressive criticisms of Cullinan's work (a tiny bit of which I can call 'our work') fascinating, not least as they help answer the question 'what is going on here?' and help to better locate my own beliefs in, and doubts about, the work. Criticism, of course, says as much about prevailing culture as it says about the subject or object of the critique. There were those who found the buildings too hairy and not well enough dressed to take their place at the Dinner of Urban Good Manners. There were others who found the work too 'wet' and too compromised to represent the Exciting Electric Future. Both were content to call him a social architect, he having signed up, after all, to a manifesto declaration that 'designing buildings was a social act'. But from such critics 'social' sounded like a somewhat patronising excuse, not the stirring call to arms that it was for us, with no division between social purpose, the pursuit of beauty and individual freedom.

In March 1986 Ted Cullinan gave a lecture at the Royal Society of Arts with the title 'Where does my baggage come from?'. In the subsequent discussion the chair, Theo Crosby, developed the theme that what mattered most in the city was

Right top Ted Cullinan at Gib Tor, his Derbyshire farm, where for him the dry stone walls represented an elegant touchstone in combining field clearance, enclosure and durability.

Right The Cullinan team on the studio escape staircase in 1976 (top left to bottom): Ted Cullinan, Brendan Woods, Tony Peake, Philip Tabor, Sunand Prasad, Claire Herniman, Mark Beedle and Tchaik Chassay; and in 1985 rear left to front right): Greg Penoyre, Frances Hollis, Robin Nicholson, Alan Short, Claire Herniman, Tony Peake, Mark Beedle, Tony Belcher, Ted Cullinan, Sunand Prasad and Mungo Smith.

Left Cullinan was awarded the Royal Gold Medal for Architecture in 2008, when Sunand Prasad was president of the RIBA.

the elevation, the visual presentation of a building to the public. At one point he challenged Cullinan, noting that, while he had shown some beautiful historic examples of entrances, he had offered no solutions to how one might make a contemporary entrance or facade. This challenge and the polite but edgy discussion that followed throw light on Cullinan's aesthetic universe and the difficulty that one facet of contemporary architectural culture has had with its manifestations. Cullinan's answer was: 'I would look for the expressive part of the programme. I would look to see how we might smash the edges of the building, how the inside might join the outside, how you might be invited into it and gathered up by the indoors from the outdoors, how you might at upper levels come out of the building and be in the open air and be partly in and partly out, and actually try to break down the edges of buildings, try to break down their containedness and closedness and bring about depth and layering in the edges and skins of buildings. If one looks to some principles of abstraction that were developed in the early parts of this century, of crossing planes and crossing members and making our parts penetrate through each other, there is a whole mine of solutions there.'

Cullinan had included in his lecture some verses of doggerel he had composed lampooning the idea of 'Englishness' in art. Perhaps provoked by this, Cecil Elsom, architect of several modern commercial buildings with London street frontages asked: 'Does the average Englishman like to live partly in and partly out?' Cullinan rose to the bait: 'However traditional you were feeling, it would be necessary to admit that today we do, for example, treat children as human beings and not as a lesser species, as they were in

the past. We tend to muck along in our houses together; we tend to move indoors and out quite frequently, through the sides of our houses; we do not treat them formally in a corridor and room-by-room sense. These understandings of our actual bodily selves moving about in our houses today are to me a source of inspiration.'

Shot from the hip, this is as good a summary as any of Cullinan's design philosophy: architecture is at one with social progress, and should manifest it physically. Buildings have the power to 'gather you up'; their forms can be open, with no defined edge; the 'moving about' of our bodies has sublime spatial potency; the abstract play of planes and members has rich architectural possibilities. All who worked with Ted Cullinan or just listened to him will have vivid recollections of such themes expansively and passionately expounded. They will also recall his commitment to and demand for compositional order and his profound understanding of the human imprint on the land.

Much of the content of the lecture at the RSA was put together three to four years earlier and published in 1983 under the title 'Red House to Ronchamp'. In Cullinan's own journey as a practicing architect the direction of travel was as much the other way. In 1954 he cycled 500 miles to Le Corbusier's Ronchamp chapel in the week of its completion and some of the building's spirit found its way into the conversion of Belle Tout Lighthouse near Beachy Head that he was then designing for his parents. The next 20 years of work – from individual houses to the Olivetti office/workshops, Minster Lovell conference centre and the first council housing projects – comprised generally free compositions of great inventiveness, with something of Gerrit Rietveld, Frank Lloyd Wright and Team 10 evident. The arts and crafts sensibility now associated with

Belle Tout lighthouse (1955-60)
Cullinan's first substantial project, the reconfiguration of a derelict lighthouse on the south coast, established a key tenet: 'copying the past insults the past'. He was first to acknowledge the irony, however, that the profound experience of visiting Le Corbusier's new Ronchamp chapel (below) had an overt influence (although the new floor was designed prior to his trip).

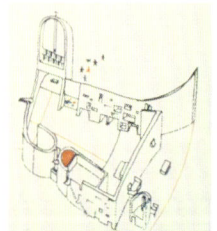

Law house (1966-68)
Recommended to the client by Denys Lasdun, Cullinan built his largest house to date, at Beacon Hill on the South Downs, from buff brick and concrete, with fascias, exposed beams, soffits and frames in timber. The L-shaped plan developed his earlier, linear house plans, setting up a diagonal that, with an open entrance portico and theatrical staircase down to the dining room, echo Lasdun's work. An annexe, designed in the office by Brendan Woods, was added in 1977.

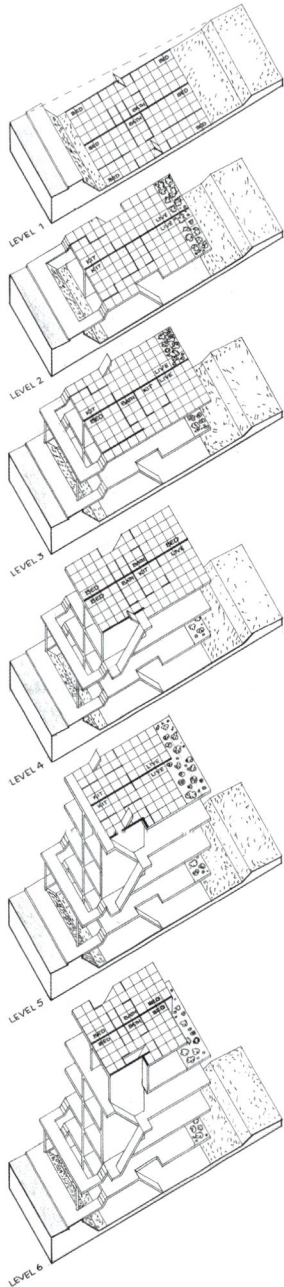

A Tale of Two Frontages (on a 900mm grid)

The largest houses occupy the lowest two levels: those for four people are 3.6m wide, those for six people 4.5m. These are the smallest widths that will accommodate the bedrooms on level 1 and the living rooms on level 2 while making houses of the same depth. The sloping site makes it simple to enter them from a pavement at level 2 direct into the living floor and as bedroom floors are larger than living floors recessed balconies naturally occur at this level.

At level 3 there is another pavement connected directly to Westmoreland Road, a further ground level again produced by the sloping site. Entered from this level are flats for two people which fit precisely over the 4.5m frontage houses for six and also maisonettes for four people fitting exactly over the 3.6m frontage houses for four below.

Stairs lead up from the pavement at level 3 to level 5, two flights, the maximum walk-up permitted by the D.O.E. They pass further flats for two on level 4.

You ask that only non-families live off the ground, so there are maisonettes for three people placed two flights up on levels five and six. They naturally vary in depth according to the 3.6m and 4.5m frontages from below but they are otherwise kept square and the same size on both floors.

By these means we have:

① Made the frontage scheme insisted on by the Bromley Council.

② Proposed houses for 122 people (six × 6p, eight × 4p, 10 × 3p, 12 × 2p), close to the minimum considered feasible by the G.L.C. for this site.

③ Followed all your guidelines concerning walk-up distances and families on the ground.

④ Produced the mix our clients would like and encouraged by you.

and it becomes clear that such items as recessed balconies and the level 5 set back are essential ingredients in achieving these ends.

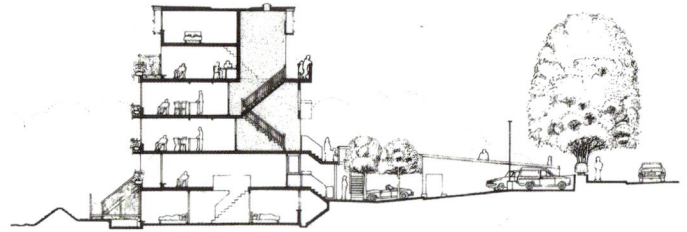

Westmoreland Road, Bromley (1974-79)

The six-storey urban block addresses the road to the north-west and a large shared garden that slopes away to the south-east. The 36 flats and apartments of six types are accessed at the front from three levels of 'pavement', where the elevation is configured as an urban facade. A looser, less formal composition of indented and projecting balconies – with 'abacus' gates made by Sunand Prasad – faces the garden.

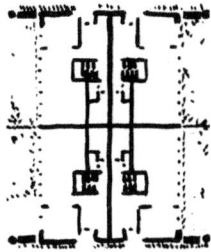

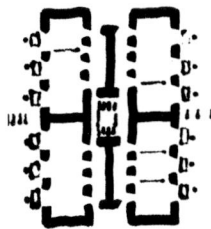

Cullinan is not evident, however. Also absent until the mid-1970s is the facade as such – that is, the elevation of a building that is significantly more than a consequence of the plan and section.

By the time of the RSA event the failure of modern architecture to create convivial urban space had long been acknowledged. Colin Rowe and Fred Koetter's Collage City (1978) and Rob Krier's Urban Space (1975, English translation 1979) provided wide circulation to ideas that had already dominated discourse at the Architectural Association school with which the Cullinan office had close contact. Westmoreland Road (final design 1976) and Leighton Crescent (1977) have the Cullinan practice's first urban facades, though located in suburban residential areas.

Westmoreland Road was quite a departure from studio practice at the time. The initial reason was Bromley council's insistence on a 'frontage scheme' instead of a lower rise occupation of the 130-metre-deep site. However the architectural response was due to Brendan Woods' advocacy of formality in the elevation facing the public realm, creating 'a theatre of appearance'. The rear would then be less formal and expressive of individual homes. This contrasted with the interlacing of public and private at the Highgrove housing scheme in Hillingdon, which was then something of a flagship.

The final (and built) scheme for Leighton Crescent, which followed shortly afterwards, was quadripartite in plan like Highgrove but on five floors, and the difference between the garden and the street facades is simply that one has steps and the other a ramp – nothing in the composition. That of course reflects the different conditions; unlike the 'through' flats of Westmoreland Road, Leighton Crescent's are single aspect.

The 1980 competition design for Worcester College in Oxford exemplifies the awakening of Cullinan's interest in the formal composition of elevations. Here study bedrooms, to be built of stone in coursed rubble with red brick string courses, quoins and window surrounds, were organised around a cloister with symmetrically composed towers at corners. Though unrealised this design was a precursor to many subsequent compositions.

The practice's then relatively recent engagement with the art of representation of buildings as urban actors formed the context for the further discussion at the RSA event during which Cullinan expressed some hesitancy about elevations: 'I agree that we are having some trouble putting faces on our buildings. We are bound to, as we move away from treating those things as objects and come to understand the city within the context of street and square. I am determined not to adopt a classical face, because that is architecture of rejection and enclosure and pompousness and it seeks to establish status.

21

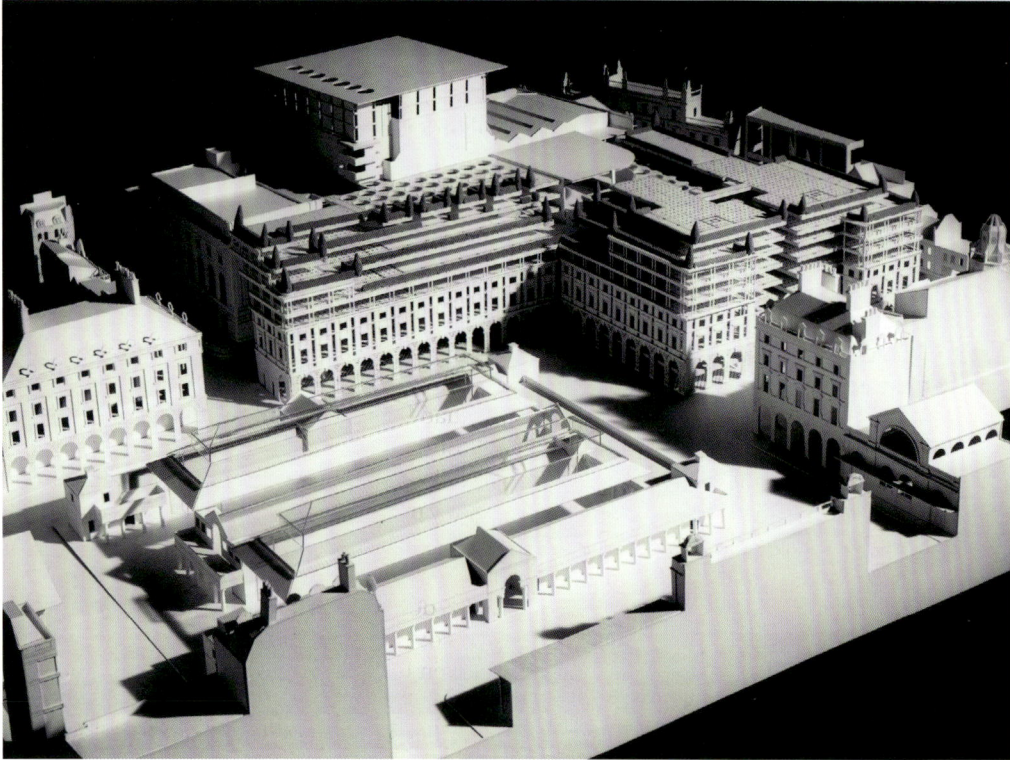

Royal Opera House (1984)
The selection of an architect for the redevelopment of the opera house at Covent Garden was eventually narrowed in four stages from 120 expressions of interest to a shortlist of four teams: Jeremy Dixon (the eventual winner, with BDP), Richard Rogers, Jack Diamond and Edward Cullinan Architects. For Cullinan's the complexity and prominence of the project presented an opportunity to develop and test ideas at a large urban scale. It also provided the opportunity to introduce a syncopated presentation method, with Cullinan drawing on an overhead projector while other team members incrementally assembled the model.

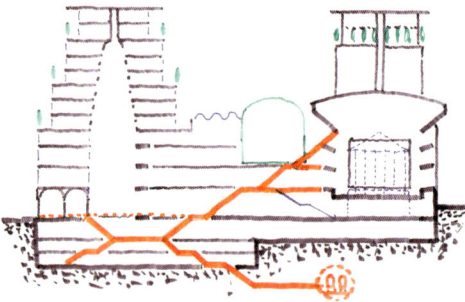

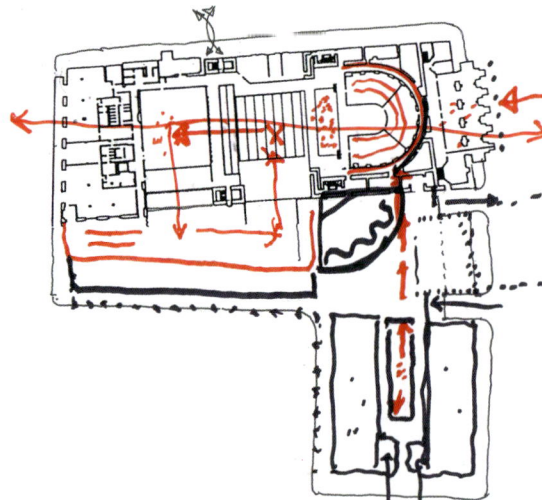

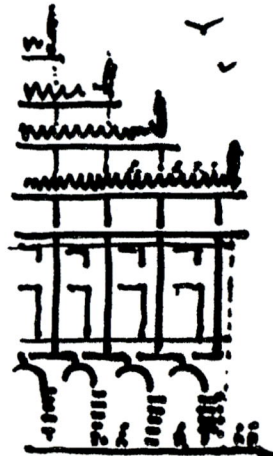

I would look for a much more populist goal in the making of public buildings and further than that I cannot go until I do one.'

There is a little context to that last sentence. In 1984 the practice had been shortlisted for the redevelopment of the Royal Opera House at London's Covent Garden, and so at last given the opportunity that Cullinan craved to show how the architectural principles developed over almost three decades could be applied to a large-scale, truly civic project. All the signals had been that the Cullinan team would be declared winners, and the loss of the project into which it had poured everything was a devastating blow. However, here was a highly accomplished design demonstrating the Cullinan way of giving a street face to a hugely significant urban perimeter block, and much more besides. It was the precursor to a number of essays in adding to the urban setting, which resulted in only one fully realised building, Ludgate Hill, in London.

At the RSA Cullinan also said that 'classical architecture was largely to do with establishing the relative status in a semi-authoritarian society of various institutions' and that 'a democratic architecture, in that sense a people's architecture, is much more interesting'. At the same time, he thought, it was no good looking for answers in most of prevalent modern architecture, which he preferred to refer to as 'recent building' and 'not architecture at all'. Rejecting 'the cold douche of a stripped-down aesthetic' he urged the prolongation of the modern tradition, then 120 years old, that through seeking out the particular, and composing with asymmetry and balance 'is expressive, and through expressiveness is decorative'.

Despite Cullinan's disavowal of classicism, the facades of the Opera House, Petershill and Ludgate in London and Morrison Street in Edinburgh, while eschewing classical orders and pediments, have many other elements associated with classicism: symmetry, rhythm, a tripartite vertical order, columns and rustication. He had decided that there was something in these elements of the pre-modern tradition that could be recovered to create a public architecture, as long as it could be combined with the ways of seeing the world that accompanied modernism in the larger, socially progressive sense. I use 'ways of seeing' in reference to the seminal book by John Berger, whose essay, the 'The Moment of Cubism' (1967), had a big impact on Cullinan, with its analysis of the few years after 1905 – years of epochal discoveries in art and science by figures that Aldo van Eyck called the 'Great Gang'.

He did not to my knowledge expressly say so, but in the design of the practice's larger new buildings of the 1980s and 90s Cullinan appears to be driven by the project of combining his versions of 'classical' and 'cubist'. Classicism, that is, without the iconography he found so oppressive, and Cubism without the multiple perspective, fragmentation and geometric tension that he did not think belonged in the practical and public art of architecture. The approach resulted in compositions that have stability and repose at the larger scale but at the level of detail the constituent elements are seemingly suspended in space, creating excitement or restlessness, depending on the viewer's own way of seeing.

Cullinan's architecture has been described as 'bricolage' (by Sutherland Lyall in 'The State of British Architecture', 1980) and the practice's constructional details criticised for being over articulated (Peter Buchanan, Architects Journal 16 Oct 1985). This tendency results from what Cullinan specifically thought was at the core of modernism's way of seeing. The discoveries of abstract art liberated architecture from representation. By seeing each part of a building, at any scale, as a thing in itself, he believed we can allow expression of its inherent elemental, abstract beauty. We need to liberate constituent parts from over-attachment to each other, instead of losing the joint in the creation of predetermined form, let alone predetermined form that then has decoration applied to create meaning. Cullinan was of course following others in this pursuit – the great tradition of Japanese joinery as well as the Neo-Plasticism of Rietveld and the timber detailing of Greene & Greene's houses, for example – but he wanted to take things further.

From the early houses onwards, Cullinan's timber detailing consistently expressed joints, which he advocated on grounds both of weathering and beauty. The beams, joists and battens (the 'sticks') passed each other in De Stijl manner, held by bolts – Cullinan had an active aversion to conventional joinery: mortice and tenon, comb, dovetail, half housing; anything that turned

something into another thing. He was a 'militant elementalist', so to speak. In steelwork detailing, open sections came to be de rigueur, expressing how the web and flange made their different contributions to the unique performance of metal in tension and compression. Elsewhere, steel was combined with timber to make flitched trusses, the steel plate and timber battening assiduously delineated. At the larger scale of building parts (assemblies), if the planning authority wanted pitched roofs, we could do them as inclined planes floating above the base, separated from each other where the ridge would normally be and so bringing daylight into the centre of the plan. External walls began to be layered, reminiscent of clothes and skin. Rainscreen construction in stone came as a welcome development to add to shingles and tiles.

Cullinan had been very taken by James Stirling's Neue Staatsgalerie in Stuttgart (1984), firstly for its urban parti but equally for the way the stonework was suspended in front of the waterproof/insulation layers with an air gap between the two, and fully open joints between the stone blocks. The stone blocks of classical architecture had become free-hanging tiles. Renzo Piano had done something similar with brick proportioned terracotta slips at the IRCAM music centre, and later developed that as discrete panels of terracotta for the housing at Rue de Meaux, also in Paris.

Cullinan developed a similar kit of parts and applied it to layered elevational compositions in steel, stone and brick. Petershill in London and Morrison Street in Edinburgh are sophisticated examples of urban place-making on a large scale and there is wit and fluidity in the architectural moves: the reinstatement of the historic Temple Bar to the south of St Paul's as both a screen and

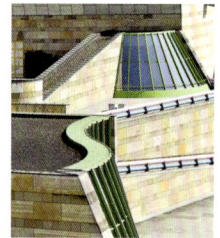

Above The Neue Staatsgalerie in Stuttgart, completed in 1984 by James Stirling, Michael Wilford & Associates, proposed an urban architecture arranged around public spaces and routes rather than monument-making.

Left Layered and lapped structure and linings at Gib Tor farm. Galvanised steel node, developed for the Downland Gridshell to allow the outer laths to slide in three dimensions and the middle pair in two, ensuring the structure's integrity.

Petershill (1989-91)

The competition to reconfigure the district immediately south of St Paul's Cathedral, which anticipated the conversion of Bankside power station as Tate Modern and the new pedestrian bridge across the river to the south, provided Cullinan and his team the opportunity to 'recapture the historic street pattern and create buildings that frame space and provide oblique vistas', undoing what he saw as the damage inflicted by insensitive post-war developments.

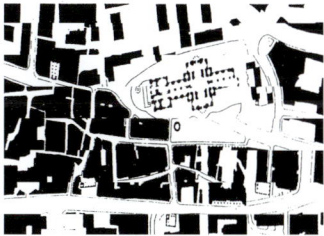

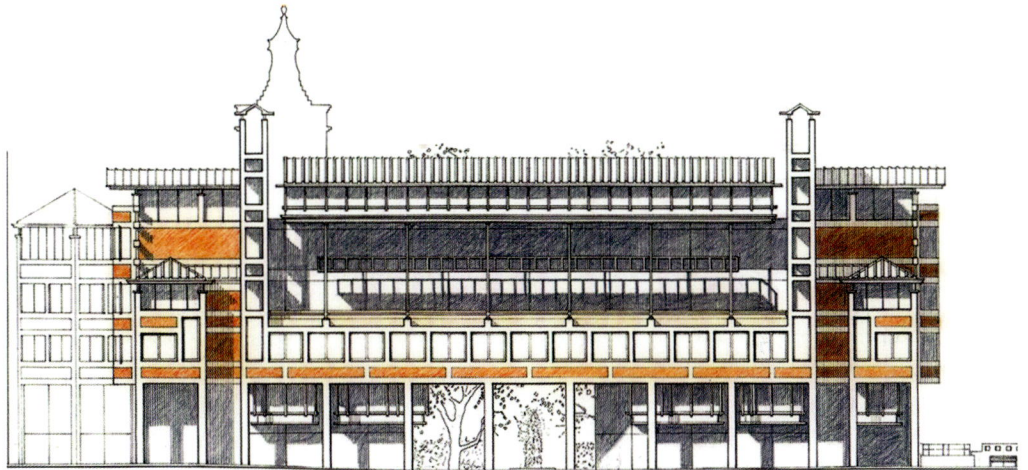

ceremonial gate; and the creation of a view to St Mary's Cathedral by eroding away most of the elevation of the new crescent at Morrison Street. But how would the elevations look today? There is a clue in the one built example of early urban-scale projects at Ludgate Hill. This project was delivered via a design and build contract where the Cullinan office's core belief in the integrity of designing and building was violated. In the event, executive architect RHWL was competent and the result, if compromised, is not unfaithful to the general design intent. However, Ludgate Hill does not represent the best and most profound in Ted Cullinan's work – it tries too hard to please. Cullinan had been scathing about post-modernism, describing it as a 'gas cloud' in comparison with the supernovae and galaxies of classicism and modernism, although from today's perspective Ludgate Hill does look somewhat post-modern, but without the naughtiness.

Whereas some in the audience at the RSA, as well as the influencers at the Royal Opera House and the judges of the Petershill competition, were perhaps looking for a greater degree of polite order from Cullinan, other sceptics expressed more factional views. At its most trenchant their criticism seems to originate in a visceral revulsion for the arts and crafts, rough-hewn character of the architecture. 'Dry stone walls so obviously hand-crafted that just looking at them is exhausting', was critic Deyan Sudjic's take on Fountains Abbey visitor centre. Could dry stone walls be anything but hand-crafted? Sudjic also found the building to have the 'fake rusticity of wholemeal bread… country-style jam in plastic pots' (Guardian, 13 August 1992). In a rather less splenetic observation, however, he touched on a more widely shared disquiet: that the architecture was 'characterised by a kind of aggressive DIY aesthetic, which celebrates with quite unnecessary vigour every bolt, batten and joist'. Sudjic, it might be noted, would not have said this about the equally wanton structural expressionism of high-tech architects like Richard Rogers or Nicholas Grimshaw. Having touched earlier on the expressive drive in Cullinan's work, however, we will return to what has been called its 'maximalism'.

Peter Cook characterised Cullinan as an architect of the 'English Wet Brigade', echoing Margaret Thatcher's description of those members of her

Ludgate Circus (1994)
The project for Ludgate Circus, won in competition by Cullinan's but taken to fruition by another architect, adopted a strategy of layering the facades with hung stone and terracotta panels to provide a sense of depth, and composing them to suggest historical continuity with the neighbouring buildings, which also allowed the floor plates to be maximised to benefit the commercial developer.

St Mary's church, Barnes (1978-94)

The reconfiguration of the parish church from ruins following an arson attack entailed a radical realignment to form a north-south axis. The tower was restored but the Victorian nave and north aisle were demolished to allow the older medieval church to form a narthex and the Lady Chapel. The space created beneath the dramatic new timber and steel roof structure, resting on retained columns, allowed for more sociable congregational gathering.

cabinet with insufficient enthusiasm for her Hayekian free-market agenda. This is of a piece with Cook's apparent disdain for the idea of community: 'I don't rate the community that highly. The irritating bit about the English is the morality with hand on heart and the barely suppressed Puritanism which is actually terribly tedious. The nutter who sits under a car mending a gasket for a whole weekend – the inventive nuttiness which leads through to high-tech in some mysterious way is much more fascinating.' (Peter Smithson, Peter Cook and Ted Cullinan interviewed by Peter Davey, AR May 1984).

Cullinan personally invited Cook ('smoked him out') to critique his newly completed (and soon to be much celebrated) remodelling of St Mary's church in Barnes. Cook had to acknowledge that the radical spatial reordering of an Anglican church in a conservative suburb was anything but wet. As for the architecture, he admired the roof and did not mind the external conservatism, but the whole left him dissatisfied. 'The aeroplane has landed and exploded the plan beneath and then… and then feet of clay or murmurs of reassurance', he wrote (AR May 1984).

He lamented the huge effort required to get anything built at all in the prevailing circumstances and blamed 'British Pragmatism' which was leading to the best work by British architects being done abroad. But that did not let off either the architect or the arts and crafts tradition, in contrast to which the real modernists that followed 'really took off, unafraid to thrust forward'. He wished Cullinan was 'a little tougher on himself and his young friends' and could face their 'comfortable decorativeness… as what it really is: a provincial and picturesque retreat into the gossip of the selective past'. And Samantha Hardingham's description of the practice's work sums up how uncool Cullinan had become for certain critics in the early 1990s: 'designed by a parking warden, and a parking warden of the kind that wears Hush Puppies'; entertaining, if difficult to parse today.

Cullinan and his colleagues rather enjoyed such metropolitan sneering, and quotations like these adorned the staircase wall in the studio. Like these critics Cullinan lived in the metropolis but unlike many of them he was also at one with the land. His childhood home had been a Nash-

27

designed house in Park Village West at Regent's Park, just a mile from the home he later built for his family in his early 30s. His schooldays were spent at the Benedictine Ampleforth College on the edge of the North York Moors, and he bought a farm on a Peak District moor to make a second home. Gib Tor also served as a continuous site for building and landscape experiments in which anyone from the overlapping family, studio and friendship circles could join.

Briefly contemplating becoming a priest like his brother, Cullinan instead studied architecture, first at the then rather stuffy University of Cambridge school of architecture and subsequently at the Architectural Association in London. There he was influenced by teachers such as Peter Smithson and Arthur Korn who were committed modernists but equally committed to taking architecture in a direction more responsive to life as lived. Cullinan was then hugely affected by a year on the west coast of the United States during the prequel to the 1960s cultural revolt – Allen Ginsberg was in the dormitory above his at Berkeley. En route aboard the Queen Mary ('riding steerage' in the cheap cabins below the water line), discussions with John Garrett, then a socialist grammar school boy who later became a Labour MP, drew him to radical politics.

While almost everyone at the AA or in practice at the same time as Cullinan (from 1959) would have described architecture as a 'social art', what distinguished Cullinan was that he found the social dimension positively exhilarating; it was not merely a duty, not what he called 'glum obedience'. The spirituality imbibed at Ampleforth had been sublimated into a political consciousness and energised by the hedonistic but egalitarian dream of freedom and the open

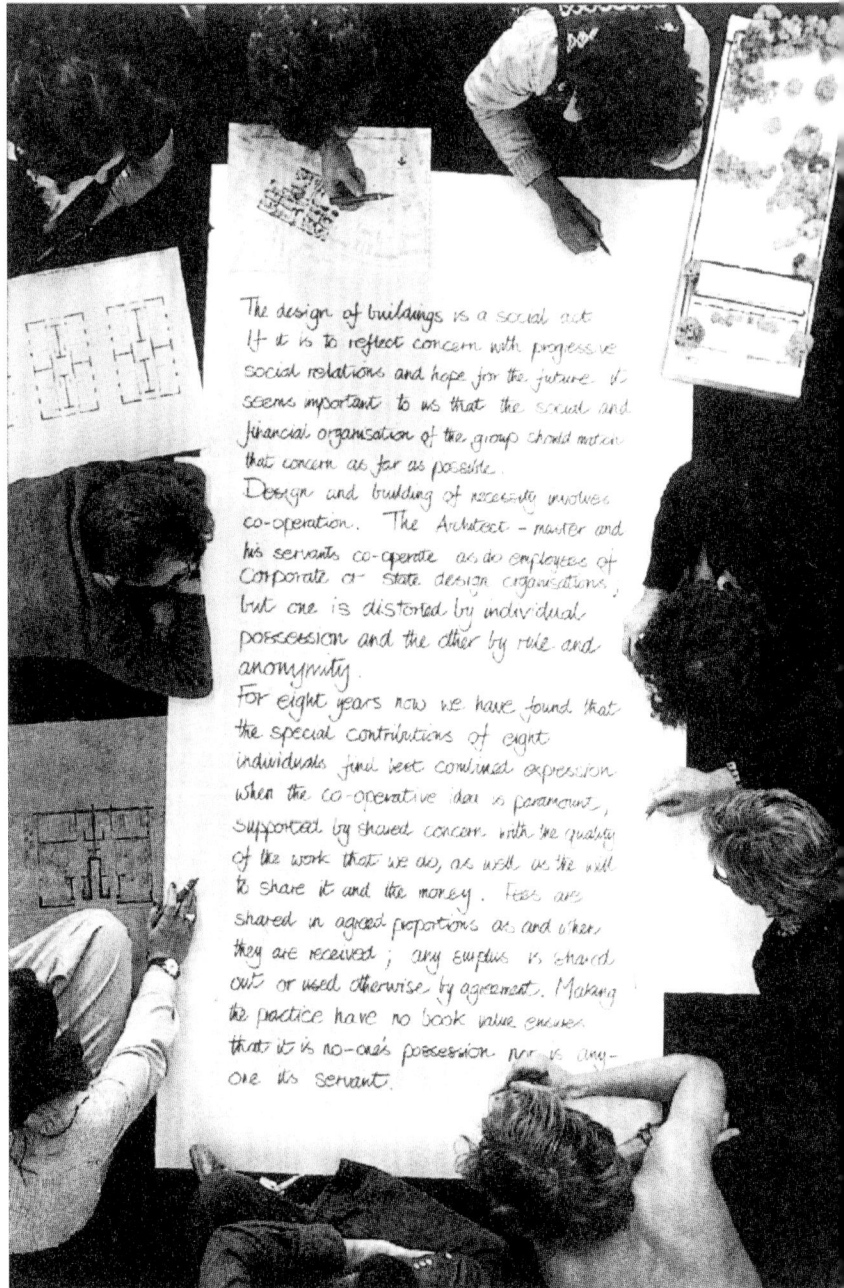

road. It found creative traction in the inventive practice of modern architecture in the service of society. And Cullinan made it his mission to find within the still young tradition of modernism a vocabulary and grammar that might bond with people in a better way than the International Style and its Miesian and Brutalist avatars.

In 1977 Edward Cullinan Architects contributed an image for the calendar of the recently formed New Architecture Movement (NAM). This depicted the members of the office gathered around a large, handwritten manifesto that opened with the sentence 'The design of buildings is a social act'. It went on to set out how the financial structure of the office, in which everyone was a partner, was a consequence of the essentially cooperative nature of designing and building.

Does the adjective 'social' suggest what the buildings look and feel like? The social imperative leads to a process of collaboration with the users, intense listening to their understanding of the project and its ambitions, then responding with propositions or amendments to previous propositions. It also leads to an egalitarianism in the studio. It does not in itself lead to a different kind, or any kind, of architecture. That is evident in the work of practices related to NAM like Support, Covent Garden Community Architects, Matrix and other committed architects for whom function and the cause always trumped intensity of engagement with the form and spatial experience of the building.

In contrast, though Cullinan frequently talked of designing with people, he also reminded his teams that it was they who 'hold the pencil'. He considered that fashioning the building was a duty the architect owed to the client, users and the public. As for egalitarianism in the studio,

he had an uncanny ability to guide and direct his colleagues towards his way of seeing while giving rein to individual talent. Until late in his career he was not only the originator of the key design concepts on most buildings but also the final arbiter of the designs.

Nevertheless, there is a way in which social commitment had an impact on 'what-it-looks-like'. As evident in the RSA event, Cullinan was very wary of any whiff of pomposity and deeply averse to the use of architecture to project power. Like other thinking architects of his generation, he considered the Modern Movement to have liberated architecture from such duties and ushered in a world of wider and fresher possibilities. These allowed an architecture of transparency and openness, of blurring boundaries, of legibility of plans, and a set of principles about urban space that now are called 'place-making' but which at the height of Cullinan's career were far from commonplace.

Egalitarianism is also evident in Cullinan's equal regard for the architect and the builder. His respect for the act of making is a facet of the socialness of the art that he considered to be architecture. Building skills were highly valued in the Cullinan office and for much of the life of the practice the 'how' of building has been integral with the 'what' of form and space. Cullinan himself never designed something he could not imagine building. The assembly of the parts was part of the parti, one might say. That and 'our actual bodily selves moving about', as noted above, over the land as well as in buildings. The affinity with the arts and crafts is not as style but as a set of principles.

In 1973 James Stirling invited Cullinan to refurbish a residential building alongside the new training building he was designing for Olivetti.

Twenty five years later the practice won the commission to design the Faculty of Divinity (1995-2000) right next to Stirling's famous History Faculty in Cambridge. Cullinan's design has a very thoughtful and clever plan and a magnificent library, subtly related to Stirling's but far better at keeping out the weather. The facades of highly articulated layers, sticks and struts were elegantly explained by Cullinan with analogy to skeleton, skin and rain, but the end result seems to undermine rather than reinforce the elegant plan and composition. The ideal of the elemental, even hermetic integrity of materials and building components – 'the thingness of things' – is made as manifest as can be. As Richard Silverman said to me in another context, this is design that looks a little like the exploded drawings that accompany the instructions for making model aircraft. Such extreme articulation is best seen perhaps as the end point in a heroic experiment of this seam of expressionism.

Cullinan's own writings, insightful and eloquent though they are, do not convey either the origin or the purpose of his architectural aesthetic, unlike his forceful expositions in the studio. These had a persistent physicality that words cannot have. The body in space, the weight of materials, the poetry of movement, the interpenetration of outside and inside; whether discussing plan, section, elevation or detail, whether working at the scale of Ordnance Survey maps, general arrangement drawings or full-size details, physical experience was ever present and illustrated with expansive gestures. The resolution of joints or of compositional elements was expounded through analogy with the elbow, the armpit and the crotch. In short, Cullinan's aesthetic was fundamentally experiential. Perhaps a phenomenological critique will be written one day, building on Cullinan's fondness for words

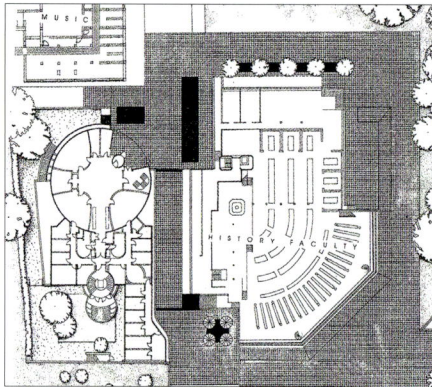

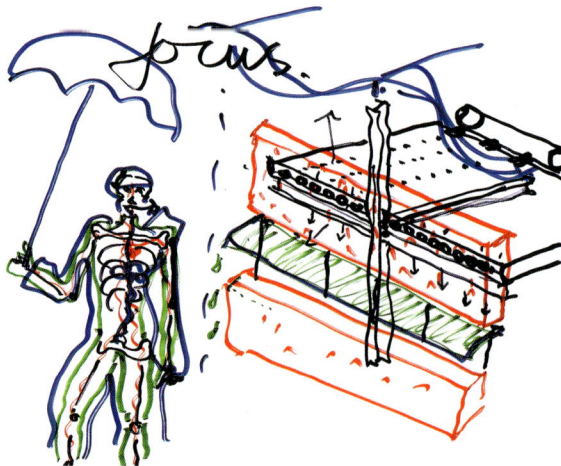

Faculty of Divinity, Cambridge (1995-2000)
Located in a former garden, the divinity building corresponds with James Stirling's celebrated History Faculty. A cut-out segment in the northerly drum form implies a shared entrance court. The Cullinan building, with a double-height library within the drum, is clad in oversailing panels and louvres for solar control.

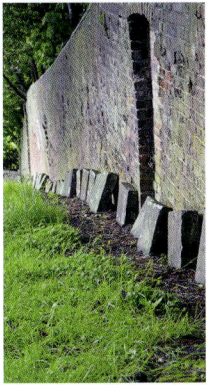

Above, right Dry stone wall at Gib Tor. Cullinan would enjoy introducing visitors to his favourite local places, including the Quaker burial ground with the graves of pioneers of the Industrial Revolution at Coalbrookdale in the Ironbridge Gorge, a simple walled enclosure set on the slope of the hillside that can be seen from across the valley; and the gardener's cottage at Chatsworth, enclosed by a stone wall embedded into the site.

like 'dwelling', 'being' and 'body', though he was no Heideggerian. For him the experiential and the visual were inseparable. He insisted that 'we are in the what-it-looks-like business' and he was a hugely skilful deviser and insightful critic of elevation and formal composition. However, plan, section and the three-dimensional assembly of materials were where his inventive energy found the ground most fertile.

The consistent inventiveness in Cullinan's work was animated by profound insights about the land and the human imprint on the landscape, for the clues they offered about how we might inhabit city and country. Cullinan's love of the dry stone wall, for example, was much more than a fetish. He was very struck by how the act of clearing the fields for crops and livestock provided the material to make an everlasting enclosure for the same fields. Not only is this a kind of a 'tuning-in' to a natural order, but also it leaves a beautiful imprint on the land. On a trip with our architecture students in 1979 he took us on a detour to point out, across a small valley, the Quaker burial ground at Coalbrookdale – a walled rectangular space, inclined at the slope of the hill as if on display to the world, containing the graves of pioneers of the Industrial Revolution. Likewise he loved the set of the gardener's cottage at Chatsworth, held in front of its yard with its curved wall created by partly cutting into the hill.

For Cullinan 'urban' and 'rural' were physically and conceptually inseparable entities that form a continuum. His vision was generous and expansive and thereby inclusive. In this light the criticisms seem partisan and relatively trivial. As global imperatives demand that we seek to reach a new accommodation between humans and nature, Cullinan's thinking seems freshly relevant and prescient.

what
made
Ted

The Cullinans' Peak District farm was both a playground for friends, family and colleagues and a laboratory for continuous experimentation with materials and techniques

Making and Playing
Robin Nicholson

Looking back over nearly 50 years during which the Cullinans transformed Gib Tor Farm, their smallholding high up in the Peak District, one can only be amazed at the energy, the invention and the determination that Ted Cullinan lavished there with the help of family, friends, members of the office and their families, especially their children – this was Homo Ludens drinking with Homo Faber!

Ted and Roz bought Gib Tor in the early 1970s having established the practice and finished 62 Camden Mews, needing another project and wanting to get away with their young family at weekends. Not that getting away was that easy as Gib Tor was more than three hours' drive from Camden, every Friday night, for which Roz would have had to gather provisions for the family and their guests; and there were always guests to help, first with the reconstruction and later with the tree planting.

Others may speculate about what drove Ted to make things but he drew and built from a young age. By just 34 he had designed and helped rebuild Belle Tout lighthouse for his parents on the cliff at Birling Gap, East Sussex, and designed his uncle Mervyn's garden house in Hampshire, building it with Horace Knight, the gardener; he had designed and built the Stinson Beach house in California for his friends the Marvins and his own Camden Mews house. Learning by doing has a long history but learning by designing and then building it yourself is particularly productive as you find that good intentions are often modified as you proceed. Along the way Ted acquired an impressive range of skills, from dry stone walling to forestry.

Writing in 1983, Brendan Woods perceptively suggested that Camden Mews 'serves as a prime source for his work of the last 10 years, where the main body of the building is established in masonry construction and the roof and balconies made of sticks exist above and beyond the primary box' ('The Art and Act of Building', Architectural Review, Sept 1983). If the experience of assembling Camden Mews, listed grade-II* in 2007, was so resourceful, Gib Tor was to be a continuous experiment, renewing the

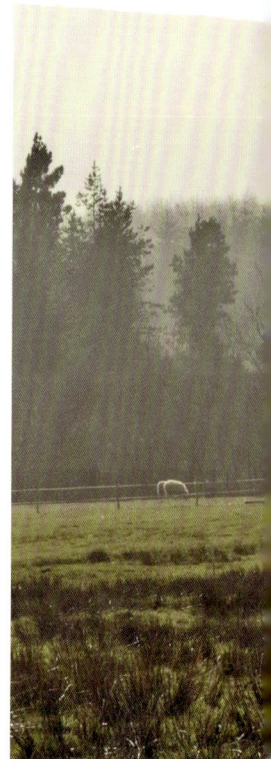

Gib Tor Farm
Located in the Peak District National Park in North Staffordshire, near the borders with Derbyshire and Cheshire and between Buxton and Leek, the Cullinans' weekend retreat of Gib Tor Farm was far removed from the 'existenzminimum' of their Camden Mews house. Rebuilt with the help of his friends and family (right), the farm project offered the opportunity for ongoing experimentation.

1841 stone barn and other structures, modifying the local environment through tree planting and growing vegetables, usually in spite of the weather. All of this was a cooperative effort with Ted imagining futures at which others might balk.

Many know Ted through his wonderfully energetic lectures, drawing how our buildings were made and how their architecture emerged through their construction. Many others have experienced his infectious belief that we could together build pretty much anything. If it was too cold you put antifreeze in the mortar; if access was difficult, children would happily climb the roof to point the stone ridge; if the planners said you had built a dry stone wall on public land you moved it; trees could be felled in Camden gardens, sawn into logs and taken in a trailer 160 miles up the M1 to heat the house; and, when it snowed, the Land Rover was jacked up and a tyre removed to drive the homemade ski lift, and igloos were built. Later, vegetables grown in cold frames on the roof of Camden Mews would be planted out into neat manure cut into the still frozen spring soil; the prolific produce was later distributed around the office.

I didn't take part in the heavy lifting of the main barn restoration, when all the stone slates were removed, rafters renewed, insulation and sarking installed and the slates replaced and pointed in freezing winter fog; the stone walls were insulated and lined with Douglas fir ply with stud and ply walls for the bedroom cells. My first exposure to this architectural experiment was before I joined the practice and just before the main barn was occupied. Fiona and I were given an angle grinder and a pile of millstone grit to start the main staircase. By the end of the weekend, under the experienced eye of Ted's 14-year-old daughter Kate, we had dressed the stones and laid the first metre of the main stair, while our children had been entertained on some other project.

The stone barn was transformed with the addition of a glass-roofed playroom, frameless Buva windows set into the stone with external ply shutters for security, massive rainwater collection tanks that hovered over the entrance hall beside a hand-operated counter-weighted lift; and then there were the shower and toilet drums. Ted held a long fascination for spun concrete sewer rings, and these appeared in projects from time to time: as water butts at Leighton Crescent and in the four-storey staircases of the student residences at Cheltenham. Confident as ever, Ted had set the circular shower tray in the floor and then stacked up one drum over it and the loo in another with the idea that he would jigsaw out holes with curved corners for the doors and then plumb

from the back. So, one weekend we set to with a huge American angle grinder he had been given; after half an hour we had barely scratched a line in the concrete. Undaunted, we spent most of the day scoring back-to-back lines inside and out. Dusty and tired, Ted inside and I outside cracked these lines with synchronised bolster blows – problem solved, but no curved cornered doors.

Below A saddle structure of riven chestnut laths and sack ties, made at the Weald & Downland Museum, was destined for the 1978 'Architectures d'ingénieurs' exhibition at the Centre Pompidou until the outdoor part of the show was dropped.

Gib Tor Farm

An eliptical belt of ash trees was planted over winter weekends to serve as a windbreak and provide wood for fuel, fencing and furniture. Cullinan told its story in a drawing that was presented to Queen Elizabeth as part of a Diamond Jubilee gift from the Royal Academy.

The largely derelict collection of farm buildings was weatherproofed and adapted for communal life. Shower cubicles were made from large diameter concrete sewage pipes.

ONE TRANSPARENT PLASTIC COXDOME.

TWO SPUN CONCRETE SEWER PIPES.

ONE ARMITAGE SHANKS FACTORY ABLUTION FOUNT'N.

The Peak District fueled so many of Ted's interests, including his love of local history and its rich legacy of monuments such as the Neolithic Arbor Low Stone Circle nearby and the natural chasm in The Roaches escarpment known as Luds Church, which new guests had to visit. Local enjoyments included rock-climbing, rambling and on a hot summer's evening a hair-raising journey in the open trailer to swim in the pool at Three Shire Heads.

The nearest village of Flash is the highest in Britain, half way between Leek and Buxton which provided a large B&Q and an opera house respectively. Its relative inaccessibility and weather ensured that Buxton had not enjoyed the success of Bath as a Georgian spa town, despite ambitious investment by William Cavendish, fifth Duke of Devonshire. The Crescent Hotel is the grandest monument but its former stables, built nearby around a circular courtyard is the more interesting as it had been domed over to house a hospital in the late nineteenth century. Ted would take visiting children to stand at the origin of what was once the largest unsupported dome in the world to hear their pinpoint echo. Of course, Ted was enthralled by the mix of uses – patients would be wheeled out in their beds onto

the upper terrace to watch the flower shows and car rallies in the circus below – one is reminded of the ward terrace overlooking the garden at the Lambeth Community Care Centre.

An early move at Gib Tor had been to build a circular earth and stone seat, five metres in diameter, around a hearth in the centre of the courtyard, framed by the farmhouse and various barns. Ted was fascinated by weather in all its aspects and the seat saw a lot of it. Over the years he planted more than 1000 trees, starting behind the barn and extending down the valley. These modified the climate in the courtyard, pushing the prevailing wind up and over the seating circle instead of swirling over the barns, allowing gatherings around the fire, whatever the weather.

Sitting opposite Ted for so many years, I witnessed the enormous amounts of planning that went into getting first building materials and later bare-root tree whips delivered, or to be collected en route to Gib Tor. Beautiful posters would appear in our office kitchen, calling for volunteers to help plant the trees and become part of this shared experiment. As with so many buildings their history is seldom recorded but now you can rent the various buildings as a 'lovingly converted unique barn conversion… (with) a wow factor all of its own'.

Visiting Gib Tor for the first time was a memorable experience for everyone, and for many it became a life-enhancing habit. Regardless of age or skill, we all became part of this 50-year architectural and arboricultural experiment. Ted tried out numerous ideas at a relatively small scale, which informed him back in the office. It was a collective experience and an opportunity for us all and especially students to spend time learning by making and playing with Ted.

Cullinan's drive to build
was grounded in robust principles
and fired by a determination
to challenge the status quo.
Mary-Lou Arscott, who worked
in the studio from 1987-94,
nurtures those lessons
in her own teaching

Ideas and Ideals
Mary-Lou Arscott

Not long after I'd started working at Edward Cullinan Architects, I was involved in a surprising and memorable incident that revealed a fundamental aspect of Ted's character. He and I had driven up from London to present our proposal for a new media centre at Cheltenham & Gloucester College. As I led the way, carrying the panels, the college principal greeted me and asked whether the driver would like a cup of tea. Ted overheard and came out with a booming laugh while I scrambled to the introductions. This, I came to learn, was typical. Ted had no affectations and no expectations for reverence. He was genuine and direct with every person he met, and a fantastic listener.

I have been teaching architecture for the last 15 years and have reflected many times on the ways in which Ted demonstrated powerful lessons without taking dogmatic positions. He showed characteristic humanity and humility, enthusiasm and inclusivity, generosity and leadership. This, while capturing all the contradictions of his hubris, at odds with the period, the rampant economy, and the evolving individuality in society.

Ted was connected to the establishment through his family and his education. The class system bestows a security and confidence on those who are deemed to belong. Ted however, used his position of privilege to raise questions and challenge the status quo. He sided with the best lefties against the Vietnam war, nuclear weapons and the poll tax. The restless searching that Ted brought to his concerns about inequality, the sustainable use of materials, how best to inhabit the world, and our climate crisis was prescient, fundamental and very unfashionable in the 1980s and 90s. Here lie the many contradictions that faced ethical concerns for architectural practice serving capitalism.

Ted held dear the principles of Mondragon, the Basque-based workers' cooperative that is now Spain's tenth largest company. The low ratio of lowest to highest paid in a cooperative business speaks of a counter cultural system to reorder societal relationships. This idealism was applied at ECA. It met many bumps in the road, and being collaborative was hard work. This structure would be seen as ludicrous in the current pay landscape

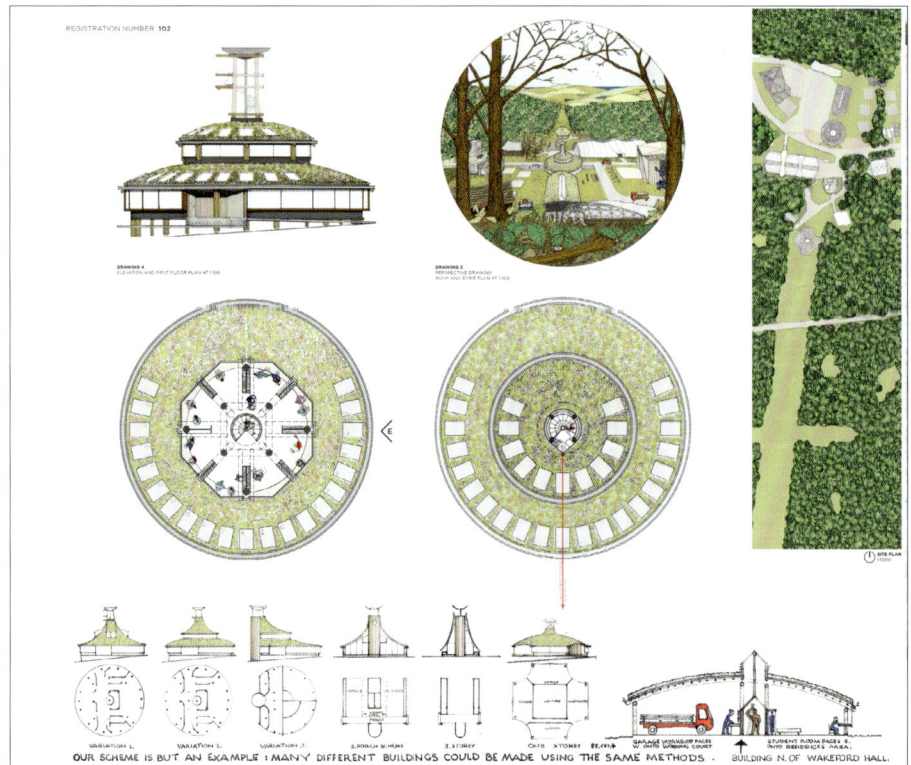

where 5000:1 is not uncommon for the ratio of chief executive to worker pay.

How can architects be in business and innovate at the same time? Though imagining professional independence, architects are service workers, generating soft costs, waiting for the email or the phone to ring. In fact, Ted's great pleasure was to be designing public buildings with imaginative clients, using experimental construction and inventive building typologies. So the precious projects for Lambeth community care, Maggie's, Hampshire schools, Purcell School, Fountains Abbey and Cambridge University all embodied principles of social justice and liberal thinking.

Commercial clients asked different kinds of questions and challenged the desire for social benefit. But Ted was optimistic and believed in the power of architecture to contribute to the public realm. The dance with the devil produced opportunities for novel detailing, a chance to create a responsive urban fabric, and I think for him this offset some of the ideological conflicts.

Ted's lecturing is in my mind every time I step up to address my students. He had such energy as a performer and somehow engaged the listeners by speaking to everyone, youngest to oldest. The narrative that he made so engaging by action drawing in the lecture format was electric, and gave the audience a sense of being involved in the development of his design ideas. We know how complex the issues are that we wrestle with as designers, but being able to write and rewrite the immensely powerful story of the architecture is where Ted's gift was centred. Never was the intractable detail decision dismissed by Ted. The detail would connect to the principal ideas and could inform the unfolding narrative. So the drawings on acetate in a lecture or detail paper in the office or a napkin in Pizza Express were genuine applications of the magic of working with Ted.

Media Centre, Cheltenham & Gloucester College
The 1960s art school campus was updated with the addition of a Media Centre (1991-93) and later student residences.

Left Competition panel for experimental greenwood houses for the Parnham Trust at Hooke Park, Dorset; ECA's Carol Costello in the window at Cheltenham & Gloucester Phase 2.

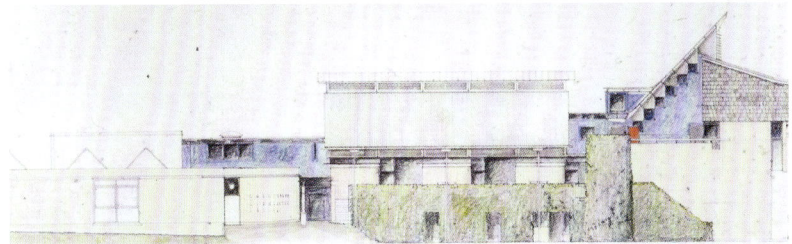

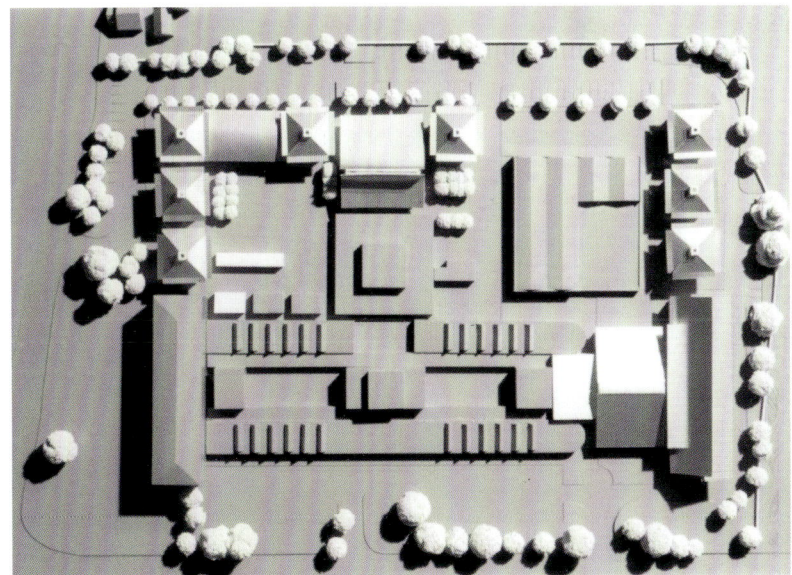

William Morris represented
a touchstone in Cullinan's
life and work, not just for his
libertarian socialism
but in his deep respect
for history and a determination
to embody ideals in the making
and expression of art

Working Ethics
Gillian Darley

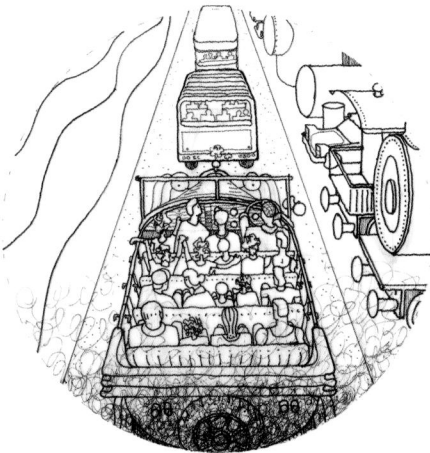

Combing through Ted Cullinan's writings and presentations, William Morris is never far off, in thought or deed. Those beliefs and driving impulses that threaded his life in practice (and out of it) are closely aligned to Morris's (and so, inevitably, John Ruskin) but architecturally underpinned by that easily overlooked and modest figure, Philip Webb. Morris was for Ted 'a libertarian socialist and incurable optimist' and refuting Marx's revolutionary socialism in 1879 he chose words 'so good [they] will make you cry', he told the Cambridge Association of Architects in 1993. If Morris's words were moving then, they bear repeating now; 'if these hours are dark… do not let us sit deedless… beaten by the muddle, but rather let us work like good fellows trying by some dim candlelight to set out a workshop ready against tomorrow's daylight'.

In his later accounts of formative influences, Ted interwove the Arts and Crafts and Modern Movements although he had already read News from Nowhere at school (Ampleforth) where he remembered being guided rather towards its idyllic medievalism, so suitable to a cloistered Catholic private education, than nineteenth-century socialism. At the Cambridge school of architecture he claimed the after-shade of Edward Prior still lingered (or did he conjure it up in later life, once he had learned of the charms in the butterfly plan?). Then at the Architectural Association he was tutored by Arthur Korn, and so found himself at only one remove from the Bauhaus and ready to be caught up in the 'energies of mature Modernism' through work alongside the Smithsons and Denys Lasdun.

Perhaps more surprising and tangible, for him and for us, was the discovery that in 1950s southern California the arts and crafts was 'alive and kicking'. Cullinan's time on the West Coast led to his high regard for the vigorous expression of domesticity, and, the antithesis, his abhorrence of 'pompous symmetries'. Philip Webb's 'relaxed formality' at Jolwynds (1873), as well as the intricate simplicity of the Red House, lead on, in Ted's pantheon, to Lutyens' Tigbourne Court (1900) and its demonstrative yet restrained trio of gables. Back in California, the Gamble House exercised its enchantment.

For a man steeped in William Morris, a devoted disciple of the work of Philip Webb and proud to have been patted on the head (literally and figuratively, too) by Frank Lloyd Wright, Ted Cullinan prioritised the humane and, then, a wider view of society. Architects, he wrote later, should listen to the users of their buildings but perhaps it was a romanticised concept of those users that was most compelling. Wright's Robie House, 'so horizontal and graceful, so developed and so complete', vied with the Prairie House, with its hints that went well beyond architecture towards a new pattern of society, towards decentralised communities and back to 'the ideal of the simple life' – a version of the Red House on the prairies? Neatly put, Cullinan considered that 'to make our future we must surely understand our own recent past and our present and seek in it and in ourselves an inspired and expressive and responsive architecture to offer vividness to the debate'. English default settings of timidity and conservativeness urgently needed a kick – involving understanding, commitment,

even an overt ego, the kind of ingredients thoughtful and engaged architects can provide.

Cullinan's socialism was William Morris's and its influence extended to the workplace, where the cooperative nature of his practice was admired but seldom emulated – it was the proof of Ted's vision, supported by his colleagues, that architecture is a 'social act'. When it came to the rebuilding of St Mary's church at Barnes, the resulting complex timber structure drew on the resonance, form and fabric of a medieval tithe barn in Gloucestershire. Great Coxwell, just six miles from Kelmscott, is the high temple for every Morris worshipper, enshrined when Barbara Castle, by then very old and but still very fired-up, memorably addressed the 1996 AGM of Morris's Society for the Protection of Ancient Buildings there, her topic being beauty, that most essential component of a just society.

No one who saw Ted, late in life and back in the Cullinan Studio, jousting with the overhead

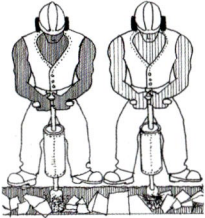

Above Cullinan shared William Morris's veneration of manual labour.

Right The medieval Great Coxwell barn – the roof structure of which inspired Cullinan's renewal of St Mary's church in Barnes – was considered by William Morris 'as noble as a cathedral'. Just six miles from the barn is Kelmscott Manor, Morris's country home from 1871 until his death in 1896, and depicted on the frontispiece of his book 'News from Nowhere'.

Opposite Cullinan's sketch for a '20s charanbanc, modern minibus and fuel cell vehicle passing transport exhibit and gridshell'.

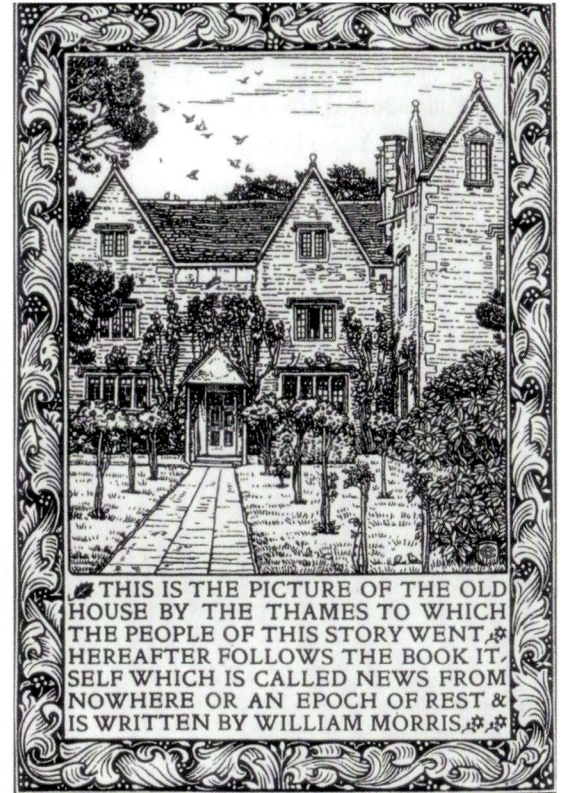

THIS IS THE PICTURE OF THE OLD HOUSE BY THE THAMES TO WHICH THE PEOPLE OF THIS STORY WENT HEREAFTER FOLLOWS THE BOOK ITSELF WHICH IS CALLED NEWS FROM NOWHERE OR AN EPOCH OF REST & IS WRITTEN BY WILLIAM MORRIS.

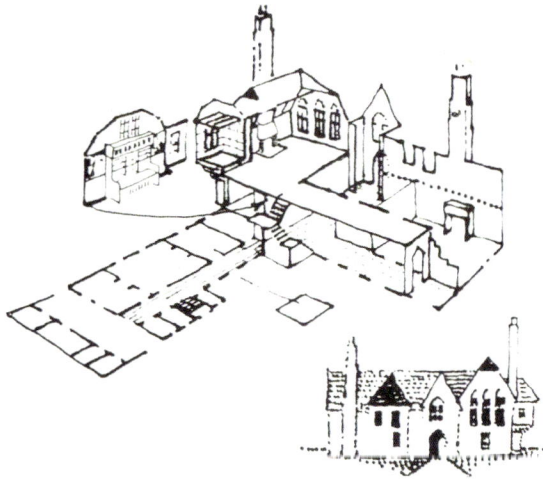

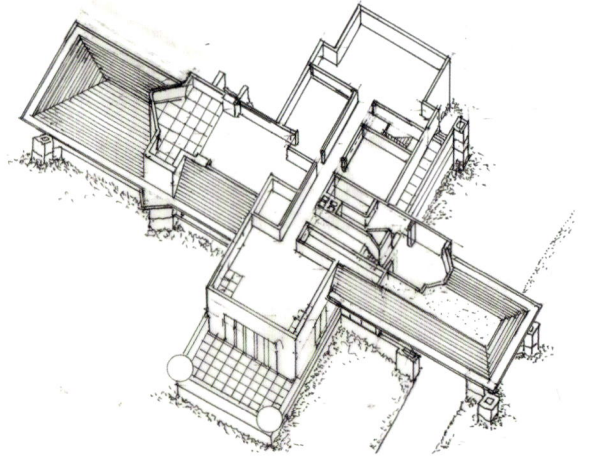

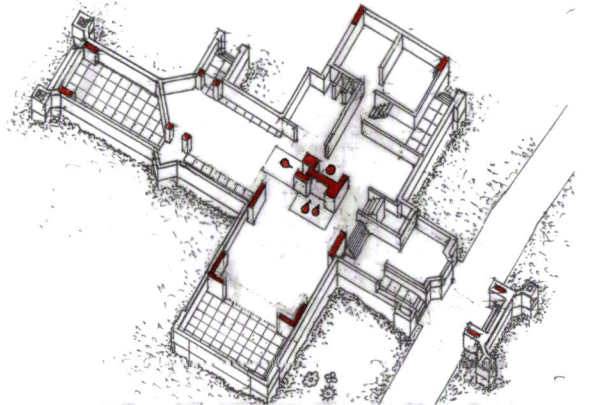

Above left Cullinan's analysis of William Morris's home, the Red House in Bexleyheath, designed by Philip Webb, whose Jolwynds (left, demolished) was among his favourites.

Above right Cullinan's cutaway axonometrics were employed to explain the interplay of spaces at Frank Lloyd Wright's Robie House.

Above Cullinan's cartoons dramatising his take on the life and work of Frank Lloyd Wright were prepared for his teaching forays in the United States.

projector as he fluently conjured up, in line and language, the former RMC buildings at Egham will ever forget his spirit. This was a fight for survival. By ensuring its listing and winning the argument, Ted's flourish of reasoned persuasion backed up by obduracy was to prove the most effective weapon in the conservationist armoury.

But, unusually among architects, Ted Cullinan thought for himself, with those strong beliefs (perhaps typical of an unhorsed Catholic?) and then a developing analytic eye. Consider how he unpicks the 1859 Red House for his audience in 1986 at the Royal Society of Arts. Enough about the precedents, 'I want to look at it in another way, in a way that will place it into the tradition that inspires me'. He walks us to towards the entrance, 'an invitation to enter', a little house that then leads to another little house, Webb's 'cupboard cum seat, to leave things in'. The

journey, up the stairs towards an intersecting gallery, just one of a series of pathways leading through and, again, out to find the well, contained by its surroundings, the garden court. 'The house is creating the situation in which it itself stands.' Once there, he examines the idea of the openings, how they impinge on the interior as sources of light and indicators of scale and, again, how they measure up on the external composition. But, for everyone who knew what William Morris represented to Ted Cullinan, this analysis is also by default a poetic exercise, exhibiting ideals in motion and practice, showing the collaborative endeavour as a transformative and organisational force, and above all, celebrating that creative contagion that comes with inspiration. All that in a modest house for a short-lived community of artist friends. The resonance that echoes on is something entirely different, both in scale and impact.

On discovering arts and crafts traditions alive and well on America's west coast as a student at Berkeley in the 1950s, Cullinan returned to Britain with a determination to breathe new life into the legacy of Ruskin and Morris

The California Connection

Mark Swenarton

Ted Cullinan emerged on the UK architecture scene in the 1960s with a series of small domestic projects, most notably his own home in Camden Mews. What distinguished him from other young architects in Britain making their name around that time (Ahrends Burton Koralek, Richard Rogers, Norman Foster, Richard MacCormac et cetera) was his adherence to the arts and crafts belief in 'pleasure in making': the belief that designing and making formed part of a single process and that architecture was a celebration of the way a building was made. By this time the arts and crafts tradition in Britain was more or less moribund but in California it was still flourishing; and it was this California version of the arts and crafts that Cullinan imported to London.[1]

The philosophy of what became known as the Arts and Crafts movement had been first developed in Britain by Ruskin and Morris a century earlier. In the chapter on 'The Nature of Gothic' in 'The Stones of Venice' (1853) John Ruskin had declared that the essential feature of Gothic was the freedom it gave to the workman to make use of his God-given creative powers in his work. William Morris was inspired by this pronouncement – which he described as 'one of the very few necessary and inevitable utterances of the century' – and, taking the viewpoint of the doer rather than the viewer, proclaimed that 'real art is the expression by man of his pleasure in labour'.[2] This he declared was 'not only the very foundation of Architecture in all senses of the word, but of happiness also in all conditions of life'.[3]

These ideas inspired architects and designers not just in Britain but worldwide. In Britain architects maturing in the 1880s and 90s – Prior, Lethaby, Voysey, Ashbee, Baillie Scott et cetera – took Morris's teachings to heart and created an architecture which relied for its aesthetic impact on the work of the building craftsman, whether in wood, stone, metal or glass. But, whatever its undeniable merits, the work that they produced hardly lived up to the epoch-making stature of the philosophy that had inspired it. In part this was because the arts and crafts ideal ran counter to ingrained British notions of class and gender, the prevailing ideas of what a gentleman does

Above Cullinan's Camden Mews house (far right) is aligned east-west, perpendicular to the street, to expose the long south elevation to the sun. The evident crafted aspect of the construction recalls the work of Greene & Greene's Thorsen House (above and top middle, 1909) and Rudolph Schindler's Jose Rodriguez House (above middle, 1942) in California.

Left Cullinan prepared drawings depicting Frank Lloyd Wright for lecture tours in America.

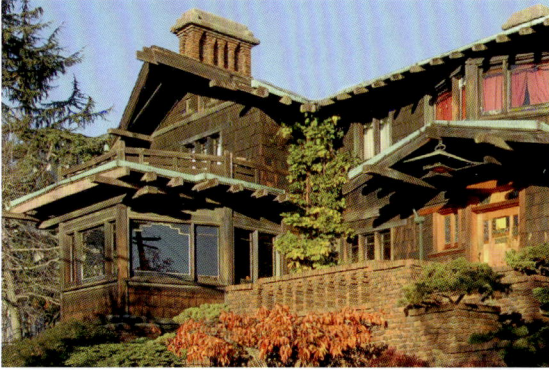

and doesn't do: gentlemen give orders and instructions but others carry them out. It also ran up against the peculiarly English culture of restraint (itself related to ideas of class): the notion that attention-seeking and display were inherently vulgar and were to be avoided at all costs. The abstemious architecture, and indeed lifestyle, of Morris's close friend Philip Webb – the idol of the architects grouped around the Art Workers' Guild – embodied this culture of reticence.

In the USA, and especially on the west coast, none of these constraints applied. In the pioneer 'can-do' culture of the west, 'do-it-yourself' was not an ethical injunction: it was a necessity of life. In California timber was abundant and, not least for its earthquake-resistant properties, timber framing was the standard method of building houses – an open invitation for an architecture that celebrated construction. Moreover English ascetism and rectitude had no place on the west coast. If you were going to celebrate construction, you were not going to do it in the puritanical manner of Philip Webb.

California had and still has a culture of its own – nowhere more so than the Bay Area of San Francisco and the University of California at Berkeley. When I was an undergraduate studying history at Oxford, my tutor, Thomas Laqueur, was completing his doctorate on Sunday schools in Lancashire in the nineteenth century. He then

got a position at Berkeley and his next book was a history of sex from ancient times to the present day.[4] You see the world differently from California.

In 1956-57 Cullinan spent two semesters at the architecture school in Berkeley on a postgraduate scholarship. He recalls that he didn't find much to interest him in the school – in fact, it bored him.[5] But California he found overwhelming: 'California really shattered me – it was just a fantastic eye-opener'. What impressed him most was finding 'the old English arts and crafts still alive in the west coast'. Two of the great masterpieces of California arts and crafts were right there, and freely accessible, just off the Berkeley campus: Greene & Greene's Thorsen House (1909) and Bernard Maybeck's 'astonishing' First Church of Christ Scientist (1910). Anyone who has seen these virtuoso timber constructions will attest that once seen, they are never forgotten. And on top of this, Bernard Maybeck, the 'exotic late arts and crafts architect… was still practising… [exemplifying] this hand-knitted arts and crafts approach that was still so alive in the Bay Area'.

If Cullinan had not discovered these buildings for himself, while he was there an exhibition took place in 1956 that put them at the centre of architectural attention in general and his in particular. Sponsored by the Los Angeles City Art Department, the exhibition was called 'Roots of California Contemporary Architecture' and formed the basis of the subsequent book, 'Five California Architects', by Esther McCoy.[6] The five were Bernard Maybeck, Irving Gill, Greene & Greene and RM Schindler. Cullinan recalled the impact of 'this great exhibition': 'I saw all that exhibition and I made sure I saw all their work too, cruising up and down in my

Ford V8'.[8] Maybeck, Gill and the Greene brothers ('who became near-gods to the young Cullinan'[9]) all belonged to the golden age of the arts and crafts movement of the early years of the century. Today we tend to think of Schindler in terms of the white planar modernism of early works like the Lovell Beach House; but in fact his trajectory was away from this towards California carpenter architecture, with a series of houses in the 1940s that were indubitably arts and crafts in their structure and vocabulary. Schindler was Cullinan's favourite and his hero,[10] not least because he loved rolling up his sleeves and getting involved on site: 'he was a great architect who loved building things himself'.[11]

Left Bernard Maybeck's First Church of Christ Scientist, Berkeley, combines California carpenter craftsmanship with Byzantine, Romanesque and Gothic Revival influences.

Right Drawing prepared in 2017 for Cullinan's Frank Lloyd Wright lectures.

This west coast version of arts and crafts architecture – so different from the workaday version in which he had been schooled as an undergraduate at Cambridge – appealed strongly to the young Cullinan. He had always enjoyed making things himself. Ever since he was nine years old, when he made a house for his then girlfriend, 'I've loved handling materials and building buildings'.[12] Here in California was an architecture based on making, on doing it yourself, and celebrating construction – but exuberantly and without inhibition, not in the abstemious manner of the English.

When Cullinan returned to the UK to complete his education (at the Architectural Association) he picked up the other attachments that were enthusing young London architects at the time: Team X (Peter Smithson was his tutor), late Le Corbusier and Denys Lasdun (for whom he went to work). These were the common currency of the day. But what he had – and the others did not – was a love of architecture as a celebration of making, not in the modest English manner but in the unabashed California manner. The Camden Mews house, as he said, was inspired by Schindler and 'Californian self-build habits'.[13] With its timber-structured upper storey jettying out over a masonry base, and the exposed timber of its interior, the Cullinan house is the direct descendant of California arts and crafts houses like Schindler's Jose Rodriguez house, built in Glendale 25 years before.

Over the decades that followed, Cullinan's vocabulary was to expand and diversify but lapped joints and exposed timber construction were to remain a leitmotif: through St Mary's Barnes in the 1970s, Fountains Abbey visitor centre in the 1980s and the gridshells of Hooke Park and Downland in the 1990s and 2000s.[14] These were virtuoso works with the same vigour and excitement as Maybeck's church or a house by Greene & Greene or Schindler. This was not the arts and crafts as it had ever existed in England, even in its heyday. It was sex through the ages, not Sunday schools.

Footnotes

1 Thanks go to Neil Jackson for sharing his insights into California architecture and to Adrian Forty for helpful comments on an early draft.

2 Quoted in Mark Swenarton, Artisans and Architects: The Ruskinian Tradition in Architectural Thought (Macmillan, 1989) p63 and p71.

3 Artisans and Architects, p71.

4 Thomas W Laqueur, Religion and Respectability: Sunday Schools and Working Class Culture, 1780-1950 (Yale UP, 1976), and Making Sex: Body and Gender from the Greeks to Freud (Harvard UP, 1990).

5 National Life Story Collection, Architects' Lives: Edward Cullinan, tape 5. All quotations in this paragraph are from this source.

6 Esther McCoy, Five California Architects (Reinhold, 1960).

7 Architects' Lives: Edward Cullinan, tape 5.

8 Architects' Lives: Edward Cullinan, tape 5.

9 Kenneth Powell, Edward Cullinan Architects (Academy, 1995), p10.

10 Architects' Lives: Edward Cullinan, tape 5 and tape 7.

11 Powell, Edward Cullinan Architects, p10.

12 Architects' Lives: Edward Cullinan, tape 12. For the arts and crafts schooling he received at Cambridge, see tape 2.

13 Architects' Lives: Edward Cullinan, tape 7.

14 Jonathan Hale, Ends Middles Beginnings: Edward Cullinan Architects (Black Dog, 2005) p217.

'In his head Ted was a historian and in his heart an environmentalist, but he loved to share his love of making things.' Cullinan was many things to many people, but even more to those who saw him as a mentor

Equal Measures
Sasha Bhavan

As a mixed-race child brought up in the prejudice-ridden 1960s I found myself as a young adult entering a professional world where there were no people of colour and very few females. Ted accepted me with open arms, encouraged and pushed me, with never a hint of anything except seeing me for who I was – this was like nothing else I had ever experienced. He gave me confidence, showed me his world of architecture and made me believe that I was really as good as anyone. He took me into the privileged white Oxbridge male cocoon (full of lovely people who became firm friends) that was Cullinan's then. Ted showed me and many others that a world without prejudice, where you can be yourself, wherever you come from, was not just possible, it was emancipating.

It was because people of all age, race and class were included that Ted's creed of 'teach by example' was so powerful. He was always the same 'Ted', whether presenting to the Royal Fine Art Commission, the public or students – all were entitled to the same level of explanation and accorded the same respect. His quest was to find an ingenious solution to every problem, so all were welcomed as equal listeners to help challenge and improve the outcome.

I visited the office as a newly-qualified part-II student, following a 'we don't have a job but come and show us your work anyway' invitation. Ted welcomed me with a glass of sherry, booming out 'Come and see this, Mervyn'. His eccentric uncle, Lord Mervyn Horder, had a desk in the corner of the office and, being a publisher, Ted thought he would be interested in my dissertation. I was smitten by Ted's openness, along with the spirit of his cooperative practice and its ethos.

This was the 1980s and Edward Cullinan Architects was a brave place of building and experiment, with ambitious, remarkable people and a culture of sharing. Everyone was a partner; decisions were made by consensus rather than by majority or dictat; pay percentages were agreed together and, exceptionally, no one earned more than three times the lowest paid member.

Right The study for Tama Forest National Park, Japan (1993), envisaged ways to enhance leisure use and halt uncontrolled development. Farnborough Grange School, Hampshire (1987-90), was designed by Cullinan with Sasha Bhavan with two south-facing classroom wings to maximise passive solar gain. Ground level and clerestorey windows are shaded to reduce summer sun but enhance it in winter.

Left The firepit provides the outdoor social focus in the courtyard at Gib Tor Farm.

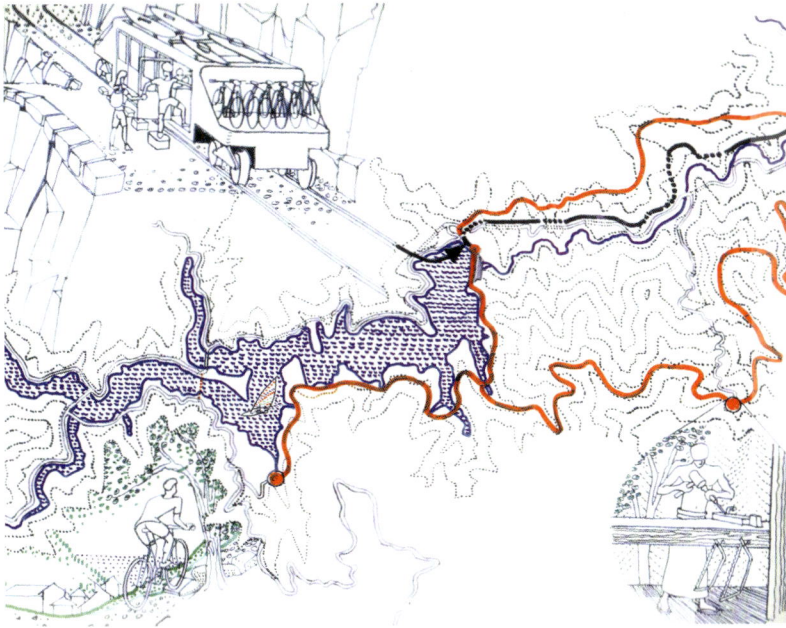

We worked with, not for, clients and with each other and we discussed the ethics of projects before accepting them. We got our hands dirty and built, both to gain an understanding of what we asked of builders and to test the possibilities of materials. This was idealistic, if not idyllic; it demanded huge amounts of dedication, long hours and complete immersion, but we tried and most of the time it worked. It included weekends building our new office on the canal, from which sprang strong and enduring friendships.

Completely fearless and with scant respect for airs and graces, Ted exuded energy and enthusiasm, but his real interest was in designing and building generous places, spaces and objects with people who shared his passion. It was contagious. Ted was the spirit of the practice and its reason for being. And his belief in the practice and all of its partners helped seed many more, including my own.

Working with Ted was a process of exploration. He taught and learned through showing and doing, physically building and feeling materials. He was always excited for the people who would use the building, imagining possibilities for them. Into the buildings were woven spaces and places to sit, meet, work, rest, study, play, party and socialise. Places for action and places for contemplation. He would frame a view out at child height in a primary school, cut a slot through a wall for the chef to see diners, make spaces on stairs and in halls for chance meetings.

Discussions were about proportions of volumes, solid to void, shifting grids, floating roofs, invisible edges and flying corners, capturing shadow and air through layering and overlapping, all intended to enhance the experience of people using the building. Remarkable solutions emerged from exciting symbiotic relationships with clients. Alongside this was a thirst for in-depth discussions on historical precedent, composition and environmental issues. In his head Ted was a historian and in his heart an environmentalist, and above all he had a love of making things. Sharing knowledge and skills to benefit the user was the norm.

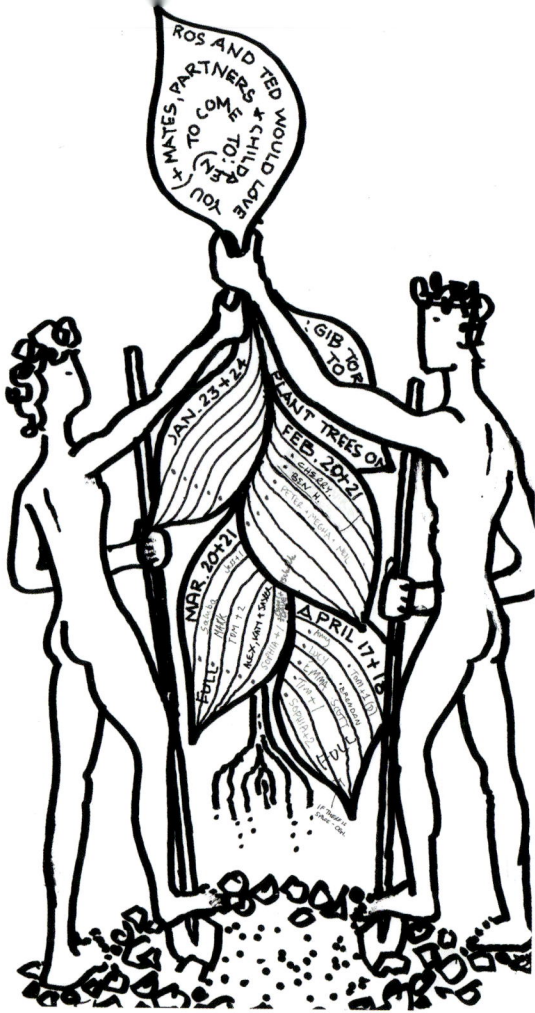

Ted was a non-conformist in a literal sense, and this was reflected in both the unconventional structure of the practice and his facility to imagine unconventional solutions. He was often ahead of his time: promoting workplace wellbeing, the institutional enrichment of happenstance within buildings, and reimagining healthcare buildings. As far back as the 1970s he was introducing concepts in discussions with clients and in his projects which a generation later became mainstream. He collaborated with his equally bold and fearless friend, engineer Max Fordham, to make energy efficient buildings way before any consensus emerged on global warming.

This pioneering mindset together with his bravery and disregard for danger made life with Ted often exciting but sometimes scary. My friend Kate, his daughter, found a letter written 35 years

ago from one of his partners, explaining how, while Ted was fearless and would walk boldly into any situation with a spirit of optimism and adventure, many of his partners were more cautious and concerned to build a more stable future for the cooperative where a regular income could be guaranteed. It is a credit to Ted that he had kept the letter, almost certainly out of respect for the contrary point of view.

It was in this vein of boldness and bravery, verging on foolhardy fearlessness that office trips became bonafide adventures. Together we journeyed to remote and obscure locations to witness the enduring human endeavour of making places of shelter and celebration such as Skellig Michael and Skara Brae. Our trip to Skellig was genuinely dangerous. We crossed a wild and stormy sea in a small open boat with plank seats, no life jackets and no ropes to hold. Almost everyone was violently sick – but not Ted. The sea was white with foam as we passed Little Skellig, covered in guano and humming with puffins and other seabirds. We finally reached the quay at Skellig Michael from where we climbed the steps carved into the rock face up to the highest point – the mist was too thick to see all the way down to the sea below. I was recently reminded of the trip when I attended a seminar for school governors about enhancing self-esteem through staging progressively physically challenging experiences.

As an intuitive teacher, Ted could spot strengths on which to build. He was open to explore solutions with whoever showed interest, cynics included. At public meetings I witnessed him persuade the most hardened, dogmatic people of the benefit of sunlight introduced through a section or the beauty in a composition of old and new. He managed to win them over with an uncompromising honesty and integrity, most

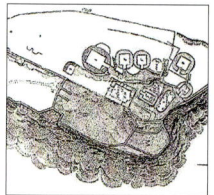

Above Office trips were made to Skellig Michael, a pinnacled crag off the south-west coast of Ireland, celebrated for its birdlife and megalithic and monastic remains. Sasha Bhavan and Cullinan at Gib Tor: 'Ted did not recognise any form of stratification, division, snobbery or affectation; he remained unimpressed by status and conventionally accepted markers of achievement. Instead he searched for our individual genius.'

Left Cullinan's Gib Tor tree-planting invitation for 2010.

Above Work and play were shared activities during the weekend gatherings at Gib Tor farm.

often through his illustrated storytelling. His slowly delivered narrative was accompanied by mesmerising hand drawings on an overhead projector, and both emerged casually, simultaneously and seductively. Few matched his charm as a public performer.

Ted particularly enjoyed and appreciated the company of young people, and this was underpinned by his determination to treat everyone with respect and engage meaningfully with them. Of many cherished memories, one of the most recent was on a freezing March weekend a few years ago, when Ted was in his early 80s, at Gib Tor, the farm he and Roz owned on the North Staffordshire moors. Kate and I produced lashings of hot carb-laden food for a team of architecture students, enticed north by the promise of 'time with Ted to plant trees'.

Working up to their knees in bog and snow, they were thrilled to be together and with Ted, sustained and injected with energy by his enthusiasm and hardiness. The task was to contribute to the planting of the ash ellipse that would provide shelter to the 14-acre farm. Ted never did things by half. The students had been recruited by my son Fergus whose relationship with Ted goes back to when he was a baby. When childcare arrangements fell through and I had to bring him into the office, Ted would fix a highchair to his drawing board and supply Fergus with a fistful of felt pens and talk to him, all the while continuing with his own drawing. Inevitably this moved on to serious discussions about architecture as Fergus grew up.

Ted's booming voice and extended utterance of 'ahhhhh' when drawing were complemented by his uninhibited resonating laugh, which could fill a room with ease. Shared humour was often what kept us going when work was grinding and unrelenting – it wasn't all roses and sunshine – and Ted expected his partners to engage with optimism and contribute wholeheartedly to his vision. You needed to stick with him.

Looking back, as Mary Beard suggests in 'Women & Power', 'helps us to look harder at ourselves, and to understand better how we have learned to think as we do'. I learned much from Ted, his unrelenting contribution as a humanist, respect for all people as equals, and a magical maker of place. At the end of his life Kate set aside Wednesday evenings to invite friends to dinner with Ted and Roz. My final memory, from a couple of weeks before he died, is of Ted organising his grandchildren and my daughter to race his wheelchair up and down Kate's living room. A week before he died, he took delivery of an electric trike: ever the optimist.

Drawing was central
to Ted Cullinan's whole being,
both as a way to communicate
and as a creative design tool,
and analysis of his technique
reveals much about his approach
to architecture and life

Drawing from Ted
Roddy Langmuir

Ted Cullinan enjoyed drawing above all else.
It was an outlet for his irresistible, creative spirit,
and the part of the day job that he loved to take
home with him. He would draw on postcards
and luggage labels, on restaurant napkins, on the
body panels of a white Land Rover in the Sahara –
in fact wherever and whenever he could. He
always 'dressed' with a black felt-tip pen in his
jacket pocket, armed to explain an idea or to
sketch out an acutely observed caricature during
a conversation. Talk led inevitably to drawing.
He loved the creative process of designing
through drawing so much that if a client rejected
his first proposal, rather than dig in and defend it,
he would grasp the opportunity to recompose it.

As a young man Ted had pondered a career as an
illustrator but he was encouraged by his mother
and uncle to turn an obvious natural ability
towards the study of architecture. His freehand
drawing of the basilica of San Miniato al Monte,
made in situ on a field trip in his first year of
study at Cambridge, demonstrates an ease with
spatial composition and an understanding of how
to balance the weight of a drawing so as not to let
the detail take over.

I joined the practice as a young architect in 1988
and was immediately sucked into Ted's beguiling
use of the sketch to float a new proposition during
a design conversation. Architects will often fumble
with words when trying to describe an architectural
idea, whereas a sketch can force the conversation
to advance, laying the idea bare on the table. My
feeling is that Ted believed a drawing brought
with it the commitment to give an idea physical
expression, line and space denying the author a
hiding place behind jargon and metaphor.

Along with this came the importance he attached
to open criticism. If Ted was unsure about his
drawing but nevertheless saw some promise in it,
he needed affirmation and would try to persuade
you to like it. If such encouragement wasn't
forthcoming he would tout it around the office
looking for support or critique to help move the
design forward. Materials were always at the
forefront of his mind – when you committed to a
sketch his first question was 'what is it made of?'

Above Caricature of fellow
architect Frank Duffy as
'Plucky Ducky'.

Left Cullinan's drawing of
his uncle Mervyn (Baron
Horder) rescuing him from
the lily pond at Ashford
Chase in Hampshire, where
Ted would later build the
Horder house.

Opposite The interior view
of the Romanesque basilica
of San Miniato al Monte in
Florence was drawn in situ
by Cullinan in 1952 while he
was a student at Cambridge
University.

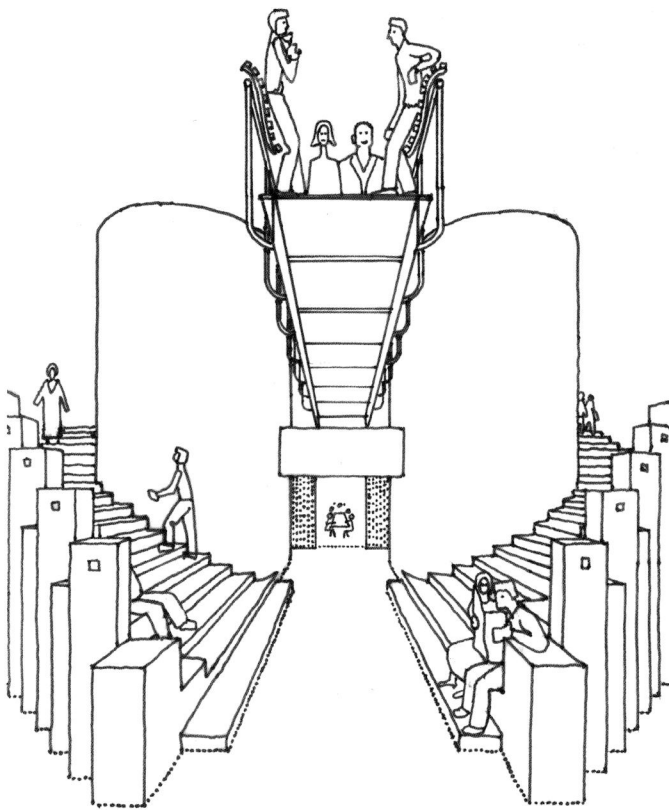

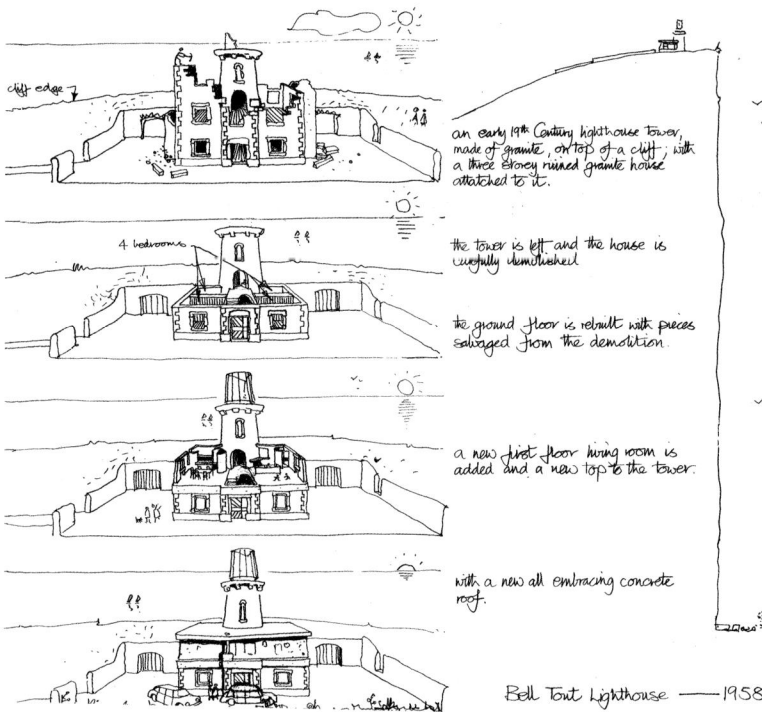

cliff edge

an early 19th Century lighthouse tower, made of granite, on top of a cliff; with a three storey ruined granite house attached to it.

4 bedrooms

the tower is left and the house is carefully demolished

the ground floor is rebuilt with pieces salvaged from the demolition.

a new first floor living room is added and a new top to the tower.

with a new all embracing concrete roof.

Bell Tout Lighthouse —— 1958

Every project had a drawn narrative that took you from an analysis of the context through a series of illustrated steps towards an outcome that, by this time, looked inevitable and – Ted hoped – irresistible. The quality of these diagrams depended as much on what was left out as in what they included. Clarity of thought required clarity of drawing, edited of superfluous detail.

Ted would draw slowly and deliberately, usually with the largest pen available, using a clamp-like grip with fingers, wrist and elbow all held stiffly from the shoulder. This gave him time to consider the drawing as he drew, and helped induce a natural tremor that gave his sketched lines an ambiguity that allowed adjustments to be made on the run. The fat pen could also be used to quell any fledgling 'opposition' that had been tentatively scratched in with a thin Rotring 0.18 pen in the hands of a young architect, by drawing right across it as though the alternative proposition had not even been noticed. Ted always encouraged others in the team to draw their ideas, nevertheless, because he couldn't bear critique without the demonstration of a positive alternative arising from it. For this reason he often sought out younger, more pliable minds to work with who might be less constrained by technical knowledge. If you wanted to shift him you needed to plant the seed, face the initial resistance, and wait. A day or two later he might seek you out to report back with a new enthusiasm for the idea he'd dismissed, and a sketch showing how he'd found a way to re-balance the whole to accommodate it.

Ted was passionate too about the form of words that went alongside the drawings, whether in a sketch for a client, in a competition bid, or in a planning statement. Words were tuned to express ideas clearly and simply, often with an almost

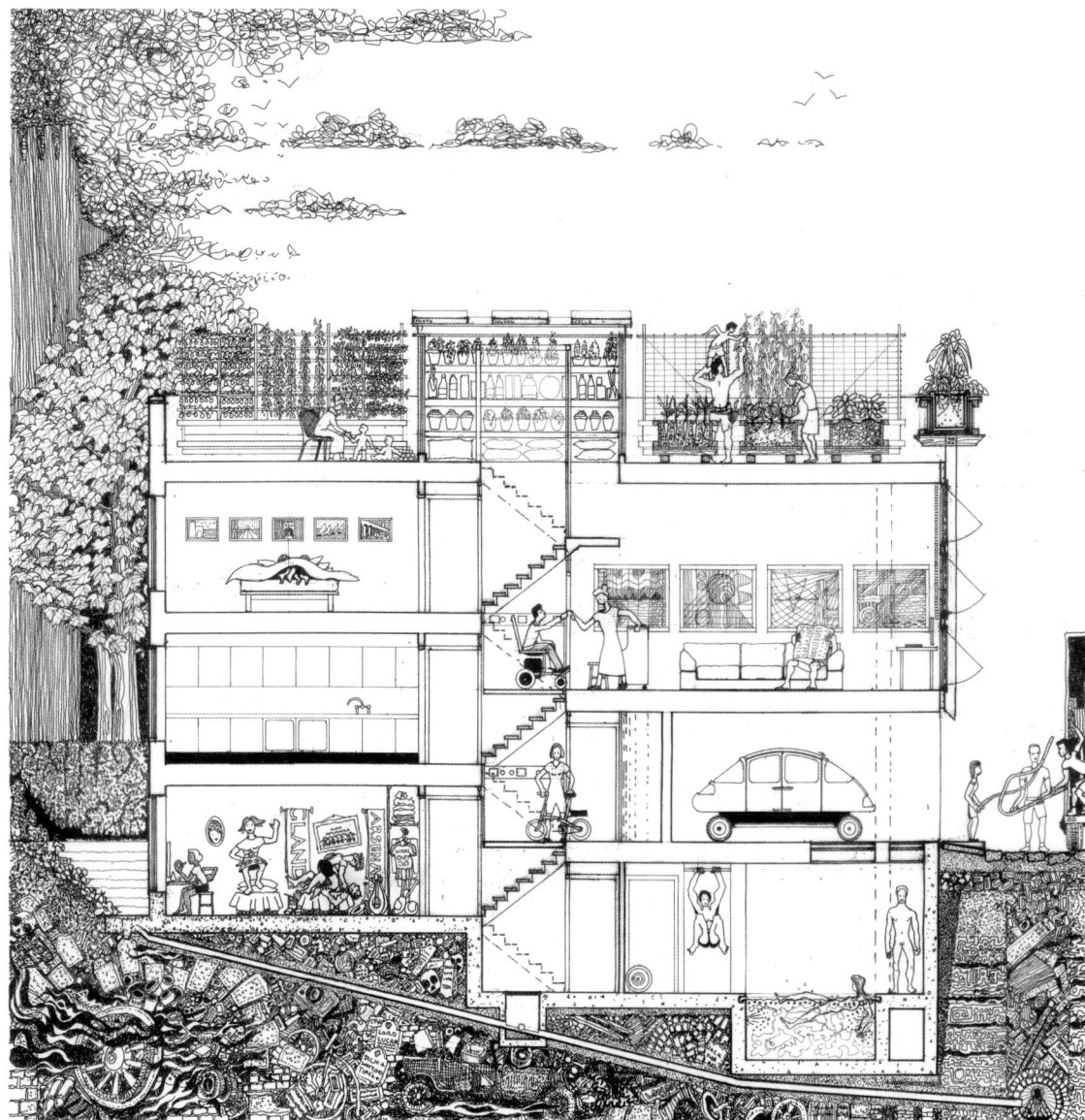

Right 'Twenty-first Century Townhouse' was exhibited in memory of Cullinan at the 2020 Royal Academy Summer Show, held online and in winter.

Opposite More than simply circulation spaces in the Nationwide's Uplands Conference & Training Centre at High Wycombe. Diagram describing stages in the reconstruction of Belle Tout lighthouse.

biblical cadence. And by describing how the building should be made, Ted allowed everyone to understand that the architecture was layered, and the expressive result of a series of physical steps that derived from its making.

Ted practiced continuous consultation with clients long before it had a name, and he would readily take the opportunity to recompose schemes to include feedback. He refered to this iterative way of working as 'hypothesis and test', and frequently made changes with a large indelible marker directly on the presentation drawings in front of a client. He was never precious about drawings per se, and his face would light up in surprise and a child-like innocence when anyone asked to keep them – giving away drawings was an act of generosity that won Ted many advocates.

Ted began each project by laboriously drawing out a grid of the site, a sort of meditative process akin to digging his garden, buying valuable thinking time as he sketched ideas in the margins. He

57

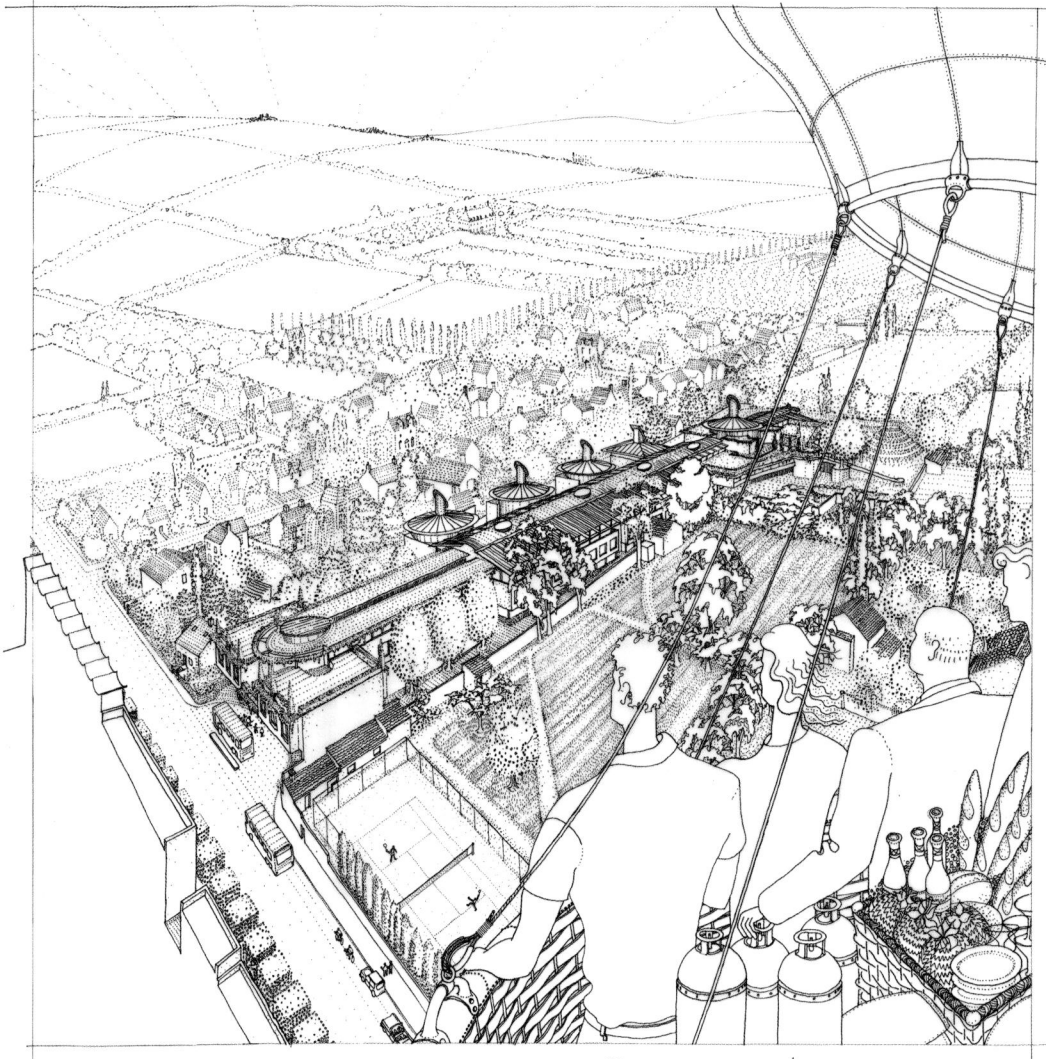

Left Aerial presentation drawing for Lagny school competition.

Below Drawing promoting the new apartments built as part of the practice's studio development on Baldwin Terrace in Islington.

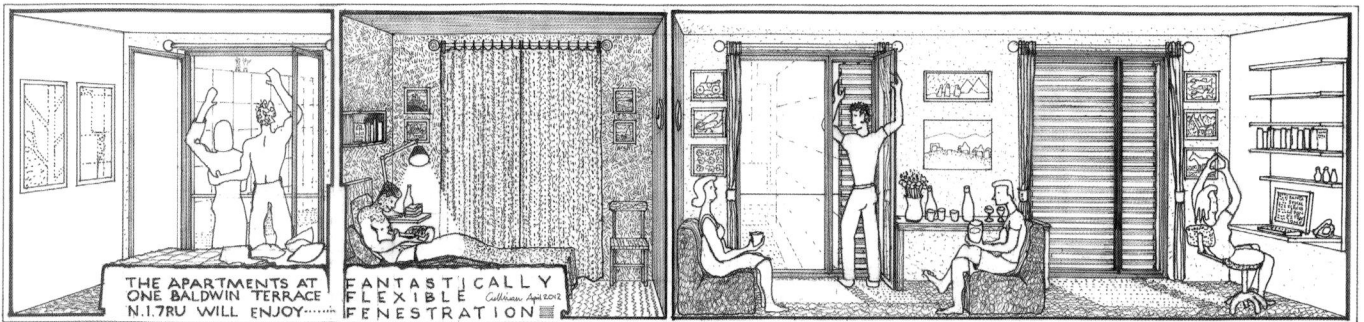

THE APARTMENTS AT ONE BALDWIN TERRACE N.1.7RU WILL ENJOY...... FANTASTICALLY FLEXIBLE FENESTRATION

would then draw out a full scheme in plan, section and elevation, acknowledging faults along the way, but getting to the end of that iteration of the design to learn everything he could, before abandoning it and moving on to begin again with a new idea. One step back to go two steps forward.

Ted never drew anything without knowing what it was made of and how it should be built, a discipline rooted in his early experience of self-building houses in California and later back in England. The resulting architecture invariably integrated an expressive constructional logic, layering materials to weather naturally, celebrating the earth and sky with grounded walls and flying eaves, and always developing the whole and the detail simultaneously. He would compose buildings as narrative journeys, as conversations with their contexts, and often imagined complete social settings which he drew out beautifully to describe the purpose of a design.

Ted used the colours available to him in the classic, four-pack Staedtler Lumocolor permanent marker set: red, blue, green and black. This was partly for pragmatic reasons – they worked well on trace and overhead projection film alike – but they also held a hidden code of a simplified world: black was usually structure, red was secondary material (often timber), green was of course nature, landscape and green roofs, and blue was both water and glass. These colours also seemed to help Ted to both envisage and communicate his ideas about architectural composition, where buildings were anchored to the earth, with floating wings and eaves that energised a relationship with the sky – coloured to emphasise their different compositional roles.

A good diagram can condense a complex design proposal down to its essence, expressing its

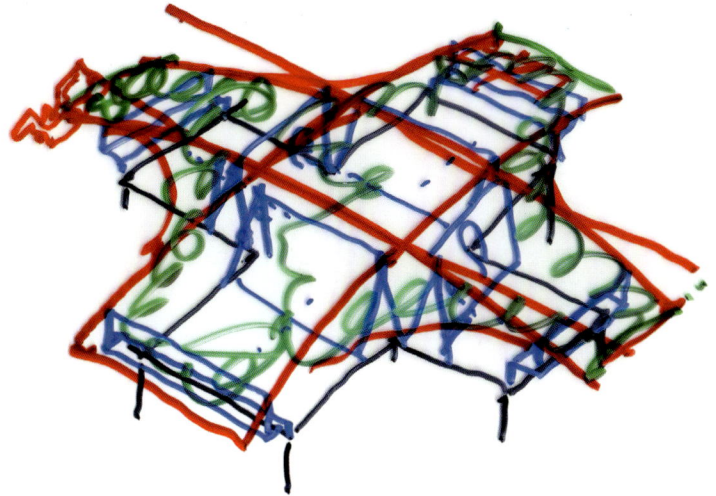

purpose, form and appearance with great clarity. In simple stages, Ted would build up a project from the existing context in a series of layers, beginning with a key vista or the facades of important neighbouring buildings, then gateway transitions would appear, massive walls, props and stick beams, roof planes and elevations, and finally the whole composition would be revealed, addressing the context. But there was more to Ted's drawings and, as if to remind us that buildings are always made for people, they would often feature specific individuals, the building user or passers-by such as a man with a child on his shoulders or an elderly couple arm-in-arm.

Ted's teaching forays in the United States led him to pre-prepare lectures in which he analysed classic works by Le Corbusier, Frank Lloyd Wright

Above Barge Arm barge in Gloucester Docks.

Top Four-colour marker pen sketch of Westminster Lodge.

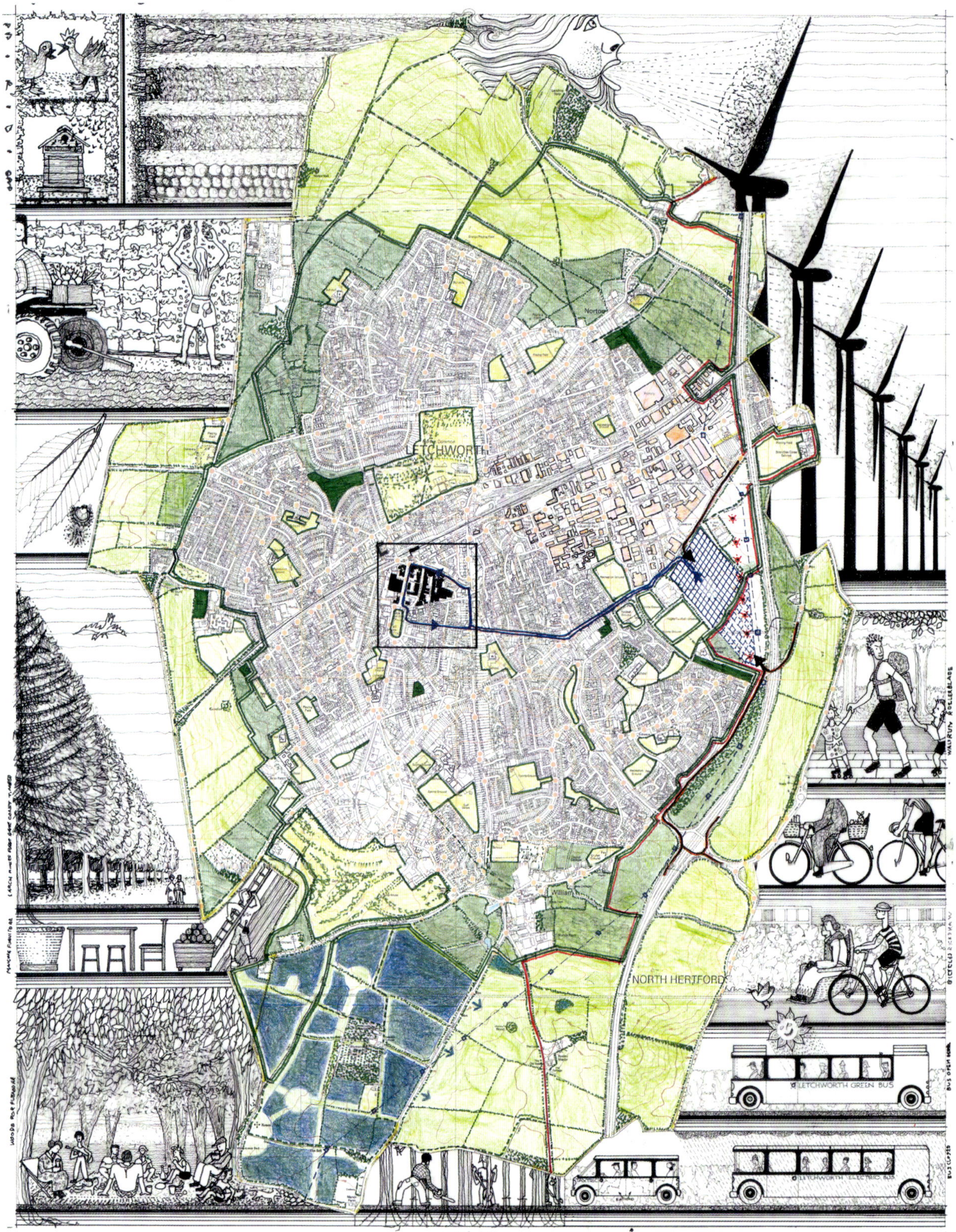

LETCHWORTH

Nortons

NORTH HERTFORD

LETCHWORTH GREEN BUS

LETCHWORTH ELECTRIC BUS

60

the map on this page is 1 : 10,000

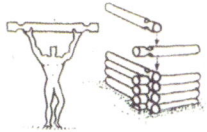

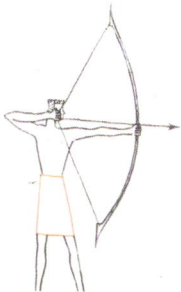

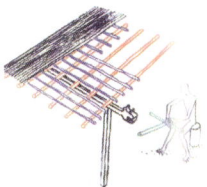

and others. By story-boarding their key elements in three dimensions his systematic decoding of the architectural compositions made them comprehensible to his audience. As Ted came to employ this technique to describe the design work of the practice, the drawings became more than mere diagrams, explaining the how and the why in a step-by-step manner reminiscent of the assembly instructions for a model kit.

History was in Ted's bones, and he loved to speculate on extraordinary connections across continents and cultures. He drew conviction from the inevitability of continuous change, believing the responsibility of the architect was to design buildings that make connections between the past and future context. He described the architect's role with the phrase 'continuers of history'. He had a particular affinity with ancient cultures, with their connectedness to the sun, to the land and to natural rhythms. Ted's drawings reflect this cosmos; the earth is moulded for shelter, it teems with life, fields are cleared of stones gathered into protective walls, throwaway timber thinnings become valuable building structures, roofs reach for the daylight, and all elements of the landscape and built form are arranged in homage to the omnipresent sun, depicted as a mandala. Our geography and our social history are never separated from the narrative.

As an intuitive communicator Ted mastered how to turn the analysis of design into a theatrical performance. By drawing live on stage his lectures built up a proposal step-by-step, switching easily between plan, section and three dimensions, and peppered with tangential anecdotes to enrich context and recount his relationships with clients and builders. He knew he possessed a powerful tool at his fingertips, one he harnessed in the service of the greatest skill

required of any architect who wants to build: the power of persuasion.

Ted's drawings are manifestations of the man. Brimming with optimism, they create settings that tell stories, inviting the viewer into the narrative. They celebrate the sun and the wind, people enjoying nature or the social life of the street. Cars are often shown topless to reveal a whole family together. People too are often topless or fully naked, and each is drawn as an individual character. The heroes in Ted's drawings are the cycle couriers, the windsurfers, the hot-air balloonists and the builders. He saw no point in drawing at all without imagining a full cast of actors, a social context and a bigger idea about the purpose of every project. Ted would scoff at typical architectural drawings that reduced the human form to stylised lollipop heads on wedge shapes – this seemed to him a complete denial of the primary purpose of architecture – to respond to our humanity.

what
Ted
made

Cullinan's first houses
made the act of their construction
and the nature of their inhabitation
into an architectural aesthetic
of clarity and wit. They set
a direction for later work
not only by his own studio,
but also by many of his students

The Aesthetics
of Buildability
Peter Clegg

All great buildings have stories to tell. They speak about why they are the way they are – and about the people, the society and the time they represent, and about the preoccupations of their designers. Ted's buildings were always very explicit about their origins, but they came to life even more vividly when he helped with the narrative. And it was Ted talking about buildings that was one of the most significant influences on my student generation in the late 1960s.

Richard Feilden and I started our architectural careers at Cambridge in 1969 during an era when it was fashionable to challenge everything and conventions were there to be overturned. Many of us felt that we needed to reinvent our profession – rethinking our role and value in society – and we were excited by the idea of reconnecting the physical act of building with the conceptual discourse of architecture. In the first lecture I remember by Ted he told the stories of the projects he built himself – the Marvin house in California, the Horder house in Hampshire and his family home in Camden. He brought with him the revolutionary garb of black jeans and black tee-shirt, the whiff of the California beat generation, James Dean and classic Ford V8 pickups, and the idea that one might be able to craft a new form of practice around both designing and building.

There is clarity and innovation, a sense of joy, but also a sense of purpose about the two first houses that Ted built. Sadly neither still exists, but from his recorded talks about them you can trace the direction of most of the next 60 years of his architecture, and the key influences that established his unique career.

The Marvin house, built at Stinson Beach just north of San Francisco, reveals the influences of his tutor Peter Smithson and Rudolf Schindler (whose work Ted knew from Esther McCoy's 1960 exhibition 'Five California Architects') in the delight of using materials in a raw and unprocessed state, and the enjoyment of the marks of construction. There is also more than a nod to Louis Kahn in the duality of the 'servant' and 'served' spaces in the plan.

Marvin house (1958-60)
Built over many weekends by Cullinan and his client, medical student Stephen Marvin, the house occupied a sloping site overlooking Stinson Beach, California. For Cullinan, the Marvin and Horder houses 'react to their specific sites and use the climate, rearranging the spaces within them from those normally associated with houses, they are concerned with the method of their realisation, and they use simple but expressive details – these ideas have interested me ever since'.

a. = dressing room (
b. = dressing room (
    with a double s
    between them
c. = w.c. and visitors
d. = entrance.
e. = study.
f. = kitchen

the hillside slopes up this way

a long gallery of rough Californian redwood, contains a bed, a hearth for sitting around and a table to eat at.

the light in the gallery is warm and ruddy and comes through windows that are like chinks in its wooden sides.

beside the gallery, a row of service rooms

the service rooms are white and brightly lit from above.

and later they will add a greenhouse.

and a guest house going on down the hillside.

and a drive goes straight up the hill like the roads do in San Francisco.

path road.

Marvin House, California – 1960

But Ted spoke and wrote about the Marvin house as a celebration of the act of living – the long gallery with a bed at one end, a dining area at the other and a central hearth with couches built in the centre. The long gallery was made out of two layers of Californian redwood; the service spaces were concrete blocks; the gallery had fixed glazing but sliding sections of wall; and the concrete boxes of the 'servant' spaces were rooflit but virtually windowless. The key aspects of interpenetrating forms, contrasting materials and a delight in daylight became lasting characteristics of Cullinan's work. What impressed us most as students however was the idea that as an architect you could spend a year building a house, with your client helping out part-time, all the while learning from the process. For us it suggested a totally new way of thinking about our professional role.

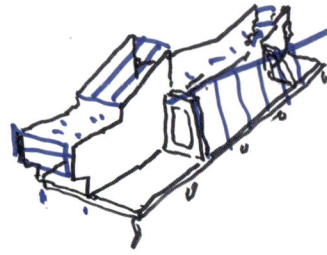

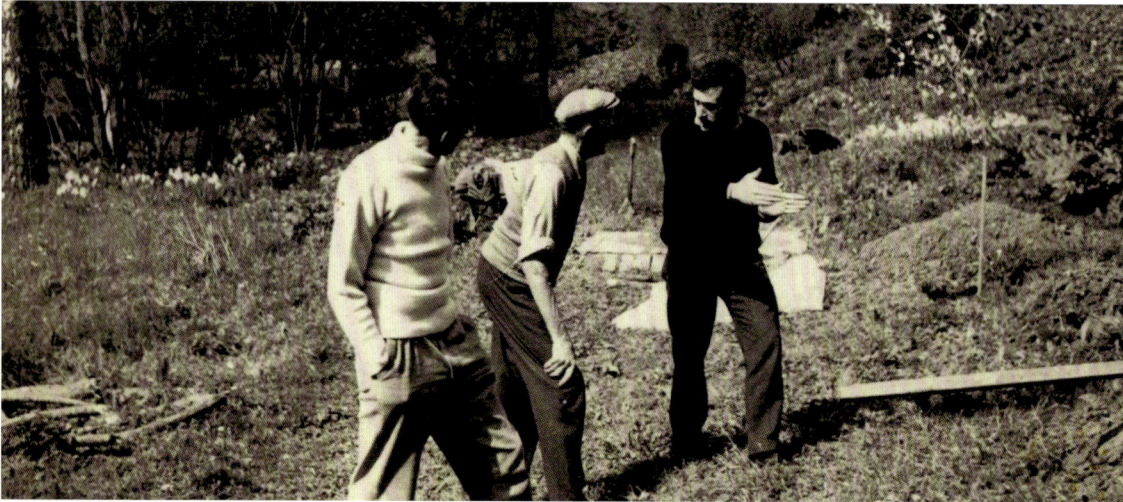

Horder house (1958-60)
Built at the edge of a wooded bank on the Horder estate near Petersfield in Hampshire, the house comprised a main living space, set behind a sloping glazed plane that oversailed the doors at each end. Sleeping areas were on 'enlarged window cills' that cantilevered from each end.

Ted built the Horder house for his uncle Mervyn in Hampshire with the help of Max Moodie and Horace Knight, a 75-year-old gardener, and like the Marvin house the building tells the story of its assembly. Concrete post foundations support precast beams and the floor (all of which were carried down to the site). Triangular concrete A-frames were then cast on the flat floor and hoisted into place – the tilt-up cast concrete that Ted had learned from his American west coast experience. Referencing Amish barn-raising, Ted brought the story to life with sheer delight in the process of building as a social activity. The frames formed the principle structure, supporting a twisted, sloping roof that ran the length of the building, and propped against this was a patent-glazed screen (which apparently worked far too well as a passive solar collector). The bedroom spaces were cantilevered out at each end of the long gallery.

The key drivers of Cullinan's later architecture are all here. He goes back to the expressionist strands of modernism, and enjoys breaking away from the rigid conformity that had come to characterise modern architecture by the 1960s. Building elements oversail or interpenetrate, roofs are allowed to slope once again, and there is a playfulness and above all a humanity which comes from the sheer joy in the process of building. Even without Ted's eloquent narrative the building exudes what he came to describe as the 'aesthetics of buildability'. This went beyond conventional tectonic expressionism, where all the joints are explicit, to a delight in the simple ordinariness of materials.

But most important of all for us as students was the way he told the stories, with felt tip drawings on an old fashioned overhead projector. The longer lectures ended up with rolls of transparent acetate decorated with colourful sketches rolling out across the floor. The slow, literally drawn-out process – punctuated by 'aaaahhs' for thinking time – engaged us with the development of Ted's ideas. We were invited in to his design process, and felt part of the story.

To build became a right of passage for the class of '69 at Cambridge. Richard and I both went off and built or rebuilt houses for ourselves before setting up our own kind of architectural practice alongside our own building company. This meant we had to operate outside the umbrella of the RIBA which didn't allow such things. But being on the fringe of the profession – as Ted certainly was – became an important part of the role we defined for ourselves. We were inspired too by the inclusive way he ran his practice, and established relationships with his clients that broke through conventional professional boundaries.

Telling stories about buildings was not just a means of presentation for Ted, but part of his design method. He would engage clients in the process by drawing the building in front of them – involving them in his thought processes and inviting them to be collaborators – though he was clearly in charge of the pen. He advocated the 'jump in and splash around' school of design, where you seized an idea and ran with it until it either came to life or withered away, in which case you started over again.

But there were personal preoccupations that ran right through his work. What started out with the Horder and Marvin houses as explorations of open and enclosed forms, oversailing and interpenetrating spaces, re-emerged time and time again over the next 50 years. His love of concrete and timber – heavy and light, solid and framed – stayed with him and was constantly reinterpreted. And he was always eager to learn, even from his own misjudgements – Ted himself was the first to acknowledge the problem of overglazing the Horder house, and he spent much of the next 50 years looking at ever more sophisticated ways of dealing with the layering of shading and designing for natural ventilation.

Unsurprisingly perhaps, the first works of many architects can be gauche, often harking back to previous generations as they find their feet. But Ted – like my other tutorial hero Charles Moore, who first built in California at about the same time – was producing work that was refreshingly original from the start. Significantly, he wasn't tempted to fill it with too many ideas, helped perhaps by the constraints of budget and buildability. Both Cullinan and Moore went on to produce architecture that was far more expressive, and sometimes the diet could become too rich – as in Moore's case when he plumbed the depths of post-modernism and eclecticism, which Ted abhorred. But both were inspirational and influential educators at the

beginning of their careers at a time when architecture had lost touch with people and the natural world. Ted's tutorial skills stayed with him throughout his life and his stories never ceased to educate and delight.

I was privileged to be taught by Ted at the beginning of my career and then to teach with him towards the end of his. For several years we would review work at Piers Taylor's Studio in the Woods summer schools, where the students created challenging sculptural installations from timber cut from the surrounding trees. Ted's critical process was to tell stories based on what he saw in the structures, to read the tectonics and – even as a less agile octogenarian – to insist on

clambering inside to examine them close up. He would insist on examining every perspective, and pulling him out from beneath the timber structures became something of a ritual. In the evening Ted would produce a talk, drawing from memory (by now on a digital screen rather than an overhead projector) on what he had seen and how it had been built, widely referencing history, philosophy and most importantly sensuousness. Ted's narrative drawings became prized mementos – and I treasure one that Piers gave me of the Camden Mews house, which Ted must have drawn for hundreds of audiences all over the world. It serves as a constant reminder of a very human story about building a life, a family, a home, as well as an architectural practice.

The directness of Cullinan's approach to making buildings that work well and can be understood represents a substantive and meaningful legacy for contemporary architecture

Sensible Buildings
Simon Henley

I first heard Ted Cullinan speak at the University of Liverpool in the late 1980s, when he came to tell us about the visitor centre at Fountains Abbey. Armed with a role of acetate, an assortment of felt-tip pens and an overhead projector, he told the story of Studley Royal and Fountains Abbey, of their geography and history, the buildings and ruins, paths and vistas, and the design of the new centre.

I recently reread his description of his four walks in the landscape of Fountains Abbey. It reminded me of the fell walker Alfred Wainwright's books. Using words and drawings, Cullinan surveys the land and its landmarks. He befriends the place. He introduces the reader to the landscape, much like he did us in Liverpool more than 30 years ago. No slides, just one extraordinarily long drawing and a story. He drew and he talked about topography, geometry and perspective, and about how in the landscape things can appear and disappear. He spoke about the legacies of the eighteenth and nineteenth centuries, of the work of William Aislabie and William Burges, and of the Cullinan practice's proposed new approach to the estate, and placement and composition of the visitor centre. The courtyard form of the new building holds the landscape at bay but also, in framing the abbey, signals its expansiveness. We understood. In the end the design seemed inevitable. It felt like any one of us would have reached the same conclusion. Cullinan's lecture introduced us to the idea that an architect might speak – think, draw, make and talk – fluently about their work, and that the work itself did not seek to obfuscate but to explain, to make sense of itself and its situation.

About four years earlier, in December 1984, I had opened my first copy of the Architectural Review, which was entirely dedicated to James Stirling's Neue Staatsgalerie in Stuttgart. Just 17 and in my final year at school, I had no idea about the significance of the Stuttgart building or the unbuilt museums in Düsseldorf and Cologne. I had a copy of Kenneth Frampton's 'Modern Architecture: A Critical History' but had so far only dipped into it. So the AR was my window into this new world. The January 1985

Calthorpe Park School, Fleet (1981-83)
The first of five school projects in Hampshire, rather than demolition, the 1960s system-built blocks were reglazed and insulated and an 'umbrella' metal roof with solar shading added.

Left Arrival courtyard at Fountains Abbey visitor centre.

issue was about the Netherlands and included projects by Aldo van Eyck, Theo Bosch and Herman Hertzberger. February's was called 'Working with the Past' and there, in among an eclectic list of projects, were two school buildings by Ted Cullinan. The first of these adapted a pair of nineteenth-century infirmary buildings to create an art block. The other was to modernise a 1960s system-built school. Perhaps it was a coincidence – Stirling, van Eyck, Bosch, Herzberger and Cullinan – but these architects and their projects were seared in my memory, not least Cullinan's Calthorpe Park School in Fleet, which was by comparison a modest commission. The original school – described at the time by critic Colin Davis as 'a loose composition of two- and three-storey, box-like buildings with steel frames, flat roofs, flat facades and too much glass' – was only 20 years old but in a poor state and in need of attention.

We tend to think that renovation lacks the clarity that comes with a new piece of architecture, but Calthorpe is clear and reveals Cullinan's personality as an architect. He takes something generic and ill-suited to the climate and transforms it into something that responds well to its situation. He surrounds the system-designed two- and three-storey science building with a fine steel colonnade which props up the 1.2-metre-wide eaves of the new roof and beneath, on the intermediate floors, above each window, a 'sun/rain-breaker' made with a sheet of blue corrugated plastic. The additions shelter the facades from the sun and rain, improving the internal environment by reducing solar gain and increasing the lifespan of the building by protecting the lightweight and otherwise vulnerable facades from the elements. The structure also introduces a liminal space that mediates between inside and outside where one can take shelter or find a place to sit. It is quite literally attractive. And all of this is done with an economy of means – fine structural sections and thin sheets of material. This architecture of adaptation simply addresses the questions asked of it and in doing so imprints the idea of climate onto the building with a new and highly expressive physiognomy.

This logic is carried through to the new building, designed concurrently for the school, but also to the timber-clad facades of the naturally-ventilated Chilworth Park Research Centre (1990) and Farnborough Grange Junior School (1990) which both share an environmental expression and material lightness with Calthorpe Park School. Realising how the practice responded to this abstract structure is to understand that the sun shines, that it rains and occasionally snows. The alterations made to Calthorpe made these phenomena tangible and beautiful.

To see where this clarity and fluency stems from, and how, when and where Cullinan developed his architectural language, it's helpful to return to his earliest works: the Horder house in Hampshire (1959), the Marvin house in California (1959) and Camden Mews in London (1963).

The Horder house was built on a south-facing bank framed by trees adjacent to a stream. Cullinan describes its site, design and construction in a series of annotated sketches:

ten posts were driven into the ground, onto which two beams are placed and a concrete platform cast to span between the beams. The platform is sheltered by a wall to the north. A 'sleeping cabin' is created at each end, enclosed by a wall to the south, with the gable between the two walls glazed – one facing east, the other west. A beam then spans between the two cabins and rests on two heavy door frames. Monopitch and shallow hyperbolic paraboloid roofs shelter the interiors. Finally, the enclosure is completed by a full-height screen of patent glazing which spans between platform and beam. The glass is inclined towards the sky and extended beyond the two doors that delimit the interior. Both of these design decisions isolate the glass wall from the other parts of the building. While today we might regard this as technically problematic it undoubtedly highlights the instrumental dimension of the wall.

In the case of the Marvin house a wall of cellular spaces serves a similar 'long gallery to live in, to eat in and to sleep in'. But unlike Louis Kahn's

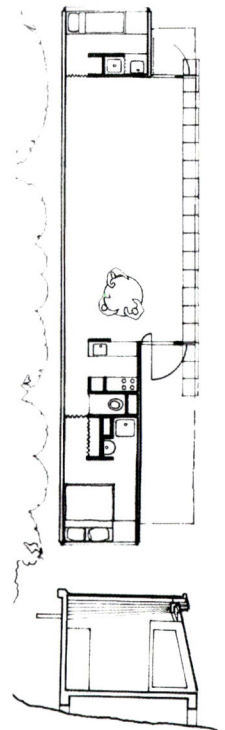

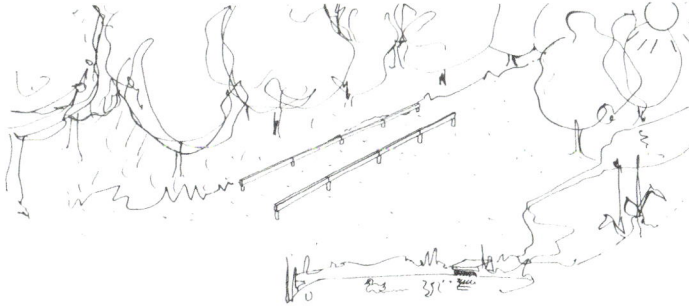

a tree covered bank, facing South,
a patch of grass and a stream,

sink ten posts into the ground and
place two precast beams on top of them.

form a precast platform between the beams
and build a long wall down the North side

A · double bed
B · two bunk beds
C · showers
D · kitchen
E · studio / living room

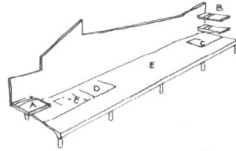

erect two strong doorframes with a beam
to join them, and two short walls on the
South side.

bolt on the windows and fix on the roof.

Horder House — 1959

Horder house (1958-60)

Combining both standard and bespoke elements, the house sits on a precast concrete platform resting on two precast beams on ten concrete-filled pipes. Two A-frame door frames were cast horizontally and tilted up (like Rudolf Schindler's own Kings Road house) to provide cross-bracing for the masonry walls, door frames, and a beam against which the oversailing screen of patent glazing leans.

Marvin house (1958-60)

Exterior and interior views and sketch plan showing the 'green rooms' for cooking, washing and storage, which open to the long living, eating and sleeping space.

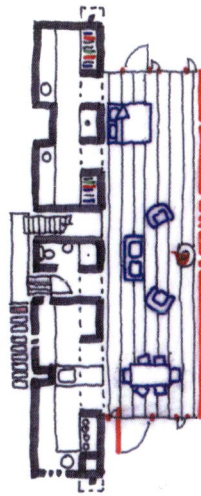

largely autonomous compositions this is explicitly outward facing. As he did for the Horder house Cullinan built a platform, and described the cells for cooking, washing and storage as 'green rooms.' In other words the platform is a stage and the house a theatre; to live here is to inhabit a stage above a landscape that it surveys. Squint at the plan and the blockwork cells form a larger single diaphragm wall which extends across the contours of the land. The materially sparse and dimensionally diminutive living room, it transpires, is 'within' the landscape. Only the space inside the diaphragm wall is removed from the landscape. The diaphragm wall fulfils a similar propositional role as the patent-glazed screen in the Horder house.

Camden Mews, the third in the trilogy of early houses, was also self-built, but for Cullinan's own occupation in north London. The parti orientates the house away from the mews towards the south west, points it at the sun and turns its back on the cold north-east winds, and dispenses with the convention of a front facing the street and a back facing the garden. While it remains in the city, the house is no longer beholden to the city and any decorum that demands. Instead it is intimately associated with the elements, and more immediately a garden that occupies the southern half of the plot.

While the situation is evidently not rural, the house has been abstracted from its urban context. Relieved of any formality and conventional notions of privacy, this relatively primitive structure sheltered the Cullinan family in magical proximity to the natural world. The architecture charges the potential between a finite interior and a similarly finite exterior in the other half of the plot. Compare it with Tadao Ando's Nakayama House (1985), which also bisects the plot to create an interior in one half and an exterior in the other. He does this by placing a concrete frame around both halves, separating them with a plane of glass. But whereas Ando thereby excludes nature, Cullinan welcomes it, and while the dimensions of the mews plot remain finite, he appreciates the countless phenomena we can perceive in the natural world.

The Cullinan house extends the scope of the architect who, living in the natural world, must build in it, and with that acknowledge that this takes time. The act of building would determine the physical properties of the building. The first robust acts of construction that unfold – laying the two-storey brick wall on the north boundary, casting the concrete frame that bisects the site, and erecting a roof that bridges between the two – all serve to shelter the later, finer and more vulnerable activities.

This trilogy of houses is vernacular, and all are designed to be made by hand. The dimensions and therefore the proportions of space depend on the availability of things. Cullinan's

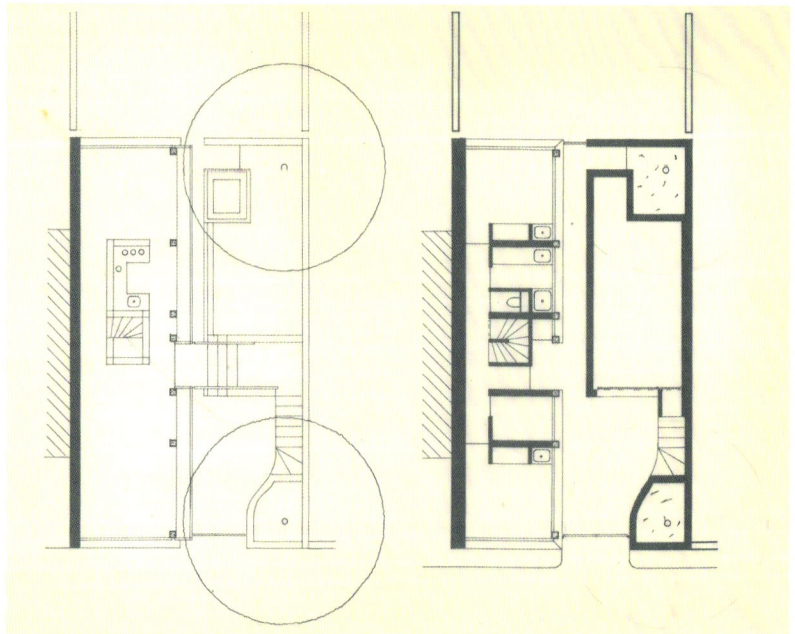

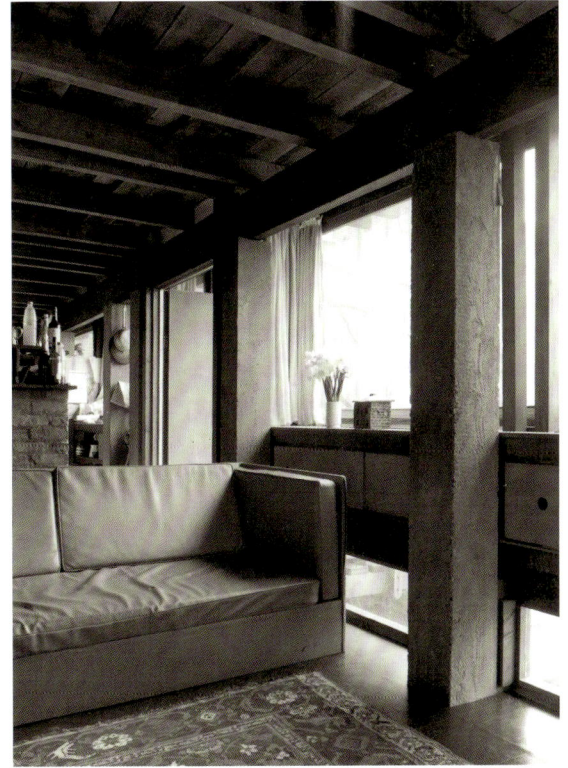

62 Camden Mews (1963-64)

Cullinan's own self-built house is set perpendicular to the mews to take advantage of the south-westerly orientation. The masonry ground floor of bedrooms and bathroom supports an open upper family space, entered via a bridge from the adjacent garage roof garden. The solid/void site parti is echoed in Tadao Ando's 1985 Nakayama House (below).

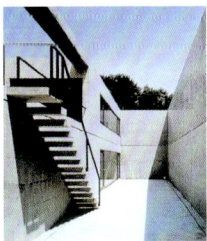

architectural references are less formal than Ando's, and the geometries less complex. Ando removes the temporal dimension of construction, conflating the designed and completed architecture with the use of concrete, which is homogeneous and ideal – there is no beginning, middle and end. Whereas Cullinan elaborates on the sequential nature of building, the relativity of elements and configuration of the detail. He doesn't set the body apart from the architecture but depends on his human strength to make it and it reciprocates by inviting the human body to inhabit it.

The brickwork and blockwork, the concrete frames and platforms, and the timber joinery used to make these three houses all comprise elementary materials, derived essentially from the earth. The spatial compositions and configurations are elementary too, each dependent on the simplest drawn gesture – the making of a line. In reality this translates into a constructed threshold or liminal space between inside and outside, mediating between and so enriching the otherwise absolute 'interior' and 'exterior'. All three houses share a basic anatomy, with a linear plan and orientation of their internal space towards a primary aspect. It is as if to build is to draw a line between inside and outside, so the architecture draws our attention to nature – like an ornithologist in a hide. By reimagining architecture as a simple binary system, Cullinan could work out what really mattered, and how this could be reflected in his work and shared with his collaborators. In time the topological configurations of his buildings would become more complex and the liminality expressed in other ways in response to different circumstances and more demanding spatial programmes.

a cross section that has in it:
A: working/sitting/concentrating strip.
B: storage and entrances related to A.
C: a walking **strip** down the building
D: carparking
E: storage and heating and elec. services etc.

the sun can enter from either side so the section can face any way,

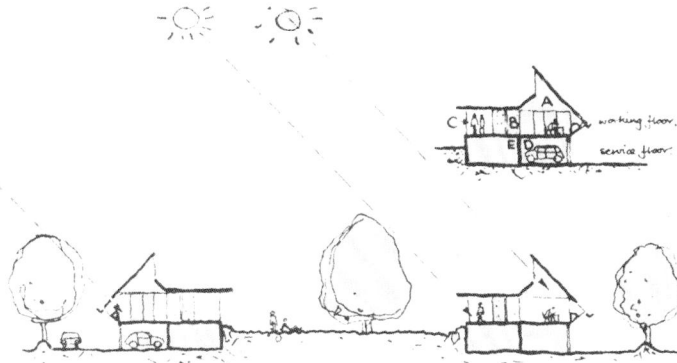

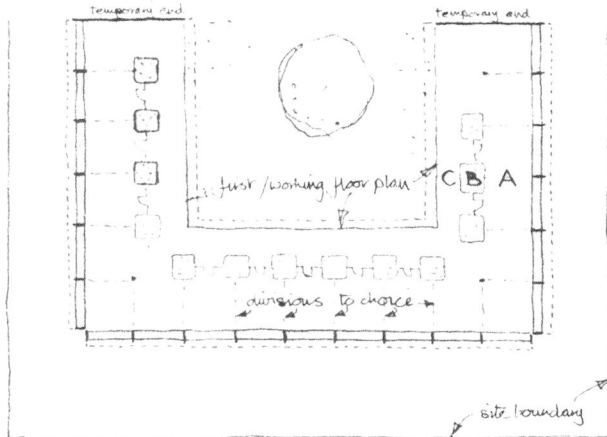

to make a plan that follows the edges of the site and can therefore adapt to any site by altering the lengths of its sides:
A: the working strip can be divided at any dotted line to make offices, demonstration rooms, salesman's depots, workshops etc.
B: the storage strip is kitted out to choice.
C: the walking strip is beside and part of an enclosed garden.

and to enter the building you come in under the working strip, up onto a half level where there is a coffee/meeting place opening onto the enclosed garden, and on up onto the working floor,

and, whatever the shape of the site the building can expand to use it,

and its internal divisions and uses can be altered by moving the (4 panel) straight divisions up + down the working strip.

Olivetti new branches - 197

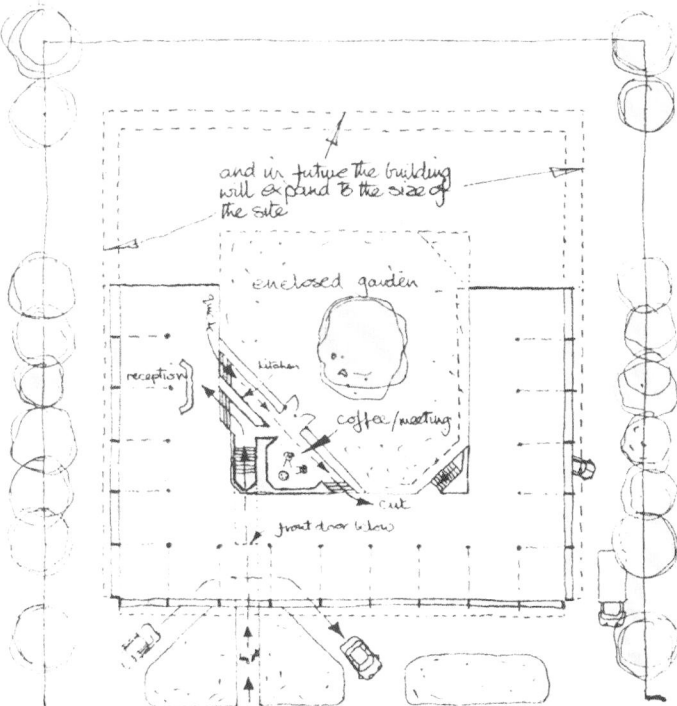

76

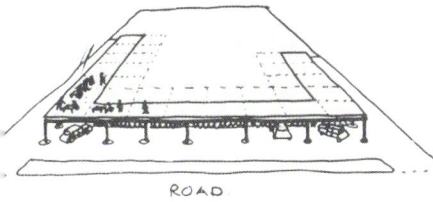

ROAD

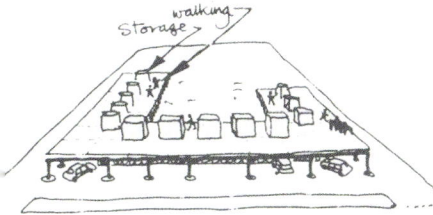

Storage   walking

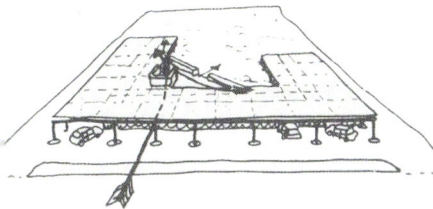

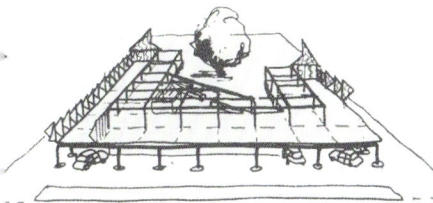

white roof.
yellow roof

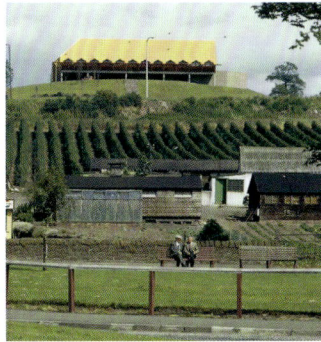

**Olivetti branches
(1970-72)**
Commissioned by Olivetti's
UK manager Carlo Alhadeff,
and following on from
Edward Cullinan Architects'
refurbishment of the
company's Haslemere
headquarters, four new
branch offices were built on
diverse industrial sites in
Belfast, Carlisle, Derby and
Dundee. The long side of the
U-shaped buildings faced the
street, leaving extendable
wings. Each comprised an in-
situ concrete parking and
service level with a working
floor above built from
plywood and steel, roofed
with insulated steel panels.

Like the first houses, the Olivetti buildings in
Belfast, Carlisle, Derby and Dundee – a series of
'branch' offices completed eight years after the
family home – have archetypal qualities: they
frame the land, capture the sun and collect the
rain. But the linear plans of the houses have been
replaced with blocks that partially wrap around
open courts. Olivetti had assumed the buildings
would need to grow so they were designed to
expand and fully enclose the courtyard gardens,
detached from their nondescript edge-of-town
context, be it an industrial or housing estate.
But the branches were never extended so remain
as built, with a shallow plan of offices, workshops,
storage and circulation defining the court. The
main floors are raised on piloti with stores, plant
and undercroft parking beneath. Creeping into
the courts are loosely planned, intermediate-
level reception/coffee/meeting spaces. Both the
architecture and the way the space is programmed
is informal. The plans are simple and, as Mark
Girouard explained, the primary floors are
'flexible, sociable, and easy to understand'.

The silhouettes and lofty interiors stem from
the section which, like the earlier Kawecki and
Garrett houses, exploits a steep monopitch roof.
But here the roof is not a separate element –
it's as if the walls and roof of a more conventional
building have been tilted through 45 degrees.
So, in lieu of walls, the offices and workshops are
enclosed by two steeply inclined planes that
converge at the perimeter of the building to form
the apex of a triangle. The roof rises to a height
of five metres to a glass-louvred clerestorey. The
perimeter is illuminated by triangular windows
cut out of the roof and the glazed inclined plane
below the eaves. The only walls are those to the
intermediate level to the courtyard and they are
glazed, contributing to the daylight that floods
into the interiors from all sides.

The construction is rudimentary, with a concrete deck raised on concrete columns, and a roof supported by steel trusses and clad in ply, like the rest of the interior. The roof sheds its water dramatically: channels direct rain around the triangular windows and into a gutter that is cantilevered from the eaves before trickling down a chain. The pipework is also confidently exhibited at the corners.

The patent glazing to the courtyard, the 'extruded' section expressed in the gables, and the overhanging perimeter facades suggest the work of Jim Stirling. The angled forms also evoke the 'Terrassenhaus' type deployed by Denys Lasdun at the University of East Anglia residences, for which Cullinan was the project architect. One also thinks of a Chinese pagoda, and the profile of the triangular perimeter windows recall Frank Lloyd Wright's late geometric works such as Marin County Civic Center.

Most of the 1970s photos of the Olivetti branch buildings – all of which have since been reclad and repurposed – are in monochrome. That was fine if you were working almost exclusively in concrete, but Cullinan wasn't. These were vibrant, futuristic, optimistic and generous buildings, and so very different to the monolithic structures that prevailed at the time. There were rich colours of stained ply, brightly painted steelwork and fenestration, and vivid yellow plastic sheet roof coverings. Looking at Olivetti Dundee on its hilltop setting, it's tempting even to see it as a biblical ark that's run aground, with its small cohort of sales and clerical staff, technicians and storemen for whom it was built.

An expanding workload during the 1970s included a number of larger housing projects for which Cullinan extrapolated ideas from the trilogy of early one-off houses. Two projects in particular illustrate the extent to which the intended experience outweighs conventions and decorum. Apart from the central front door to the apartment building at Leighton Crescent in Kentish Town, north London, the openings in the facade are evenly distributed. And in each there is a pair of French windows with a balcony. Inside the shallow-plan flats had demountable partitions, giving the residents the freedom to reconfigure their space. The one constant however is a consistent and generous series of apertures to the street. Whatever the space standards and the arrangement inside, it is the wall and the ample doors in that wall that qualify the interiors.

The Highgrove housing, for the London Borough of Hillingdon, employs a similar quadripartite plan to Leighton Crescent, but in a low-density scheme of back-to-back semi-Ds. Much like Camden Mews there is no front or back. Instead the front door, toilet and (in some types) a garage are on the gable elevations, freeing up the wide-frontage kitchen and living spaces to spill straight out into the garden. The 'Christmas tree' section – a series of three monopitch roofs descends towards the garden – culminates in a low eaves that (before re-roofing) dropped even closer to the ground at each corner to a water butt, at the same time giving the family a little extra privacy where they might feel otherwise exposed. Neither Leighton Crescent nor Highgrove look shockingly new but they both once again direct the residents to their outside environment.

Cullinan's office completed the Ready Mix Concrete headquarters in Surrey in 1990, when I was on my 'year out', and I remember poring over the drawings in the Architects' Journal. Like most of the practice's buildings the design is a very particular response to its situation, but otherwise

Lambeth Community Care Centre (1983-85) Commissioned intentionally because the practice had no track record in healthcare design, and therefore no preconceptions, Lambeth comprises a row of in-patient wards in the steel-framed, south-facing upper level and cellular consulting rooms in the brick base.

Below Leighton Crescent, exploded axonometric of lower floor; Highgrove housing, section and lower floor plan of typical house, four of which constitute a cross-walled cluster.

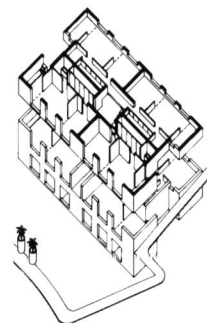

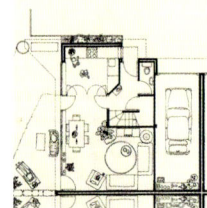

GILBERT ROAD

it's quite unlike anything else to date. Instead the RMC headquarters makes an architecture of gardens, and its seeds can be found in two community health buildings in London.

The first, Lambeth Community Care Centre (1983-85), sought to place healthcare in a domestic setting, and the design is again explicit about its relationship with the outside world. A brick base, part submerged into the ground, houses the daycare facilities and forms the foundation for a pavilion of small wards and a south-facing terrace that overlooks the garden. This arrangement – together with a direct access by staircase – brings the plants in the garden close to the patients sitting out on the terrace. Like an awning over a veranda, the fine roof reaches out to protect the fully-glazed bedrooms and to shelter the terrace. The roof liberates the wall, tempering environments inside and just outside the wall where residents may become absorbed in nature. The second, the Whittington Centre in Streatham (1985), fully occupies its site with a single-storey structure, but for a small round tower containing a caretaker's house. Here the architecture is again orientated towards a garden, but this time a central, circular court is cut out of the plan, on axis with the corner entrance, and overlooked through fully-glazed perimeter walls.

With hindsight both these fine healthcare buildings – perhaps constrained by their suburban settings, limited programme of uses and potential for spatial complexity – seem comparatively unsurprising. That's not so with the RMC headquarters, which reverses the polarity between built form and landscape. There were three houses on the site: the Georgian Eastley End and Meadlake houses, and the arts and crafts-era Grange, next to a lake from which gravel had once been excavated for concrete. Various additions

and outbuildings were removed. The original garden walls extended and a low-rise 'mat' building envisaged, and this extended east from the Georgian houses almost as far as the Grange. Out of this were cut three courts, one in front of each Georgian house, and a third one in between.

Here 'figure' becomes 'ground' to create an architecture of gardens, not buildings. It's an idea that introduces a context that the original buildings never had but always craved. It harnesses the latency of the historic buildings and the landscape and makes sense of them by projecting specific axialities out from the original houses and cross axes that link the gardens with a sequence of paths and staircases. It is an accomplished composition in the spirit of Webb, Lutyens and Stirling, all of whom Cullinan admired. With its more complex spatial requirements we can see how the architecture continues its association with the natural world while at the same time creating morphologies that reflect the range of activities and the social and communal dimension of the work.

The RMC interiors are naturally lit by continuous screen walls of glass and skylights. A concrete 'table' supports the metre-deep soil and gardens overhead, creating enough thermal mass to make natural ventilation a possibility for the offices, dining rooms, laboratories, lecture theatre and swimming pool. But this needed the glazed walls to be shaded.

This – as well as other issues such as guarding the edge of the roof garden and concealing the roof construction and an otherwise ungainly fascia – was cleverly resolved by raising a hedge border above the ground. The hedge is planted in a steel trough supported by fine circular steel columns. The white-painted steelwork, which recalls Queen Anne details and the cast iron structures of nineteenth century glasshouses, is detached from the heavy concrete structures used to support the earth. This simple innovation solves a multitude of problems and opens up a liminal space between interior and garden, ultimately becoming the architecture itself, having cast the concrete into a benign role.

RMC headquarters (1986-90)

This complex, ambitious and innovative project incorporates three existing buildings, listed walls and protected trees. A rich landscape of courtyards and rooftop gardens is introduced with linear office wings accessed from a new entrance and central facilities building to the south-east, containing a pool, restaurant and squash courts flanking the main circulation route. The focus on landscape, low-energy design, worker amenity and the weaving of new and old – far removed from the norm for office buildings in the 1980s – proved hugely influential. Extracts over the pool and cafe in the form of giant chess pieces injected a dose of Cullinan wit.

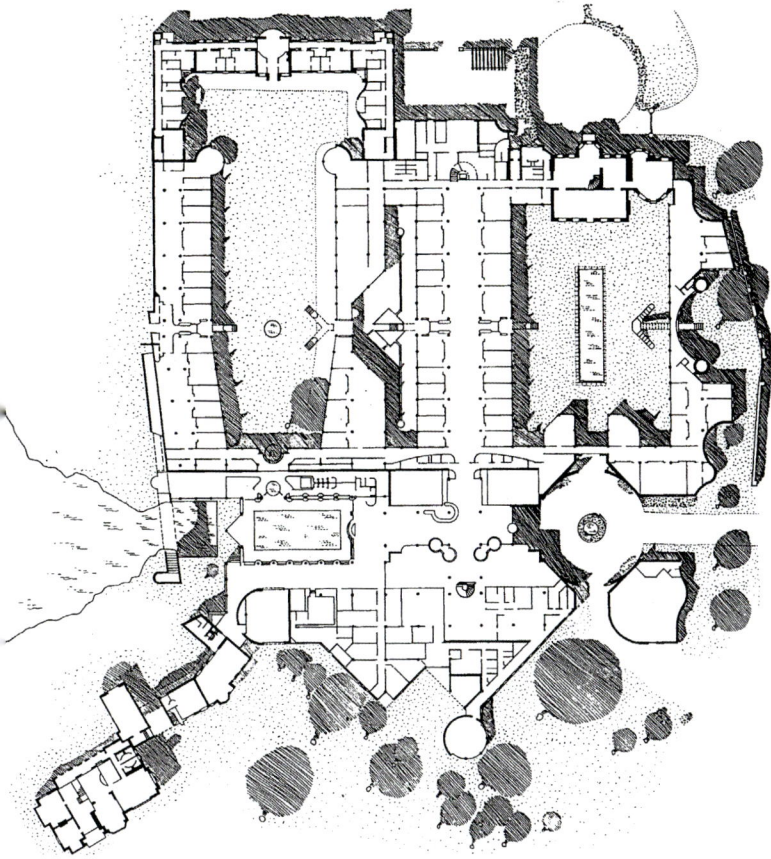

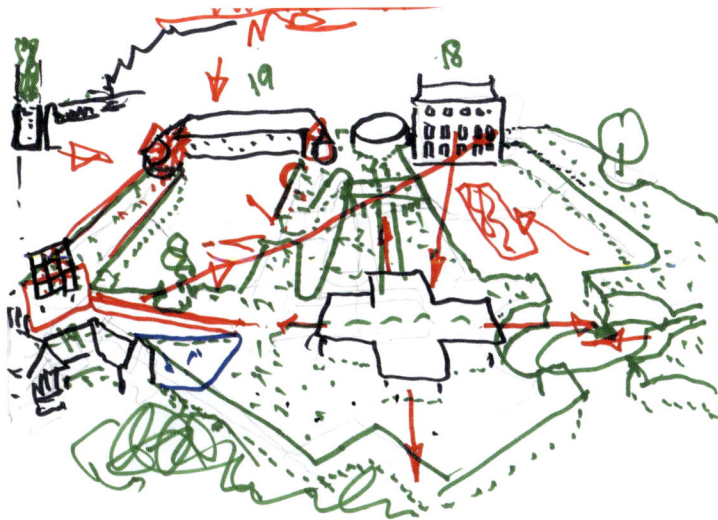

Richard Gooden, who worked with Cullinan on RMC, compared it to Lambay Castle, where Edwin Lutyens encircled a group of existing but unrelated buildings with a new wall that formalised their previously incidental arrangement. Listening to engineer Max Fordham talk about the RMC headquarters it is evident that the project brought together the intuition of the architect and the science of engineering in response to the environment. Natural phenomena were made perceptible. Three decades on, it is clear that this project has influenced a generation of environmentally conscious architects whose work relies not on complex forms or technological systems but on natural phenomena.

A recent study led by the University of Exeter Medical School highlighted a correlation between people who had been 'reconnecting' with nature and behaving sustainably. It isn't surprising. Consciousness breeds conscience. For more than half a century Cullinan's buildings have been reconnecting their occupants with nature. This has been possible because his buildings associate them with their situation and express the manner in which they respond to phenomena in the environment. He spoke of 'a tradition that concerns itself with particular conditions and particular situations; a tradition that composes with asymmetry and balance; is open in form and is expressive, and through expressiveness is decorative; a tradition that uses industrial production in the service of particularity...'

Cullinan admired Team 10 – the loose group of European architects, including his tutor Peter Smithson, who broke from CIAM and its doctrinaire approach – because its members had variously responded to their environment and

Above The rich landscape of courtyards and roof gardens at the RMC headquarters. Ventilation and extract cowls are modelled as giant chess pieces (right).

situation, to physical and human geography, and to the anthropological potential that the inhabitants and their activities might generate rather than the reductionist functionalism of pre-war Europe or post-war commercial modernism. In the 1980s it was quite apparent, even to me as a student, that Cullinan had more in common with Aldo van Eyck and his Dutch colleagues than with postmodernism or high-tech. Cullinan was not interested in built rhetoric, obfuscation or abstraction, and his was 'quite the opposite kind of architecture to the generalised, enclosing skins of the Mies boxes at the Illinois Institute of Technology' (RSA Journal, Jan 1987). Rather, he chose to find art in the practical requirements of building, and this was underpinned by his appreciation for the Arts and Crafts Movement, for Greene and Greene, Wright and Schindler, Lutyens, Rietveld, Corbusier (for both his early white plastic purism and his post-war primitivist work), Lubetkin, Aalto, Scharoun and others that represented what Colin St John Wilson termed 'The Other Tradition of Modern Architecture'.

Cullinan was concerned with the idea of shelter because it was born out of self-sufficiency and common sense. For him being outdoors, in the countryside, walking in the mountains, standing in the sun, were not abstract ideas but things he enjoyed, his pastimes, things he wanted to do, experiences he cherished and wished to share with others.

It was apparent early on that Ted's predilection for building walls reflected a curiosity about all forms of construction. Many architects, lacking such curiosity, never find the confidence to build, and just draw. Nowadays, largely due to hugely complex regulations, the plethora of manufactured construction products and systems,

and the complex interfaces that these create, the perceptible or recognisable aspects of construction are often difficult to comprehend, let alone harness. Building is increasingly hard to grasp. So Ted Cullinan's record of mediating between the tempered interior and the elements, and the ways he chose to configure and construct his architecture to make buildings that we can quite literally understand, leaves a vitally important legacy.

The directness and pragmatism of Cullinan's architectural approach was grounded in the hands-on experience of building small houses for friends, family and himself

Building Blocks
Ian Pickering

Ted drove my first wife and I home from our wedding in the back of his Morris Minor pick-up, and he insisted on lying down across the threshold so I would have to step over him, carrying my new bride. Caro, who I met when I started at the Architectural Association at the age of 25, had known Ted's wife Roz for some years, and soon Ted and I become good friends too. I had some experience in a local authority architects' office and Ted, who was then working for Denys Lasdun, needed occasional help with the small private commissions that were the beginnings of his own practice. Producing the drawings of the Marvin house in California introduced me to Ted's extraordinary ability to integrate construction and spatial organisation, and I learned valuable lessons.

About this time Ted started to build his house in Camden Mews and every Sunday friends would gather to help out. Ted's highly original concept was to avoid the tradition of the mews house as a continuous terrace, turning the house sideways the length of the plot to capture the sun and view, placing the daytime living accommodation at first-floor level, which also gave a degree of privacy. Like the Marvin house, it was a manifestation of the economy and sequence of its construction.

We didn't commit to every Sunday, but whoever turned up, irrespective of experience or age, Ted would accommodate them. When it came to cast the first-floor beam on top of the columns, he had my seven-year-old stepson walk along the shuttering to vibrate the concrete. There was a party atmosphere, with music and food. We helped to locate the large timber beam along the top of the first-floor concrete columns to support the roof rafters. Each column had an upstanding bolt cast into the top and the beam had a series of matching holes, and I was involved in placing one end of the beam in position. There were setbacks – some of the shuttering collapsed as concrete was poured for the stair, and all hands were needed to help locate the first-floor windows, held by a rope tied to a column in the next door house – but Ted remained typically unphased.

I worked for Ted intermittently during my studies, first in his mews flat in Regents Park, then in Camden Town as he started his practice, and later (when he was still working for Lasdun) during a year out from the AA as his assistant in Henrietta Street, Covent Garden, then still a thriving market. While giving me what felt like complete freedom in the design of a print works, workshop and offices in Whitham in Essex, Ted had an acute sense of when to step in and help.

Conversations in the office were mostly about architecture, and I learned much, but it was also fun. Ted was a judo enthusiast and disagreements over design or detail were occasionally and jokingly resolved with a bout in the next room.

Although I wasn't involved with Ted in any professional sense after finishing at the AA, I grew increasingly aware of his influence on my thinking as I started to teach in architecture schools. Some time later David Wild invited me to join the part-time course at the University of the South Bank, and he also asked Ted, Sunand Prasad and others from the office. Later, when I taught in Glasgow at the Mackintosh School of Architecture, Gavin Stamp organised a series of Friday afternoon lectures and invited Ted. We had lunch together beforehand and I was asked to give a vote of thanks. I am not sure that Ted was aware of it but he showed one of my drawings very early in the talk and I mentioned it. It was the drawing I did for him in my first year, of the Marvin beach house in California.

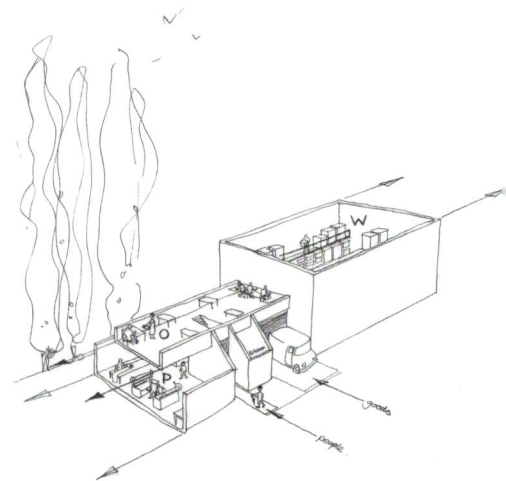

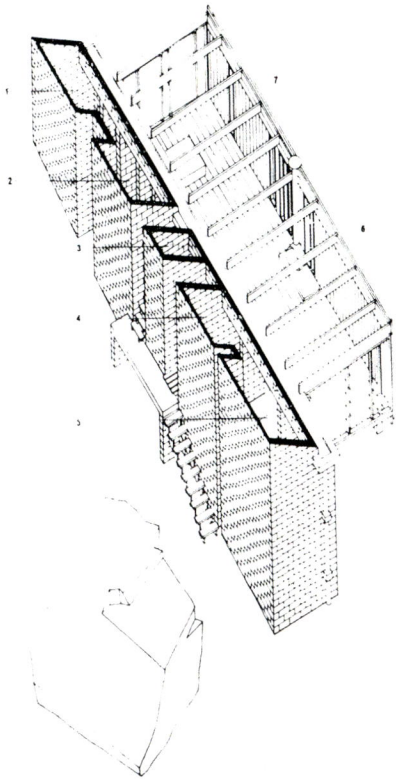

Marvin House
(1959-60, demolished)

Built with Cullinan's friends, the Marvins, at Stinson Beach, California, a series of top-lit, concrete-block 'green rooms' serve a 'stage' of Californian redwood. The green rooms provide two dressing rooms with a shared shower, a guest shower and toilet, an entrance, study and kitchen.

Left

Cullinan on site at the Marvin house, cutaway perspective of the print works at Witham, Essex.

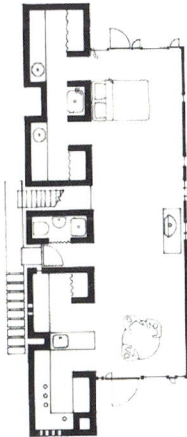

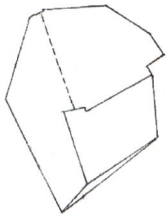

Ideas applied in a series of seminal housing projects in the 1970s were rooted in Cullinan's first one-off houses. Brendan Woods, who worked in the office at the time, considers how these early concepts were fused with social and urban concerns at a larger scale

Towards a Pragmatic Utopia
Brendan Woods

When I arrived at the Cullinan office from Cambridge in the late summer of 1973 the Highgrove housing project for the London Borough of Hillingdon was in the early stages of development and each member of the team was allotted a role in the detailed design.[1] Tchaik Chassay and I were asked to work on the roofing/ceiling system – an ingenious system made by ICI called Purlclad, which seemed a sensible successor to that used on the practice's Olivetti buildings – a system, however, that was to prove vulnerable to circumstances out of our control.

The Highgrove project is based on an idea that might be described as a multiple of 62 Camden Mews – Ted and Roz's own self-built house – and also, I understand, Ted's proposal for the 1967 Runcorn housing competition, with 133 houses set back-to-back and side-to-side as a low-rise carpet in four rows, separated by hedges, paths and roads. It bears some similarity to Frank Lloyd Wright's Suntop Homes inasmuch as each basic unit comprises four corner houses. And Highgrove can be seen to be imbued with the same spirit that inspired Wright's Broadacre City – a new way of living together, but in the suburb of Uxbridge rather than the American Midwest. We all knew about Ted's legendary meeting with Wright at Berkeley when the grand old man had stumbled and regained his balance by grabbing hold of Ted's shoulder – a laying on of hands, or passing the baton perhaps, and Ted was surely up to the task of translating American optimism into English pragmatic utopianism.

The houses adopted a section that perhaps evolved out of Victorian flatted factories, Gino Valle's Zanussi headquarters in Udine, Jim Stirling's Cambridge History Faculty and Patrick Hodgkinson's Foundling Estate, whereby a continuous cascading section/elevation was created. There's a precursor too in Ted's 'house for a ploughman', designed in the 1960s on a Buckinghamshire farm, where the builder had said: 'Good God, you could build them end-to-end and back-to-back', which of course Ted did. But his ingenuity at Highgrove was to use the timber window framing as the structural support to the roof. This was possible as the Purlclad

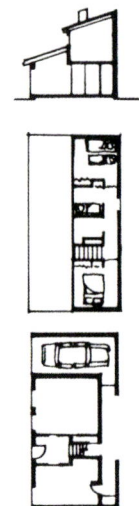

Above The 'house for a ploughman' was the sixth in a series of early, one-off simple dwellings built by Cullinan in the 1960s. The sectional design, combining lean-to and monopitch roofs, was later deployed at Highgrove and other larger-scale housing projects.

Left The angled extensions to the original roofs at Highgrove delivered rainwater to concrete water butts for gardening.

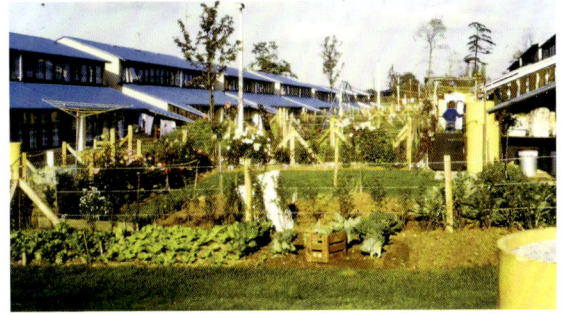

Highgrove housing, Hillingdon

Dwellings are entered from interstitial alleyways that run perpendicular to the vehicular streets, dividing the rows of houses into clusters of four homes. Four parallel rows of houses run south-west to north-east, intersected by the alleyways and efficiently served by just two roads.

Above Project architect Tchaik Chassay and Ted Cullinan.

system was only 55mm thick overall and relatively lightweight – the financial constraints on architects designing council housing in the 1970s were severe indeed. Ted's innovative idea also derived from the Olivetti workshop buildings where a not dissimilar roofing system had been developed with two sheets of plastic-coated corrugated steel with urethane foam pumped in as insulation. At Highgrove it comprised Plastisol-coated corrugated steel, made by British Steel and formed by PMF in Cheltenham, with 20mm of urethane foamed onto the inner face by ICI and 9.5mm plasterboard glued to the underside.[2]

I stress this technical aspect to remind how Ted's early work was ground-breaking. The Olivetti works are assured essays in combining an architectural idea about 'community' with an engineering idea about 'economy of means': a principle that seems sadly lacking today, where if you can model it on a computer you can build it! And the results are incoherent, inelegant and bizarre examples of what used to be referred to as creations of 'monkeys and typewriters'. As others will attest, Ted was imbued with both an inventive spirit and a passionate social conscience, virtues that grew out of the Victorians' desire to create a humane architecture out of the maelstrom of the late Industrial Revolution (cf Ruskin, Morris et al). For Ted that was transformed into what can be understood as a humanist version of so-called 'high tech', but with a dose of witty DIY derived

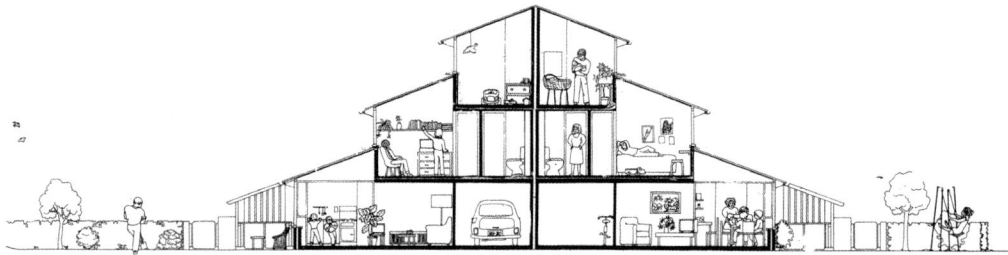

Highgrove, Hillingdon
Section and plans of the type-A house.

Below The 'pinwheel' plan of Frank Lloyd Wright's Suntop houses, like Highgrove, allows for four homes each with two party walls.

Right 'On a recent visit I was taken aback by the re-roofed, re-fenestrated and re-painted houses which now resemble a rural community of Homes for Heroes rather than the colourful essay in a new tectonic for suburban dwellers that I had worked on. But perhaps that sense to it was always there in Ted's mind. And the unkempt hedges have considerable charm. Sadly, the reroofing resulted in the loss of the elegant termination to the roofs, the rainwater butts, and the resulting intrigue to the thresholds.'
BW

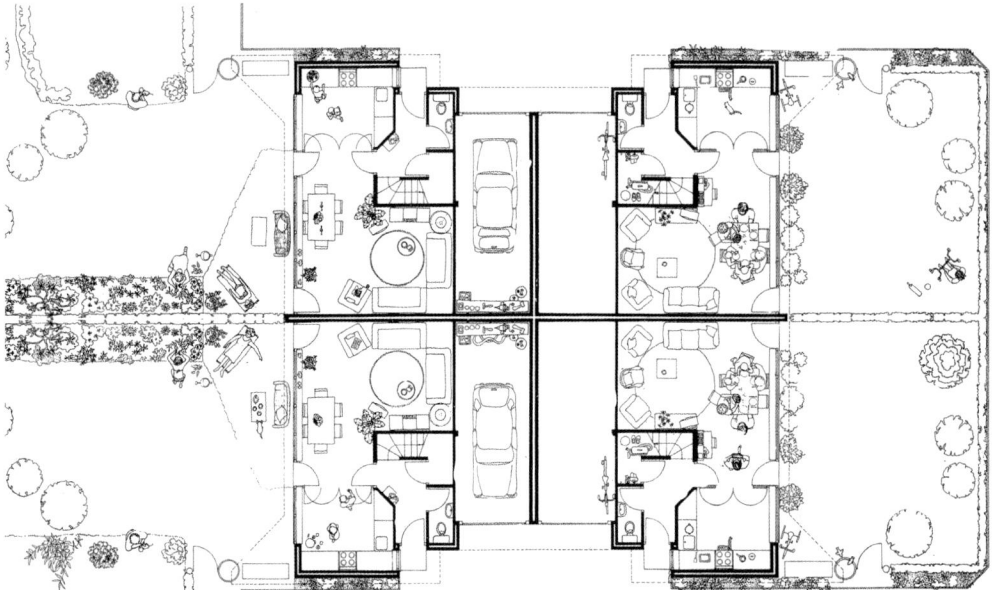

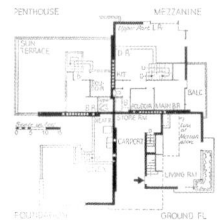

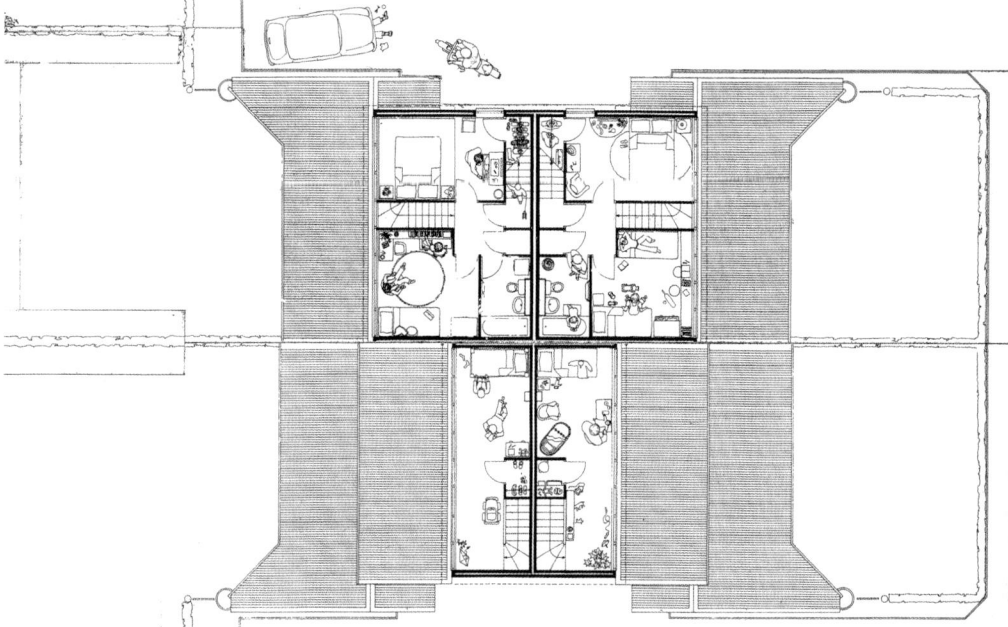

from his own weekend building projects. The Highgrove housing had that with its rainwater butts, improvised from concrete drainage components, that beautifully resolved the cascading blue roofs. Ted's use of these concrete rings reached a particularly poetic resolution in the shower at Gib Tor.

At Highgrove, however, the roof/ceiling system was compromised when, during the 1976 heatwave, the Plastisol topcoat migrated to the underside of the steel coils awaiting pressing at PMF in Cheltenham. ICI's advantage of self-foaming the urethane onto the corrugated steel started to delaminate and a new top coat had to be adopted which in turn produced problems with the tolerances to the joints between the 900mm-wide sheets of plasterboard, and condensation ensued. It was a tragic outcome for an innovative prefabricated system that enabled a house to be roofed in an afternoon, and perhaps one factor in explaining some of the more conventional construction methods in Ted's work in the early 1980s.

The Highgrove houses also employed an ingenious way of making use of standard components in their section. The requirement for habitable rooms to have a median height of 2.3 metres meant that 2.1-metre-high doorsets could be used to set the lower datum of the sloping roofs. The 2.1-metre ceiling height proved overly restrictive when it came to manoeuvring large pieces of furniture, however, but this was solved by incorporating trap doors.

As a reminder of the prejudices still operating in 1970s Britain, Highgrove initially had to overcome being considered as 'back-to-back' housing, a typology that at the time was not permitted, but Ted hit on the idea of describing it, more accurately, as 'corner-to-corner' and the problem was spirited away.

Reflecting on the 'genius' of 62 Camden Mews, it is in its ability to take a site where the old pattern of fronts and backs is set aside and a type – perhaps similar to farmhouses in Normandy – is adopted where orientation allied with a concern

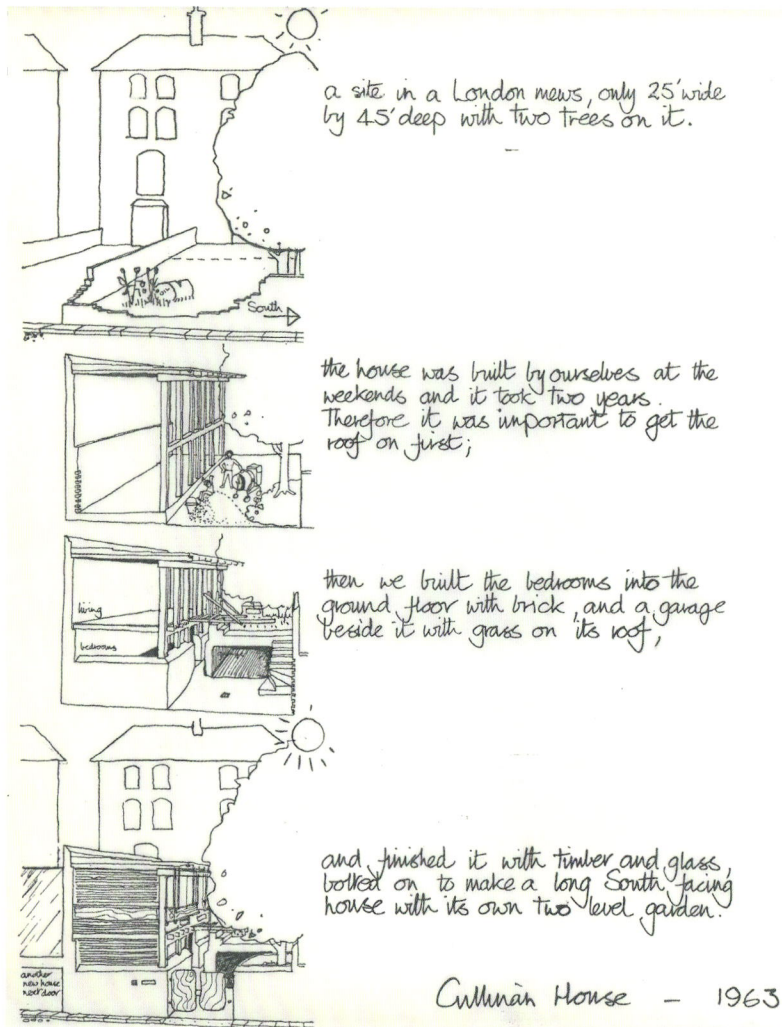

a site in a London mews, only 25' wide by 45' deep with two trees on it.

the house was built by ourselves at the weekends and it took two years. Therefore it was important to get the roof on first;

then we built the bedrooms into the ground floor with brick, and a garage beside it with grass on its roof,

and finished it with timber and glass, bolted on to make a long South facing house with its own two level garden.

Cullinan House - 1963

Camden Mews

The Cullinan house exploits its constrained site with an arrangement perpendicular to the street, unlike most mews' precedents, which allows for a long, south-facing main elevation.

for privacy produces an architectural synthesis which is extraordinary in its richness (something I experienced in living there for a few weeks in the summer of 1976 while Ted and Roz were at Gib Tor). Camden Mews cleverly turns the plan through 90 degrees and creates an entry sequence from a front forecourt protected by a double gate. The bedrooms are at ground level, accepting the lesser need for light, while the living spaces are on the upper level. Of course, a mews might well be the ideal place to experiment in a sub-urban partis, and while it does translate successfully to the site in Uxbridge, single-aspect housing has its disadvantages. My flat faces east and while I appreciate the morning sun, my well-being would be drastically affected if I couldn't also enjoy the late afternoon/early evening sun streaming through the tiny west-facing kitchen window. The movement of the sun is an essential part of the daily cycle, of one's circadian rhythm, and this perhaps contributes to the success of Leighton Crescent where Ted and Phil Tabor further developed the corner-to-corner partis and where each flat has windows on two sides.

Ted was adamant in his opposition to narrow frontage dwellings and I know was disappointed in finding no alternative in the scheme that he and I designed with Sunand Prasad for Solon housing association on Westmoreland Road in Bromley. The project was funded by the Housing Corporation and administered by the GLC, who would have been happy with a terrace of narrow frontage family houses. However, this would have made limited use of the extraordinary site that Solon had acquired in the early 1970s. Solon had other ambitions and encouraged us to design a building with a range of dwelling sizes so that the democratically-governed community created would be enriched by couples living alongside small and large families. The pressures were such that some of the dwellings ended up with a narrow 3.6 metre frontage, exactly what Ted had tried to avoid throughout his career. We did, however, achieve a good mix of dwelling sizes and types, with a garden that seemed almost utopian, with a children's playground, a lawn for picnics, allotments further down the site irrigated by rainwater from the roof of the building, and a

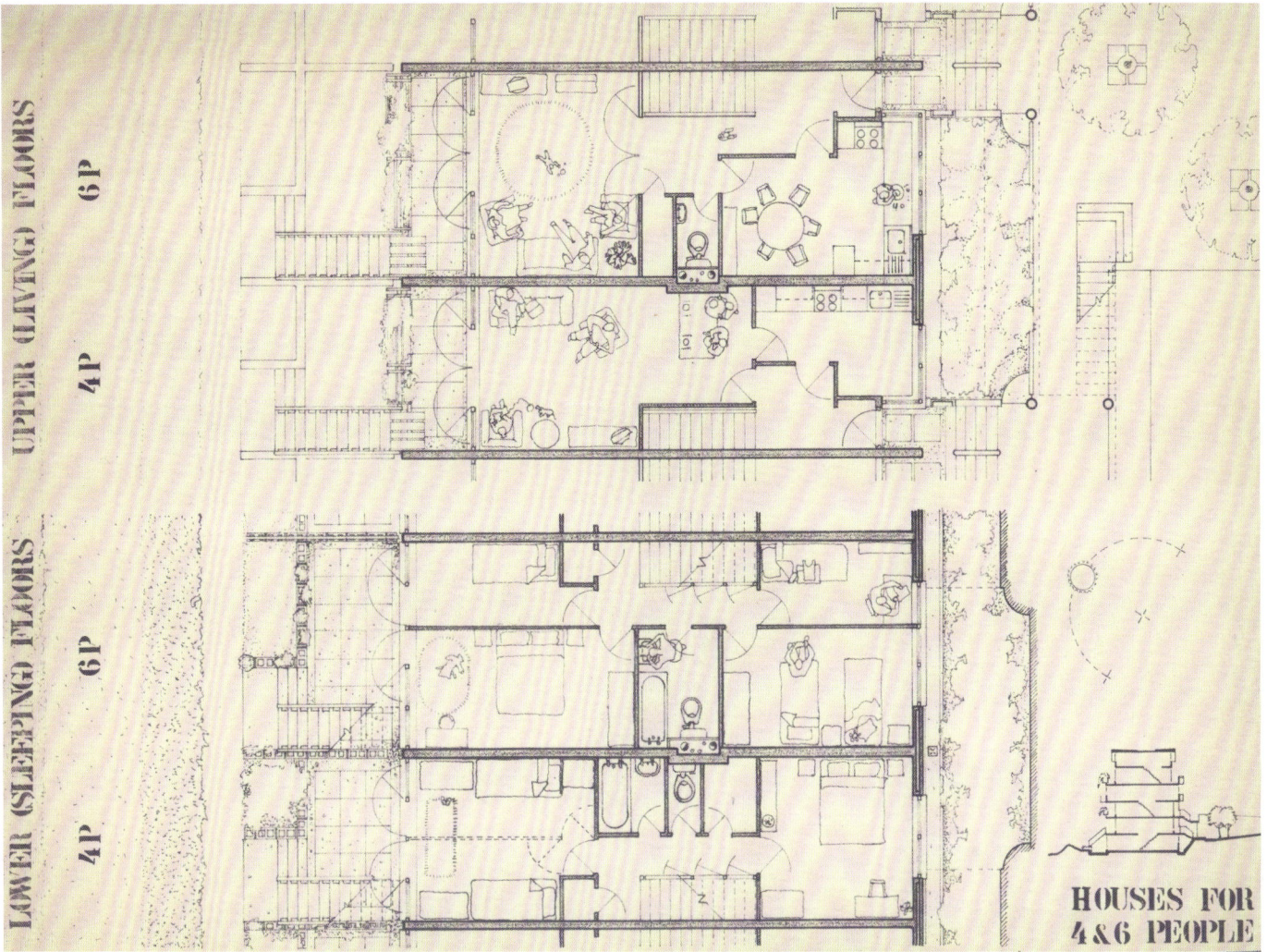

UPPER (LIVING) FLOORS

6P   4P

LOWER (SLEEPING) FLOORS

6P   4P

HOUSES FOR
4 & 6 PEOPLE

Westmoreland Road, Bromley (1974-79)
The sectional design, with external stairs and ramps, allows a high density of dual-aspect maisonettes and flats on six floors, without the need for costly and often anti-social lifts.

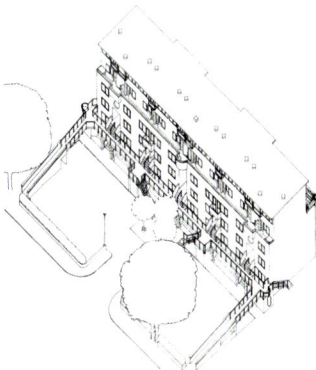

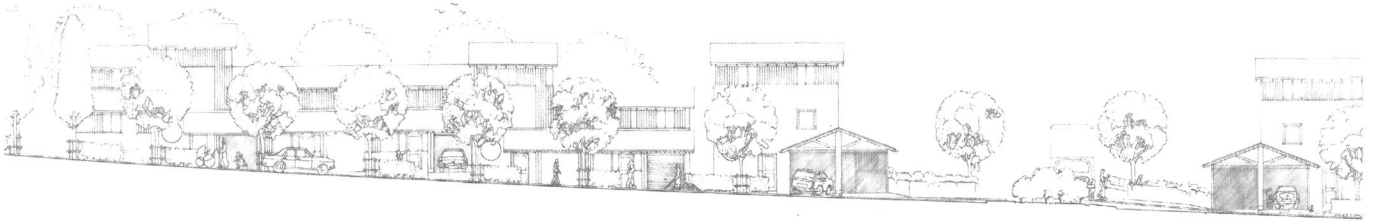

WEST ROAD

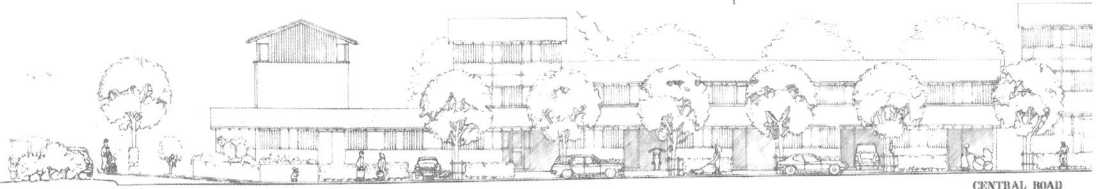

ELEVATIONS SCALE 1:100

CENTRAL ROAD

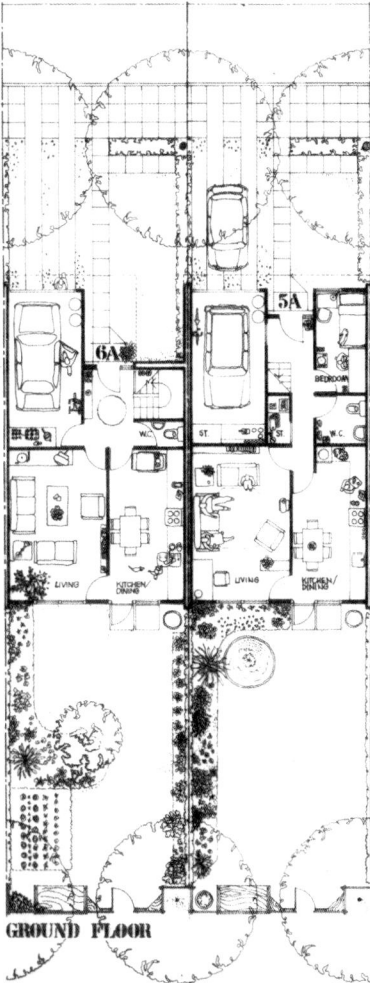

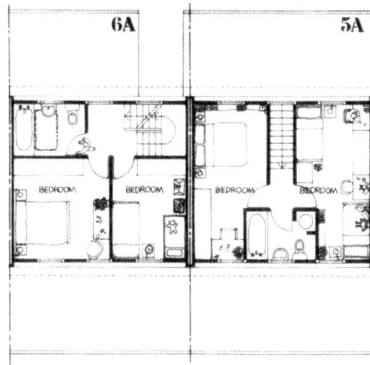

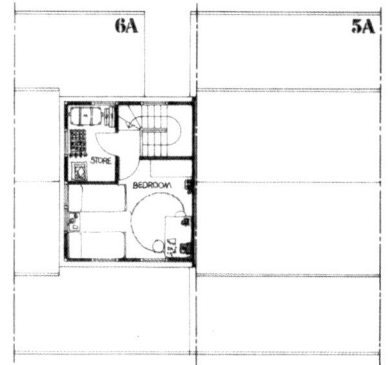

GROUND FLOOR

FIRST FLOOR

SECOND FLOOR

**HOUSES
5A & 6A**
SCALE 1:100

92

Bradwell Common 2, Milton Keynes

Working within the given parameters of the Milton Keynes grid, the project provides a variety of house types than define and reinforce the site plan and exploit the sloping site. The East Road is shown soon after completion, and the West Road recently.

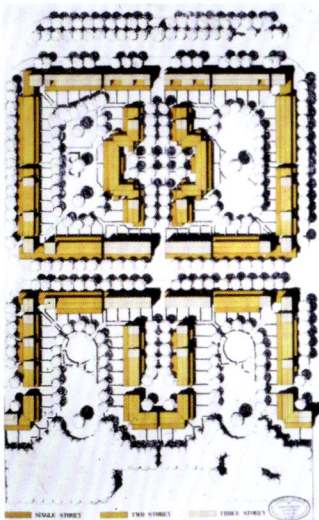

small lake at the end of the garden (kept free of weed by Green Tench).

And the section created – given the southern aspect of the garden front – achieved a more public face to the building with its forecourt and clever use of ramped access. A public arena of arrival was established, beyond and behind which the inhabitants could get on with their private lives. Westmoreland Road acknowledges the tradition of 'fronts' and 'backs' that Steen Eiler Rasmussen identified as quintessential in his wonderful book 'London: The Unique City'. Developed in the office at the same time, and also for Solon, Selhurst Road was more consistent with Cullinan's ideals. It demonstrates another recurring theme – the 'cave' and the 'bird's nest' – ie that which is solid and perhaps 'carved' and that which is constructed/modelled (a distinction that originates from Vitruvius, I believe). The carved element in architecture – via Adrian Stokes – is almost something discovered, autochthonous, and laid bare, while out of this arises the modelled element – the ego-defining object – for example, the upper floor of 62 Camden Mews with its De Stijl-like timber work and minimally framed windows.

At Bradwell Common in Milton Keynes Cullinan returned to more traditional ways in that both the layout and characterisation were clever adaptations of the terrace house format. However, by combining slightly different types and enjoying the slope of the site the resulting conglomerate form provides a richness that turns the terrace into a reinterpretation of an English village street, full of carefully composed incidents.

In the course of 15 years or so the practice had gone from attempting to translate radical construction and prefabrication systems, for example the blue roofs of Highgrove, via essays in brick, as at Selhurst Road and Leighton Crescent, to embracing a more conventional interpretation of what a house in a street looks like, but as always with a vigour and passionate commitment to place-making and muscular and idiosyncratic construction that was the hallmark of Ted Cullinan as architect.

Footnotes

1 Prior to working with Ted from 1973-78, I had met him just once, in 1968, when we had an intense fireside chat at 90 Westbourne Terrace where I shared a flat with Tchaik Chassay – I assumed Tchaik had recommended me as a possible collaborator. The office, then comprising Ted, Tchaik, Tony Peake, Phil Tabor, Mark Beedle, Deborah Strother and myself, occupied the middle floor of a warehouse building off Jamestown Road in Camden; engineer Max Fordham was based upstairs and various others were downstairs.

2 As part of the research into ICI Purlclad for the Highgrove roofs we prototyped the material in the refurbishment of Germaine Greer's house in Cambridge Gardens, a project that came into the office via Tchaik Chassay. For quite a few years afterwards, when travelling on the elevated Westway into London, one could see the bright blue roof, sailing above the line of nineteenth-century cornices.

A focus on the creative potential of the cross section enabled Cullinan to employ simple construction techniques to achieve legibility and complexity of form and space

Template of Ideas
Bob Allies

The clarity of thinking that underlies each of Edward Cullinan's designs is immediately apparent in the building's section and plan; each drawing reads almost like a diagram of an idea. Invariably, it is the section that most eloquently expresses this idea, a key section that acts as a sort of three-dimensional template from which the more complex forms of the building may then develop, but not one by which they are restrained. Cullinan rationalised and ordered the relationships within the building in order to achieve this key section, and he did this for two reasons: first because it facilitated a modular, repetitive system of construction, and second because it planted the seed from which a variety of spatial inter-relationships could then begin to grow.

This fascination, on the one hand for the use of new constructional systems and on the other for the intricate manipulation of space, points to Cullinan's firm roots in the architectural philosophies of the Modern Movement. But to Cullinan, as important as the philosophies themselves was the force of the social responsibility and concern that accompanied them, a view reflected in his personal commitment to the design of low-cost housing, to maximising the physical return to be gained from very limited financial resources. It is interesting also to note that Cullinan set up his office as a cooperative.

Where Cullinan moved beyond the Modern Movement was in his particular response to the need for simplicity of technique rather than simplicity of form. He adopted straightforward and additive, rather than refined and reductive,

methods of construction, partly because of his own experience of self-building, but also because he believed that it was through the manifestation of its construction that a building gains its particular meaning. In much of his early work Cullinan retained a conventional masonry structure at the base of his buildings, but the solidity and permanence of this part of the construction then gave way to a lighter, more flexible structure towards the roof. Paradoxically, it was the base of the building which was formally most fluid and relaxed while the lightweight structure above was very rigidly defined and ordered; ultimate flexibility necessitates preliminary restraint.

These primary elements – base, wall, roof – then receive an accretion of secondary elements – decks, entrances, porches, planting boxes, rainwater butts, balustrades – modulating and ornamenting the facade. Each building has one, or sometimes two facades, consistent, linear and open-ended. The facade commands the external space before it in the rather formal relationship of building to landscape, house to garden. These traditional relationships Cullinan respected, as he did the conventional values of the prospective occupants of his houses. But while endeavouring to embody these traditional relationships and conventional values, Cullinan was equally committed to experimentation, invention, to the search for new ways of building. His work continually evolved, lessons were always being learned. But many of the ideas and the principles originally developed and expressed in the design of his first, small, private houses he carried with him throughout his long career.

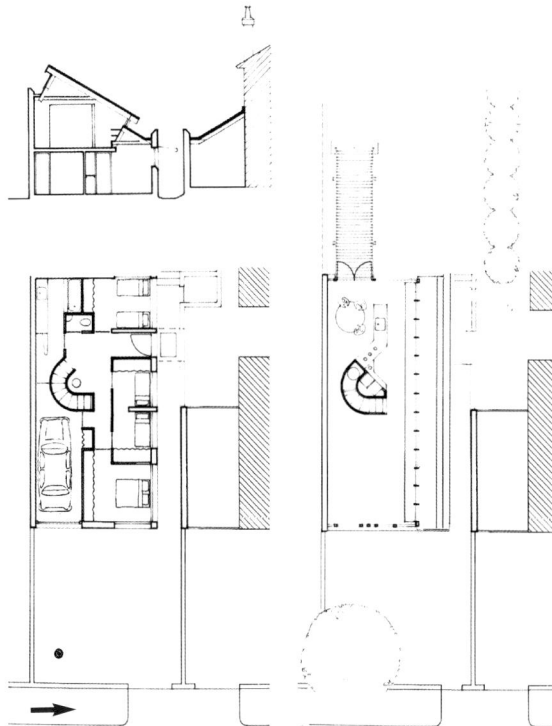

Garrett house

Built in 1966 on an infill site in Eltham, south London, for Wendy and John Garrett, later a Labour MP who Cullinan had met when they crossed the Atlantic on the Queen Mary to start graduate studies at the University of California. The project, extended beneath the ramp to the rear by Cullinan in 1973, originally included the neighbour's garage (now demolished) with a reciprocal sloping roof. Reclaimed stock bricks, exposed internally, were used for the ground floor and stair enclosure, with timber frame above.

Opposite Garrett house street sketch; Lambeth Community Care Centre sketch section. Bob Allies' text is based on his entry on Cullinan, written in 1980 for 'Contemporary Architects'.

While the Cullinan office became well versed in the design of flexible homes for contemporary living, Leighton Crescent was among its first housing projects to also address issues of order, symmetry and urban responsibility

Urban Ambitions
Philip Tabor

Around 1972, not long after starting to work at Cullinan's, Ted asked me to join him in designing a building in Leighton Crescent for the London Borough of Camden. I followed the project through to final approval but left the studio before construction. It exemplifies two Cullinan principles: architecture is the art of solving real problems enjoyably and, to quote Ted, 'good architecture needn't cost a bomb'.

The client, a progressive public authority open to architectural experiment, was perfect. But the brief changed frustratingly several times, starting as a complex of maisonettes to settle finally as a cluster of 12 one-storey flats and four two-storey houses. This long pregnancy allowed the studio time to develop, through discussion and experimentation, a distinctive approach to 'residential typology' which also informed several roughly simultaneous projects, especially those at Highgrove and Westmoreland Road.

The underlying ambition of all these projects was to transform what was rather disdainfully called 'housing' by inventing new plans and sections which would allow those living in them a more free and generous use of space and a more dignified and contemporary representation of themselves. Leighton Crescent in particular allowed us to confront, at first nervously, a rather new challenge: how to insert a new building into an old urban context whose formality, scale and architectural language fit uneasily with modern life and sentiment.

Our context was indeed formal. In the nineteenth century five blocks of brick terrace houses had been arrayed in a crescent around a green semicircle. The central block, now demolished, defined our site. The solution, obvious to anyone today, was to replace the 'missing tooth' with a block similar in volume and fenestration to its neighbours. But this was the 1970s. Overall symmetry, clearly mandated by the site's centrality, disturbed our modernist sensibilities, and Ted was allergic to 'hole in wall' windows. 'Many have died', he told me, 'to defend the strip window' – Le Corbusier's sacred *fenêtre en longeur*.

Leighton Crescent
Designed in 1972-7 and built from 1979-80, the compact block of four duplex and 12 single-floor apartments provides the missing infill centrepiece of Leighton Crescent in Kentish Town, north London. Vertical metal poles, set one metre in front of the facade, rise from the ground, supporting the prominent cornice and continuous horizontal rails at each floor where small balconies allow the French windows to be fully opened while ensuring a sense of security. The grid of verticals and horizontals serves to modulate and 'scale-up' the facade as befits its prominence in the crescent.

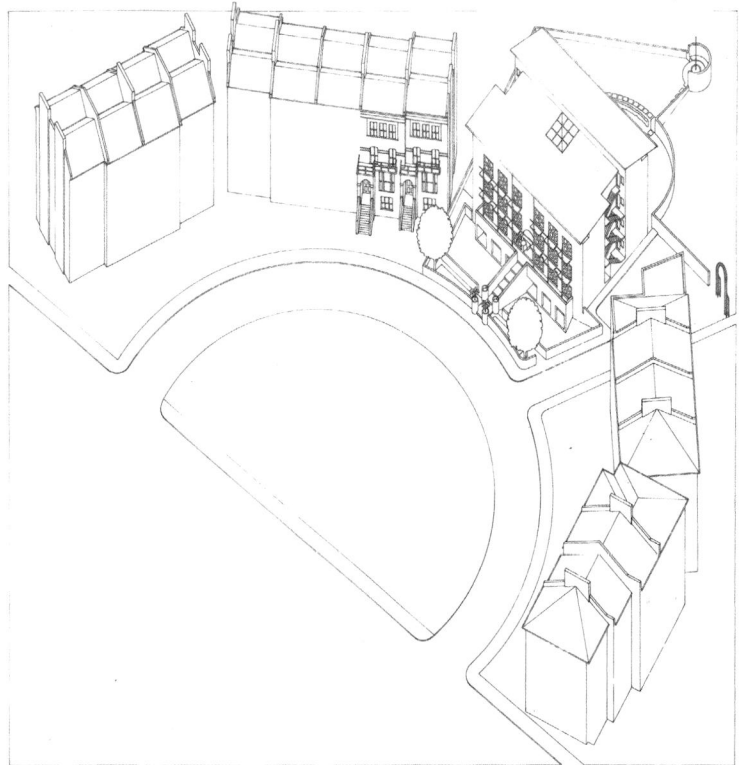

In the end, in an audaciously proto-post-modernist move, we conceded that our building had to address the crescent symmetrically and have hole-in-wall windows. So as not to replicate the heavy appearance of the neighbouring blocks, however, we gave the topmost flats a wrap-around strip window to separate the building's brick base from an over-sailing roof. My reference was the *liagò*, a roofed loggia, sometimes glazed, that is a feature of some Venetian palaces. Ted's, I'm sure, was Frank Lloyd Wright's Prairie houses.

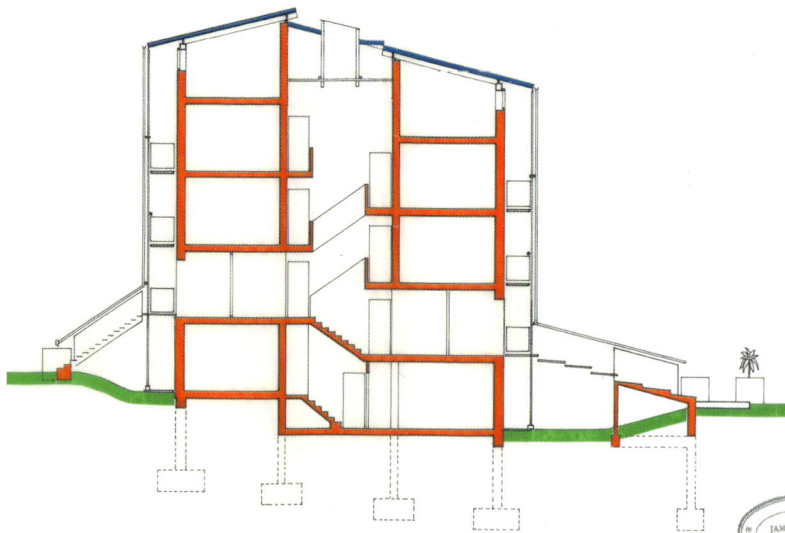

Compared with houses built before the twentieth century, those built later can seem positively mean. The standard size for a cottage in the thirteenth century, as decreed by King John, is said to have exceeded that laid down for post-war publicly-funded houses, still more for an average speculative private house. Ceiling heights too had been steadily reducing. But whereas many tenants once climbed four or five flights of stairs to reach their accommodation, the expectation now is for two or three flights at most. Lifts are expensive and can be abused, so are best avoided. It's no surprise, therefore, that new urban houses often look and feel mean and pinched compared with their older neighbours.

So to match up to the four Victorian storeys of its neighbours the building needed five twentieth-century storeys. But no front door could be more than two-and-a-half storeys above ground level, and we could afford no lift. We therefore sunk the building half a floor below pavement level, and flew a gently sloping bridge up to the front entrance, thus establishing a new ground floor one storey above the lowest floor. We then put the front door of the top flats on the floor beneath them. This way we achieved the necessary five-storey height with nobody, having entered the building, needing to climb more than two-and-a-half floors to their front door.

The other scale problem concerned the facade. Had we done the normal thing and made each dwelling stretch from front to back, the facade would have been four flats wide. If each flat had had the usual two windows, the facade would have been eight windows wide, which would have

looked tight and crushed. Instead we turned the flats through 90 degrees and gave each of the lower ones not cill-height windows but three large, widely-spaced French windows.

Inside, because through no fault of the client the floor areas were less than generous, we planned each flat like an Elizabethan long gallery with screen-like partitions which opened up all three rooms (bedroom, living room, kitchen) for a more open-plan life. The top flats also opened upwards, into the lofty sloping roof space.

We'd inherited from the 1920s the simplifying tendencies of modernism. This was perhaps partly caused by a moral shift – modern society

Leighton Crescent

A central ramp rises from the pavement to the first-floor front doors of the four duplexes that occupy the lower two floors of the quadripartite plan. Each duplex overlooks its own hedged-in private garden. Beyond the first-floor front doors, the route leads on out through the building to a circular barbeque that terminates the entrance axis. A central staircase serves the upper three floors, each with four flats, arranged in pairs on the staggered section.

The wide frontages allow the apartments to have 'gallery' plans that the residents can change by moving one or two identical partitions between the main rooms. They also allow each to have three large, evenly spaced French windows. This accords with a compositional system that introduces a large scale to the elevation intended to measure up to that of the adjacent buildings on the crescent.

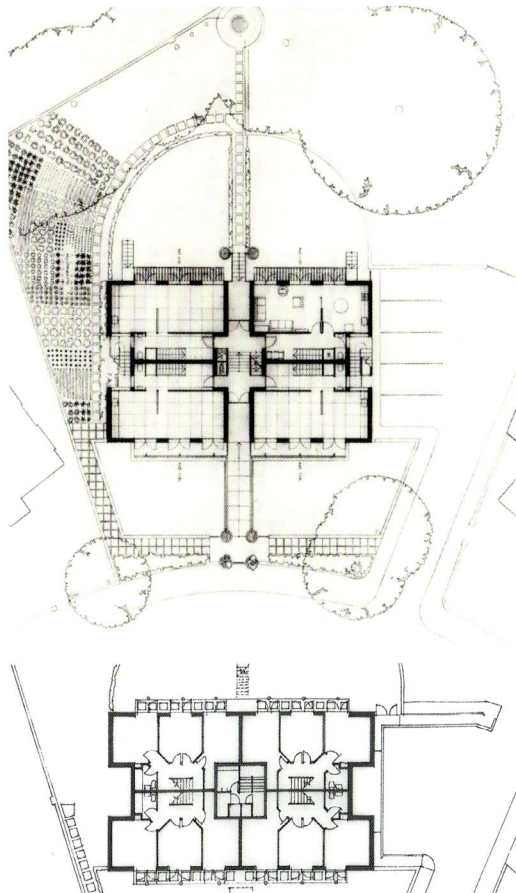

spent less on architecture than preceding generations – and partly by an aesthetic impulse towards abstraction and geometric simplicity, and away from representational detail and visual complexity. Like many studios at the time, Cullinan's sought ways to counter this impoverishment of architectural language without losing its coherence or, indeed, costing a bomb.

For Leighton Crescent we basically built a big, simple brick box. This matched the massive qualities of its neighbours and, in any case, was all we could afford. But to give this box the proportional refinement found in a Georgian facade we designed the elevation on a 90cm grid. The windows were all exact 180cm squares, separated by brick widths of either 90 or 180cm. This grid dictated the plans – at zero cost.

We then added a relatively cheap simplifying element: an outrigger system of tubes and wire mesh forming balconies to the French windows, balconies which extended the flats in summer and provided somewhere to grow plants. The poles and the mesh, being set out from the facade, offered complex parallax effects and cast an intricate, ever-changing shadow on the facade. The parallax and the shadows, too, cost nothing.

To maintain generosity of scale the balconies were supported by one vertical tube, not two at the corners as you might expect. And the vertical tubes, combined with the horizontal handrails continuing from balcony to balcony, formed a counterpoint mega-grid of 270cm squares. We'd originally intended rainwater from the roof to come down the balcony supports, travel along the balcony handrails, then swoop down the handrails of the bridge and gush into rainwater tubs by the pavement so that people could water their plants with it. For hygienic reasons, sadly, we were prevented from doing this, so had to add two downpipes over the entrance. A similar strategy informed the interior. The plain plaster of the stairwell was enlivened by a shadow-throwing timber trellis, which supported planks for accessing the skylight for cleaning. It too cost almost nothing.

The backlash against system-built highrise in the 1970s led Cullinan to develop new housing types based on inhabitants' real needs. Tony Peake worked in the studio on projects ranging from four flats at Selhurst Road to 158 homes at Bradwell Common

Homes and Humanism
Tony Peake

Selhurst Road (1976-78) is a small scheme of four homes on a restricted site at the junction of two streets of substantial suburban houses at Norwood Junction, south London. Our ambition was to make a 'full stop' building of four storeys to correspond to the scale of the streets – 'a building which adds to a corner that counts', as Ted would say.

We felt we could achieve modest gravitas by putting two pairs of maisonettes on top of each other, but this immediately created a problem of how to make the climb up to the second floor acceptable for the upper residents. We dropped the lower floor by about 90 centimetres into the ground, and contrived steps, a fairly long ramp, more steps and a change of direction to rise to the upper entrance. We hoped that avoiding a tall, external single stair would ameliorate the psychological effort of ascending.

With a low budget, the floor plans are simple and repetitive, with south-facing balconies for the upper maisonettes, apparently suspended from the flat roof but actually concrete cantilevered from the floor slab. The brickwork stops at the cill level

of the top floor with a band of timber panels and windows beneath an overhanging eaves.

We were delighted to be asked by Milton Keynes Development Corporation to design 158 homes at Bradwell Common 2 (1979-81) – the practice's biggest housing scheme to date – as it offered a real opportunity for 'placemaking'. Ted and I worked hard to discover the special rules and requirements for the New Town's housing projects. Each time we presented a fresh, laboriously hand-drawn proposal, Keith Revell or Stuart Mosscrop, MKDC's liason/bulldogs who controlled the architects, explained that we had transgressed some crucial rule about how the dwellings must be planned – so back we went to Camden Town to start over again. Ted described the swathe of government, Department of the Environment and MKDC requirements as 'a knee-deep river of jargon'.

Our houses were arranged in terraces with 'ends' and 'middles' along the pre-established roads, and with a 'mews' running north-south through the centre of the site. We had 17 different types of

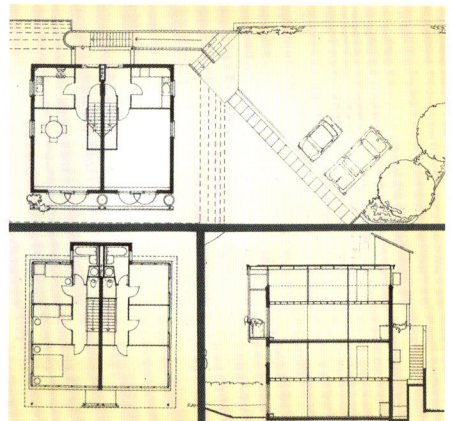

'Back in the early 1970s we were at the Huckleberry Finn end of architectural practice and we had a huge amount of fun. Life was so much simpler and less regulated, so site cock-ups were far easier to sort out as far less contractual aggro was involved in making buildings.

'In 1965 I saw Minster Lovell conference centre in the Cotswolds and was at once enchanted. Ted had generated a gloriously flowing plan, handsomely cloaked in timber and stone, simply detailed to express its structure and to celebrate how all the pieces joined together. It was a completely fresh and consistent interpretation of traditional construction, with nothing remotely pretentious or false, just an absolutely beautiful and harmonious place. As the projects became larger and more complex, our built solutions owed much to the brilliance of this early work, though with very different means and materials.

'We all believed in fairness and a more equitable society and tried to express this through a humane architecture. For 14 years I worked closely with Ted as the practice's 'token Tory', and due to his generous spirit we worked well together despite my 'other life' of traditional rural pursuits. Ted always wanted to work co-operatively, and one day our professional indemnity insurance broker, baffled by our explanation of how we worked, said to him 'Ah, I see, you are a Soviet!'.

'I was never sure whether Ted wanted the international respect accorded to some of his contemporaries, or to be left alone with a small team to work out 'meaning in a new architecture for all'. In reality, I believe he wanted and achieved both.'
TP

homes, generally two storeys and rising to three at corners, to meet both the brief and our own urban design ideas. We were blessed with a south-sloping site which opened up the heart of the perimeter plan to sunshine and views. All the dwellings had private gardens which led into shared, park-like areas with playgrounds.

In keeping with the focus on landscaping throughout the new city, we made sure that our scheme was fully planted. A network of 'footways' linked up throughout the site, with no dead ends. Maintenance of the gardens has been pretty good over the years and the trees have matured to reach a good height.

We built the houses using contractor Llewellyn Construction's own timber-frame system. Large wall panels and roof trusses were made off site, erected fast and had basic waterproofing which allowed good progress to first fix. The set-back upper floors were simply structured by means of spandrel beams between the party walls. They were clad in brick up to first floor with unplaned timber boarding above, stained in cheerful colours which are easily overcoated for maintenance.

At Cullinan's we were always interested in how rainwater reaches the ground, the final flourish of all displuviate roofs. We insisted on the avoidance of 'swan-neck' downpipes, instead having rainwater pipes dropping vertically from the overhanging eaves gutters. This necessitated the use of long horizontal brackets – dangling gutter brackets or 'DGBs' as we called them – rather than fixing the downpipes to the face of external walls. Llewellyns' managing director bet me a decent dinner that most of our DGBs would be smashed within two years. The rainwater goods have survived for 40 years – proof perhaps of Ted's mantra that people will respect something that looks good.

Left Bradwell Common 2 (1979-81) exploits the given Milton Keynes grid square to provide a variety of linked house types around perimeter boulvards, inner closes and communal gardens.

Opposite Selhurst Road (1976-78) comprises two pairs of stacked duplex maisonettes, each with a floor of living spaces and three bedrooms above. Tony Peake with residents.

A rigorous interrogation
of constructional elements and
details ensured that each part of
a Cullinan building was developed
both in its own terms as well as for
its role in the overall composition.
Mark Beedle, a member of the
studio from 1970 to 1995,
considers how the parts
became the whole

The Dialectics
of Construction
Mark Beedle

'There's what to do, and there's how to do it.'
With these plain words Ted Cullinan summarised
an entire architectural philosophy. It was an
attitude of mind founded on a deep knowledge
of historical example and precedent, a fascination
with geography, climate and environment, and a
hands-on, practical familiarity with the nature of
building materials and process.

Cullinan came of age at a time of transition
between the arts and crafts and modernism,
during the period after the second world war,
with its circumstance of materials shortage,
make-do-and-mend and new technologies, in a
cultural atmosphere of idealism and the drive to
reconstruct and to build a new society. Trained
first in the UK and later in the United States,
he was grounded in both the traditional and the
more innovative approaches to construction, and
with an awareness of the influence that the means
of production has on architecture.

Neither the work of Ted by himself nor later of
'Cullinan's' was preoccupied with delivering an
'ism' or responding in a generic house style.
Instead, energy was directed at seeing in each
project the opportunity to make a clear-headed
investigation of its subject, arrive at an agenda,
develop a design concept and, importantly, evolve
an approach to construction and detail that
would deliver that core idea with clarity, thereby
literally and metaphorically making the point.
The objective was to tailor responses to answer
the needs, and bring out the potential of each
project for the benefit and enjoyment of the user,
while at the same time contribute to the context
in which they were to take their place.

The body of Cullinan work can thus be seen
as the findings of open-minded research into all
manner of subjects and places and techniques,
translated into form as manifestoes. Their
appearance does not result from an a priori
need to be photogenic or in keeping, but
from a concern to achieve an implicit sense
of inevitability. They are dynamic, interactive
compositions that combine archetype, proportion,
feel and touch, to be both seen and experienced
through the prism of a Cubist sensibility.

Right
Horder house (1958-60),
Camden Mews (1963-64),
Minster Lovell (1967-74),
Olivetti Derby (1970-72),
Highgrove housing (1972-
77), Leighton Crescent
(1974-79), Uplands
Conference Centre (1980-
84), RMC Headquarters
(1986-90), Weald &
Downland Museum
Gridshell (1998-2002).

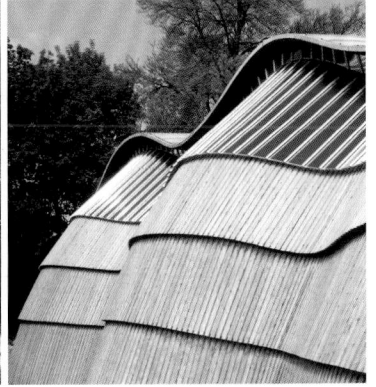

It was an architecture of elements – major, minor and miniature – that could be carefully evolved, composed and articulated to embody the core design intentions. Its antecedents lay in the work of Philip Webb, Le Corbusier, Rudolf Schindler et al. For, freed from making standard or habitual responses to building type and the limitations of relying on received wisdom, the value of working from first principles, drawing on the wealth of knowledge to be gleaned from examples of the past and exercising imagination could be harnessed productively and brought to bear.

This was a compositional approach, savoured and vividly communicated by Ted many times in presentations. He would gradually 'build the building' before the eyes of the audience, by drawing in multicoloured marker pens each accumulating layer, explaining its role in the whole and revealing the underlying rigour and rationale at play, beyond the mere picturesque.

Cullinan's lifelong love of drawing was rooted in what the process of drawing involves – the concentrated looking that allows seeing into what is to be drawn, and noticing. It is from this that the essential nature of things can be understood and recorded. And when imagining possibilities in the mind's eye, the process of drawing provides the means to record, test and investigate their substantiveness, and to revise and edit.

Cullinan belonged to the tradition that saw architecture very much as an applied art, to be pursued and developed for the benefit of the greater common good. Accordingly, the overarching objective was to actually deliver the outcome of deep thought and investigation about how lives might be improved by the built environment.

'The Tradition of Change'

St Mary's church, Barnes
Cullinan surveying the ruins following the 1978 fire; strategy for taking the past into the future, incorporating surviving and salvaged materials and features.

Right
Parts and language evolved for reconstruction: delicate pieces poised in space.

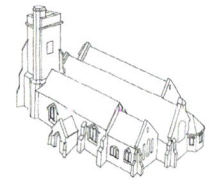

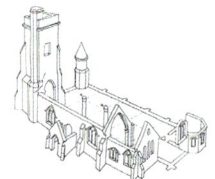

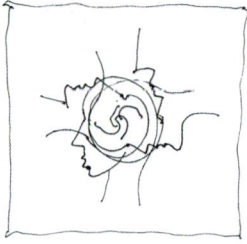

A like-minded team gradually gathered which, both in its organisation as a cooperative and the way the work was produced and carried out, echoed the elemental architectural principles and approach to which it was committed.

It was akin to the culture and dynamics found in a jazz ensemble, where a basic tune is chosen, a key is called and the leader invites band members to explore and contribute section arrangements, variations, substitutions and solos that expand on the initial theme to produce a whole greater than the basic proposition and the sum of the parts. For this to sustain, the players must be in concert in their sensibilities and be able to intuit and recognise the direction of the piece as it unfolds, and to be secure in the process of exploration towards a shared goal and coherent resolution.

So it was with Cullinan's. In architectural terms this meant that coordinates of plan and section were explored to determine and fix relationships of occupation, space and light, and their integration to context and terrain. These were then corroborated by how the building was to be built.

Decisions needed to be made regarding the appropriate constructional nature of the parts, how they related to one another, and individual and overall performance needs. So we considered how heavy or how light, how engaged or disengaged, how tidy and resolved or collaged and layered, how thick or thin, how smooth or 'hairy' as Ted would say, whether connections should be expressed or concealed, whether materials should be finished or left raw, how generic and how site specific, and how colourful.

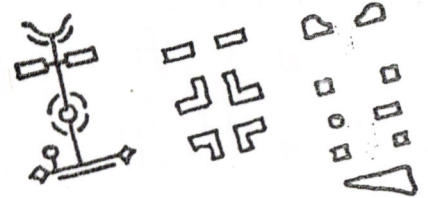

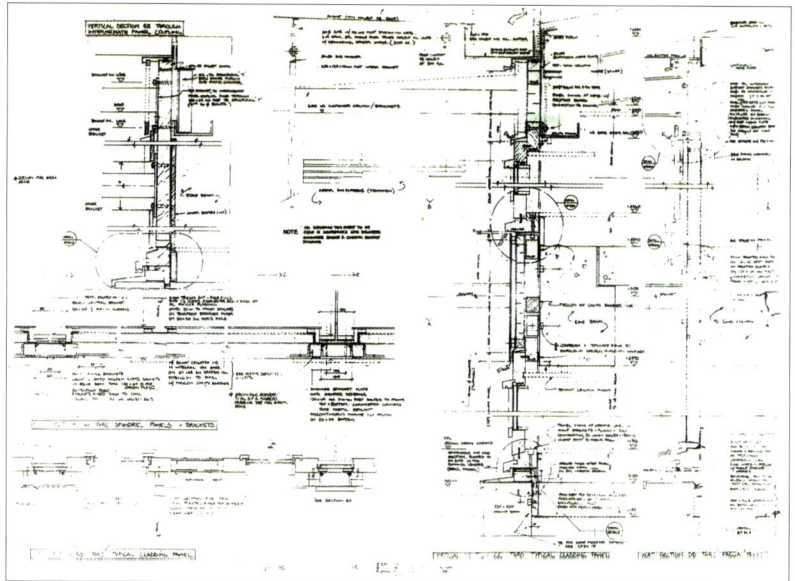

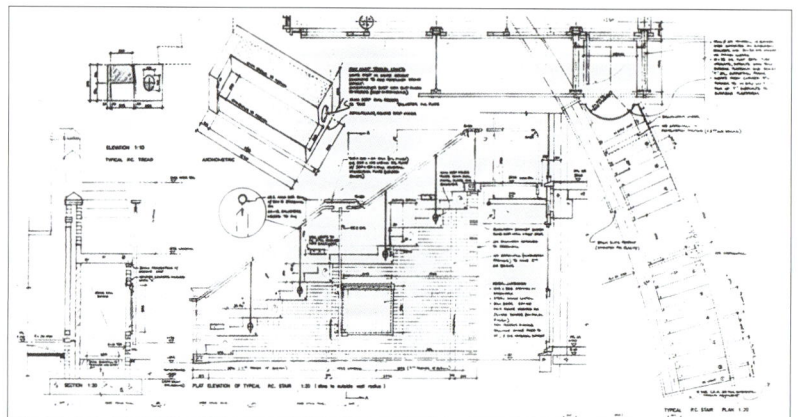

Making a 'There', 'There'

Chilworth Park, Hampshire (1988-90)
Study for the extent of sunscreening (right); a composition of buildings and landscape – rhythms, counterpoint and repose.

Left Site and strategy: circulation, pavilions and park; detail drawings of key building elements.

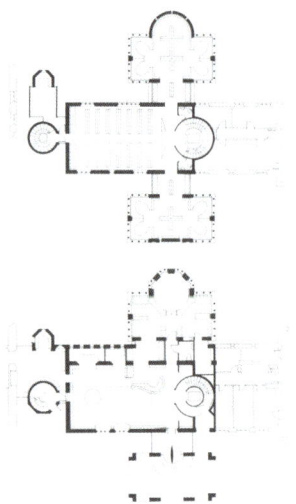

'Without Pastiche'

St John's College Library, Cambridge
Study of elevation facing the College Chapel;
construction sequence within the constraints
of the court.

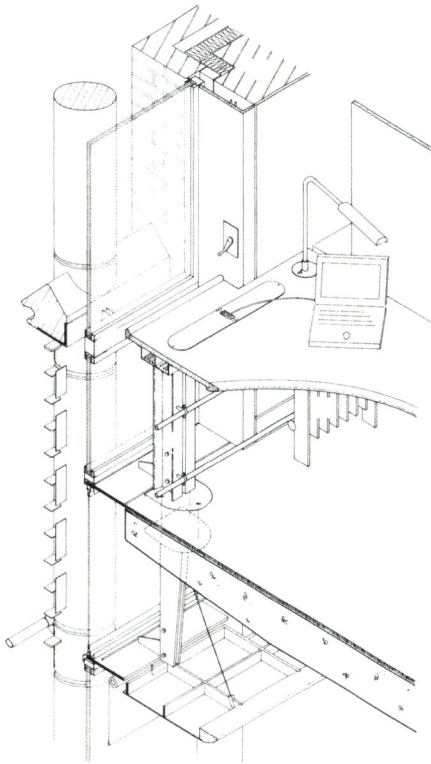

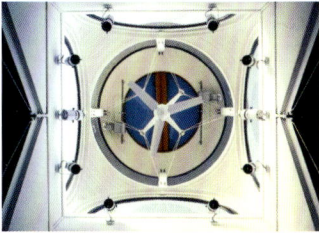

The approach allowed for each component part to be developed on its own terms and then be reconciled to the role that it played in the whole composition. This provided great flexibility for the introduction of emphasis, complexity, simplicity and wit, as variously desired or required to communicate the intended overall outcome.

Such detailing and production work on projects at Cullinan's involved a rigorous process of hypothesis and test in order to bring the entire proposition to life elegantly, proportionately and apparently without effort. All this was achieved by collaboratively developing a language for each project in turn, in a shared spirit of endeavour where authorship was secondary to seeking authenticity in the architecture.

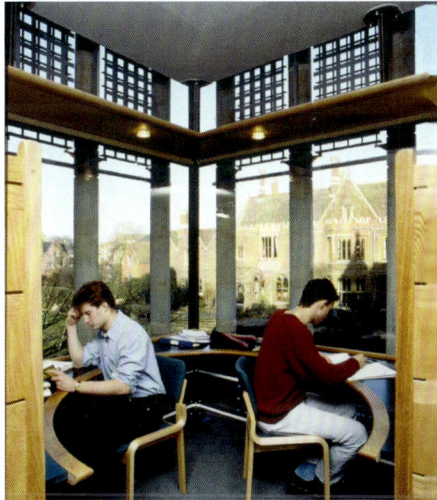

It was an architecture built piece-by-piece, where each piece is carefully chosen and judged to count essentially to the balance of the whole design, socially, visually and technically.

And, whether we were together across the drawing board, 'On the Road' visiting the pueblos of New Mexico, team-teaching at MIT or grappling with gritstone at Gib Tor, these were our shared preoccupations. A deep commitment to not just 'tell it like it is', but to 'tell it like it could be'.

Above Ventilating lantern over the crossing of the plan; bay window study carrel – the layering of parts.

Right On the Road: Ted and Roz Cullinan at Taos, New Mexico, in 1976.

The Cullinan studio was underpinned by Ted's ability to act as both teacher and colleague, a role that proved critical in collaborative competition entries with the scale and ambition of the Royal Opera House and Leeds Playhouse

Working Together
Greg Penoyre

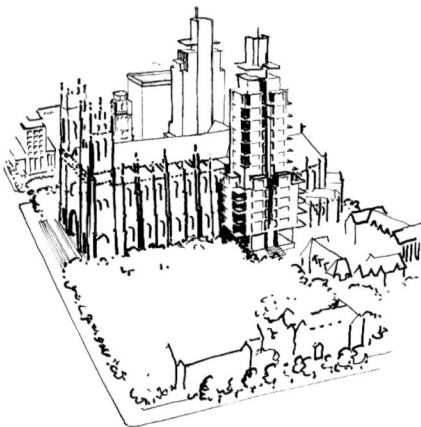

In 1976, during my second year at the University of Sheffield, Gerry Adler and I invited Ted to give a lecture in our student-run series. I don't remember the lecture but I do remember the angle grinder. Meeting Ted at the station I offered to carry his luggage. Sure, he said, and handed me an innocuous bag containing a heavy petrol angle grinder which I stubbornly hauled all the way up the hill. It was a typically immersive start to a relationship that was to become an intense working companionship with Ted and the team at Cullinan's. I later found out that I had 'met' Cullinan before when, as a teenager walking in the Hampshire woods, I came across a strange, glass-fronted structure. It was the Horder house, a kind of modernist secret that had remained lodged in my mind until it appeared on a slide in a talk and then of course became a well-aired early work which summarised a number of Ted's core principles.

Cullinan was a visiting critic during my final year at Sheffield and we had vigorous discussions about my work – not always in agreement. He taught me then to look for the essential reasoning in design decisions, and later he would demonstrate that things get done if you work to clear and quite selective principles. For example, in dry stone walling there are two fundamentals: always have more material around you than you need so that you can chose the appropriate stone for the wall; and always place the stone so that it is at rest, with three points of contact. It worked then, empowering the young amateur to do satisfying work that did not fall down, and it still works, designing and making now.

Work for Ted was about focused concentration, but it was also about being with other people, doing things together, whether learning to windsurf together or building walls together or designing buildings together – always talking about it and always in a clear and infectious shared language – finding the first principles of anything. It is perhaps paradoxical, despite this commitment to the essential in design, that in the middle period of Ted's career when I was at Cullinan's the designs became increasingly complex and rich, not simpler.

Royal Opera House
The studio spent much of 1984 working on the four-stage competition for the redevelopment of the opera house at Covent Garden, as the entries were narrowed from 120 to four: Jeremy Dixon with BDP (the eventual winner), Richard Rogers Partnership, Jack Diamond and Edward Cullinan Architects. Beyond the technical requirements of the brief, ECA proposed an escalator link to the adjacent tube station, reconstruction of the Floral Hall, commercial offices around an atrium and flats above the fly tower.

Left 1978 competition entry by Edward Cullinan Architects for New York's unfinished St John the Divine cathedral, with a hospital in the north tower and affordable flats in the south tower. The winning proposal by Santiago Calatrava remained unbuilt.

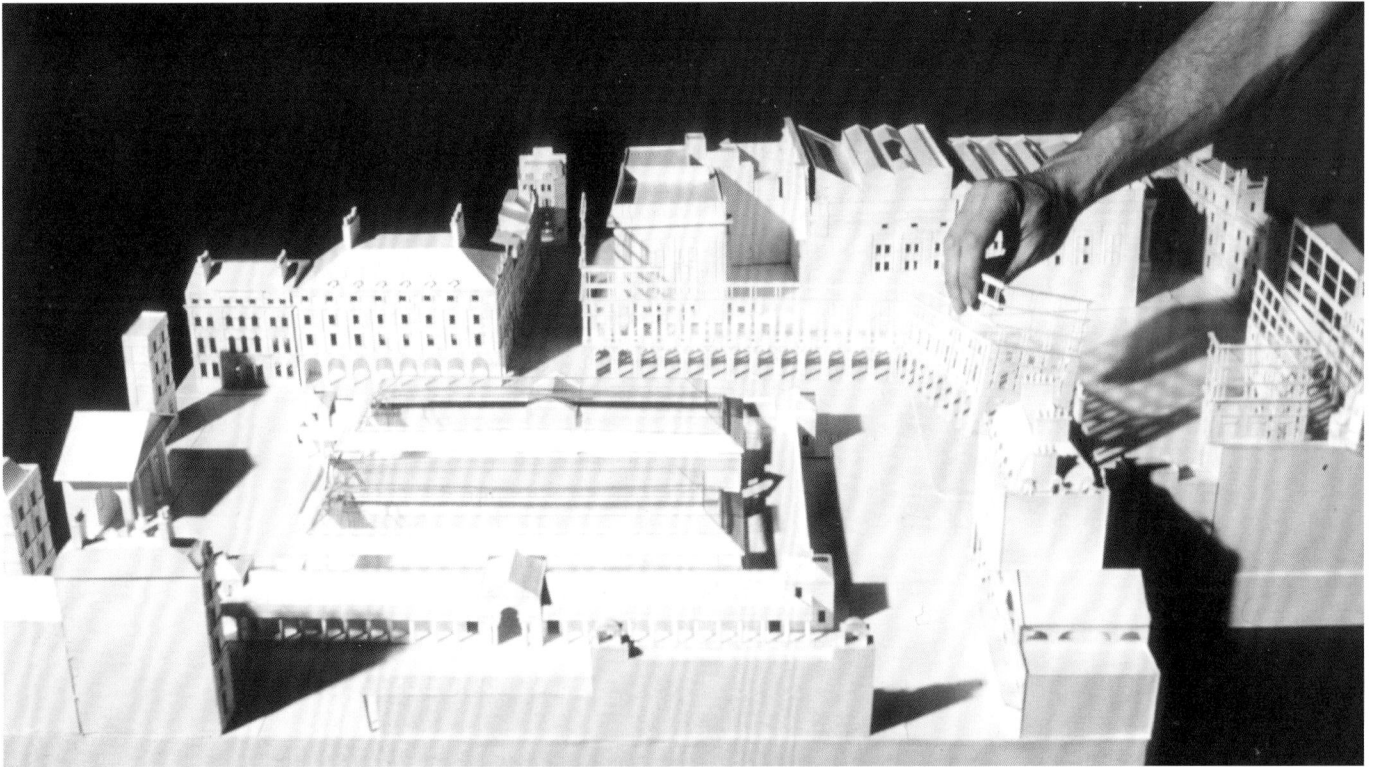

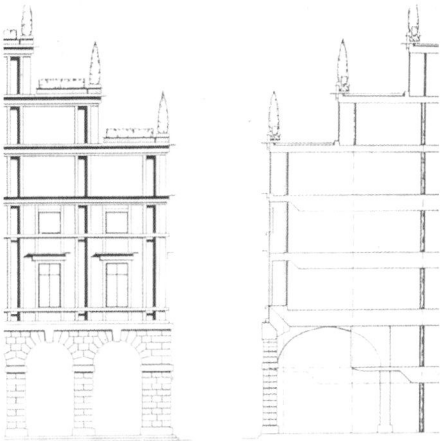

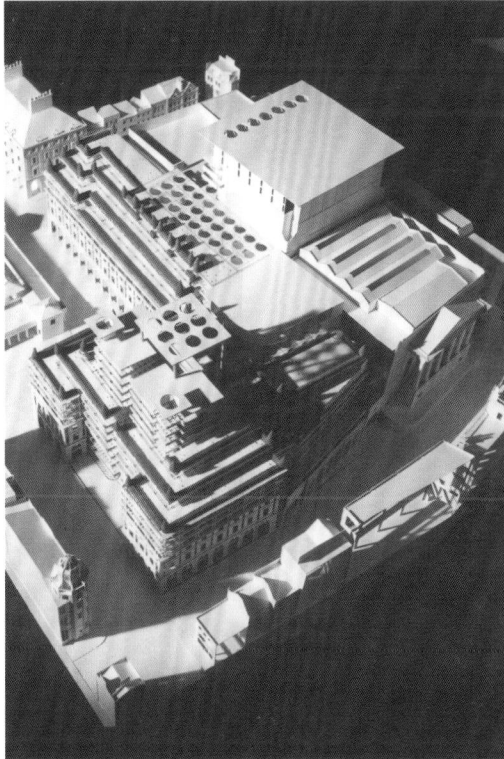

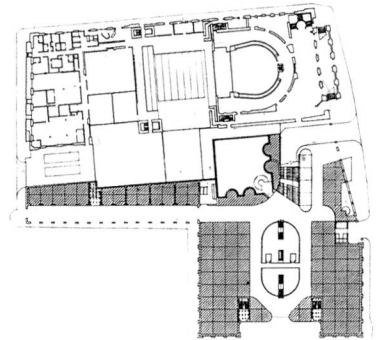

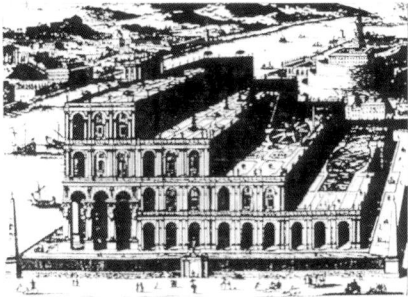

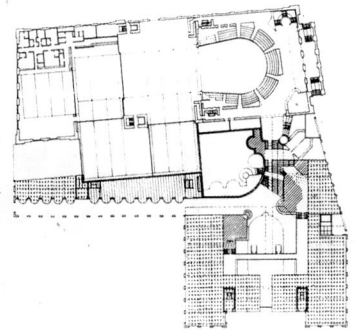

Ted would hold two parallel stories in his mind while designing, one being the physical qualities of the place and how the building might be made in response to it, and the other his empathy with and love of the human interactions and activities which would go on inside the building. These two lines of thought, occasionally conflicting but usually compounding to good effect, drove much of the discussion and intense exchanges, whether in the office, in the car, or sketched on napkins in Stella's cafe.

The first is a sort of given – Cullinan was a designer and builder who loved how things are made. He would usually start a project, armed with a Rotring pen and a razor blade for scratching out, by laboriously and silently drawing the site plan with all the contours, trees and even drains as a way of immersing himself in the new challenge. Knowing how quickly Ted could strike on a scheme I think he was using this time to hold it back and test it in his mind before exploring it with us. The second is more complex, arising perhaps more from a love of people and their behaviour than from a wish to be directly guided by them. Fortunately Ted was a good listener who loved conversations about seemingly the most ordinary interactions and these he would reflect back to users and clients to their delight. But although the activities of people were a vital part of how he described a scheme, the designs themselves seldom sprang from consultation, and more often it would help validate and refine an already developing strategy.

In the early to mid-1980s we worked on a number of competitions that raised the scale and ambition of the projects in the office, including the Royal Opera House renewal (1984) and the new Leeds Playhouse (1985). Being competition entries, these lacked client dialogue and could be seen at odds with the highly iterative design methods of previous schemes. But they involved just as much imagining of quite ordinary activities and interactions – how two people might sit opposite one another in a window embrasure, how a corridor might widen to allow space for conversation or how a sheltered cloister might encourage sitting outside whatever the weather.

The large-scale competitions were a departure for Cullinan's, requiring a huge effort and dominating everything in and out of the office. A lot depended on these more civic projects coming into the practice and not surprisingly there were stressful times. Ted's unstoppable energy for design meant he kept going, developing detail when one might think a well articulated strategy would have sufficed. The project for the Royal Opera House was based on a simple, clear strategy for reorientating the circulation and public access, but it also entailed an elaborate and detailed study of the workings of this vast institution. Its location at the corner of Covent Garden Market was a stone's throw from the practice's first office on Henrietta Street, so was close to Ted's heart. The dense urban context would raise different concerns for us than previous, typically less urban sites. Ted approached and described the proposed scheme from the outside in – that is from the make up of the elevations, with their historic references woven into modern frontages – before describing the design from within, its plan, its workings, its sectional logic, as had been the habit. Leeds Playhouse also had a beautiful, lyrical plan and it was also conceived as a significant object in the civic landscape of Leeds.

Notwithstanding these concerns with external appearance, Cullinan's design methods can be seen as classic modernist stuff – with the plan as a direct and concrete description of the life in

Leeds Playhouse (1985)
The Royal Opera House proposal was followed by a series of three unbuilt competition projects, in Leeds, Edinburgh and south of St Paul's cathedral in London), in which the practice developed an approach to placing substantial buildings in urban contexts, based on a thorough understanding of the history and existing condition of the site. At Leeds the theatre was located on Quarry Hill to accentuate its prominence and align with key streets. A lost square was reinstated by the placement of the smaller auditorium, while extensive glazing enhanced legibility and enlivened the visitor experience. The competition was won by Appleton Partnership.

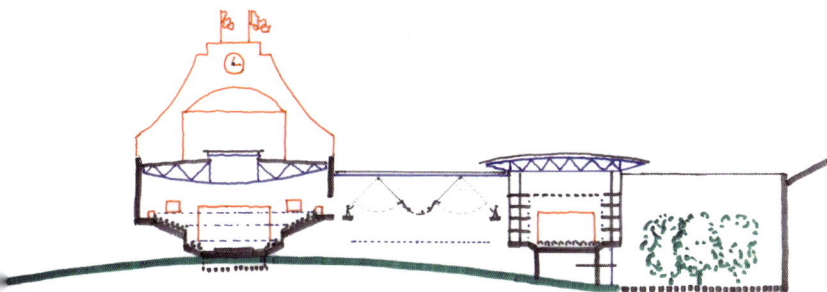

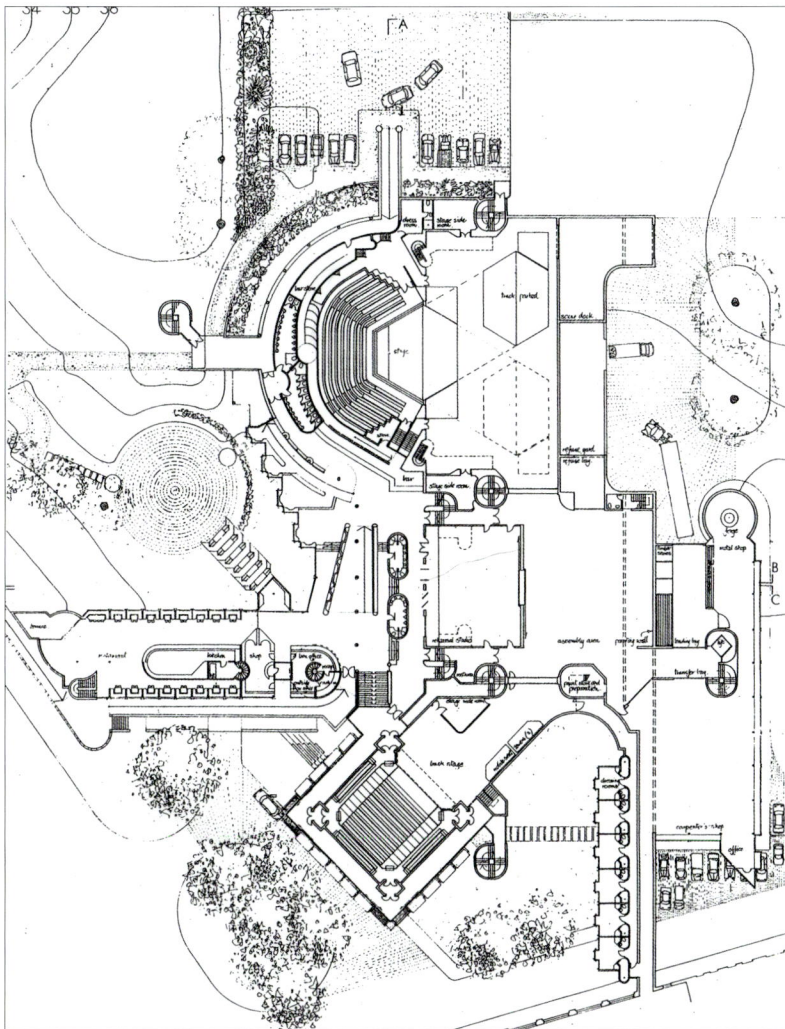

the building, with room shapes arising from the activities and rituals that happen in them and circulation as processional, social spaces of importance. The plan was fundamental to all of the schemes, and was often set down in diagram on day one. The section, with the principles of hierarchy of heavy to lightweight, of sheltered and daylit spaces, might take a little longer – but not much. It is a credit to Ted's ability to share his thinking, however incomplete, that as collaborators we felt a shared sense of purpose and ownership of the design.

And alongside these preoccupations Cullinan was exploring others. There was the story telling – rich narratives involving characters and references welling up from his memory, his imagination and his way of seeing history. These would surround the emerging design, with stories sometimes lasting weeks and involving quite mischievous wordplay bouncing round the office.

He had an almost sentimental attachment to decorative embellishment – perhaps springing from painting roses and castles on narrow boats in his teenage years – which would take us by surprise and I think may have fed the tendency for complexity. At its best this served to create a wholly justified richness, as in the layered elevations built up of enclosure, solar shading, access and planting, such as those we explored in the schools for Hampshire County Council and more formally in the facades of the Royal Opera House.

Working with Ted was about conversations and shared activities, but it was also about drawing. Drawing to explain ideas in front of other people, even while the idea is still forming in the mind, has become a lifelong habit thanks to his example and to his openness to others doing it too.

How people inhabit buildings
was a central concern
of Cullinan's architecture,
so his design approach
was focussed on moderating
the external environment
to enhance their comfort
and wellbeing

Utility and Joy
Brian Ford

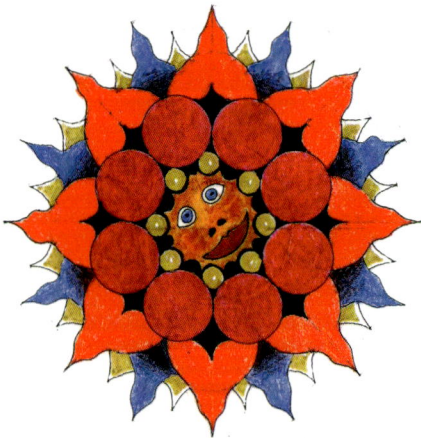

Architecture is made for people to inhabit, and to be successful it must meet the requirements of utility as well as experiential delight. Different activities require different types of space, and how our bodies define, occupy and move within space was a key starting point for Ted Cullinan.

Cullinan saw the occupants of his buildings as active participants in their environment rather than just passive recipients, and he was keen that they should engage with them and enjoy the opportunities they provided. This would include encouraging casual encounters within transition spaces, providing points of reference to facilitate navigation and enjoyment of the route, and interacting with the building to modify the internal environment. The utility and joy of inhabitation is exemplified by the people that occupy his delightful drawings.

Cullinan's awareness of the environmentally immaterial (light, air) was as strong as his awareness of the material, and its impact on the wellbeing of the occupants of his buildings. This included an understanding of the apparent movement of the sun around the building, the provision of daylight to deeper parts of the plan to enhance utility or to create drama, and the promotion of natural ventilation for air quality and thermal comfort whenever possible. In adopting this approach he would seek to exploit and enhance the particular character of the location and uniqueness of the place.

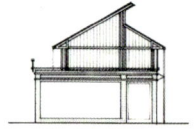

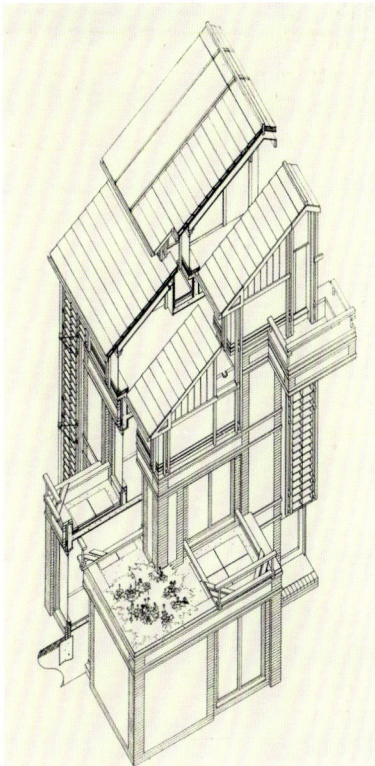

Uplands Conference Centre, High Wycombe
Built for Nationwide Building Society, new wings containing study bedrooms are arranged to form quadrangles that reinforce the focal point of the existing country house in the landscape.

Left At Minster Lovell a range of run-down stone buildings beside the River Windrush was adapted and extended to provide a residential study centre.

This is especially evident in the early project for the conference centre at Minster Lovell in Oxfordshire (1967-74). A series of new buildings was added which extended and made connections to the existing barn, malthouse and mill, showing great respect for the original Cotswold stone buildings and their setting along this stretch of the River Windrush. The steeply pitched forms of the barns were exploited to create new spaces that celebrated the big volumes. In a manner quite contrary to the architectural orthodoxy of the time, the new buildings represented a contemporary reinterpretation of the existing, fitting seamlessly into a 'highly prized historic place'.[1]

In a similar manner Uplands Conference Centre (1982-84) respected the form, character and setting of a late nineteenth-century house on a hill near High Wycombe. Here, the new additions retain the main hall as a centrepiece, picking up on the knapped flint and brickwork of the locale. The new buildings are characterised by shallow plans, with top floors exploiting the roof space to bring daylight via clerestorey or ridge glazing to the centre of the plan. The extensions to the north of the existing house introduce light through glazing along the ridge of the big new pitched roof. This light dramatises the central axis, allowing sun into the heart of the deepest part of the plan. Even under (typically) overcast sky conditions, this device provides approximately three times the amount of light per square metre from the zenith compared with vertical glazing at the perimeter. Light from above also increases the three-dimensional modelling of objects, and therefore drama, in these fine spaces.

The opportunities and risks of bringing daylight and (with care) sunlight into buildings were everyday challenges that were strategically significant in much of Cullinan's work. He described how the first houses he designed and built – the Marvin house in California and the Horder house in Hampshire (both 1958-60) – 'collected the sun'. The linear, narrow-section plans, highly glazed on the south and almost opaque on the north, can be regarded as pioneering in that they anticipate the passive solar houses of the 1970s. However, while they did both have masonry north walls and concrete floors in the bathrooms and bedrooms, which would have helped keep them cool, they were largely timber frame (so lacking in much thermal capacitance), and the glazing to the living spaces was mostly unshaded, so were likely to suffer overheating. Cullinan learned from this, and the overhanging roof and upper facade of his own house in London (and subsequent housing projects at Westmoreland Road and Leighton Crescent) protect the glazing and throw rain away from the elevation.

The environmental benefits that were derived from an evolving vocabulary of overlapping timber construction became even more evident in the series of school projects (new and refurbished) for Hampshire County Council in the 1980s. Concerned with the problems related to its large stock of system-built (SCOLA) schools – overheating in summer, underheating in winter, and deteriorating fabric – the council involved the Cullinan office (with engineer Max Fordham) in a number of projects and studies to find solutions. One of the first was at Calthorpe Park School in Fleet, where the team addressed these problems by providing a ventilated cover over the existing roof of the science laboratory building and fixed shading to reduce glare and solar gain. New buildings for mathematics and drama adopted the same vocabulary of elements. The results were applauded at the time: 'the upgrading of the science block is a transformation, not just of its technical performance but also of its architectural character. This new improved building system, with its added architectural ingredient, is then used to construct the new buildings.' [2]

The project at Fleet was followed by others at Church Crookham (refurbishment) and Farnborough Grange (new build), both of which adopted a radical approach to improve the internal environment by manipulating form and fabric to avoid overheating and enhance daylighting and ventilation (this was important not just to improve air quality, but because the additional insulation needed to reduce heat loss

Calthorpe Park School, Fleet (1981-84)
Rather than demolishing or stripping back the existing poorly performing buildings to their structural frames, insulation was added to the walls and roofs, and oversailing roofs added with steel structures supporting solar shading.

Church Crookham School, Fleet (1984-87)
A seven-point strategy for the refurbishment of the classrooms included reducing the extent of perimeter glazing and adding hinged insulated shutters. These open against triangular storage units during daytime to form pinboards. Rooflights with rotating shutters were added to enhance daylighting at the back of upper floor classrooms.

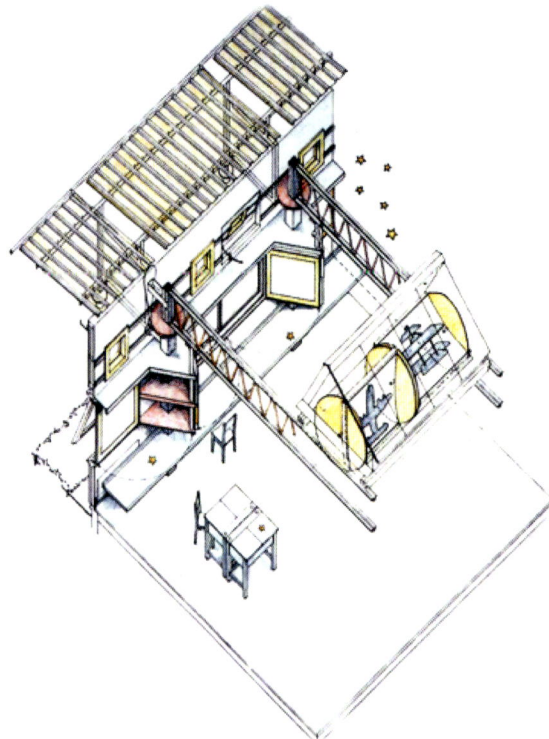

in winter increased the potential to overheat in summer).[3] At Crookham Junior school a seven-point strategy was adopted to upgrade the classroom environment.[4] This included the installation of internal insulated window shutters which acted as cupboard doors and pin-up space during the day, and folded back against the glazing at night to reduce heat loss. Parents collecting their children at the end of the day would often walk around the perimeter of the school to view the artwork framed in the windows.

At Farnborough Grange Junior School the cross section of the new southerly-oriented, single-storey classroom wings was crucial. An asymmetrical roof arrangement bounces indirect daylight deep into the plan via opening clerestorey glazing, which also ventilates the rooms and helps prevent overheating. The walls and roofs were well insulated and sunshades incorporated on vulnerable facades, providing classrooms with an internal environment far better than their 'beyond repair' predecessors.

Cullinan's Hampshire schools proved influential in demonstrating that relatively modest improvements to the design of the building fabric could provide dramatic improvements in the learning environment for both staff and students while reducing maintenance and running costs.

This approach – in which the architect's responsibility for achieving an optimum internal environment is explicit in the design – continued to be a guiding principle of the practice, and it has been refined and applied in many projects of different types. Lambeth Community Care Centre (1980-85), for example, took advantage of a southerly aspect while using the roof overhang to shade the first-floor day wards, with clerestorey windows to light and ventilate the deepest part of the plan and an exposed intermediate floor slab to moderate summer temperatures. And Chilworth Park Research Centre for the University of Southampton (1990) employed a vocabulary of overhanging roofs and an external structure supporting both vertical and horizontal shading devices, while shielding top-hung windows which ventilate the office spaces behind.

While the facade might be read as the 'visible expression of the environmental agenda'[4], Cullinan Studio's awareness that a successful environmental strategy is equally dependent on plan and section is clearly illustrated in a series of projects at the University of Cambridge.

At St John's College Library (1993), the key to achieving natural ventilation – not the norm in library buildings – was the use of a central stair tower to promote stack-driven ventilation. Fresh air is drawn from perimeter opening windows, through the open book-stack areas, to the central glass and steel lantern above the stair. This air-flow path is coupled to the thermal capacitance of the existing structure, which helps to moderate summertime temperatures. A grid of sunshades, supported on external columns further helps to reduce the risk of overheating.

In the Faculty of Divinity (2000) a cylindrical drum accommodates major public spaces, with a double-height library on the top two floors and lecture theatres in the basement. The library, with

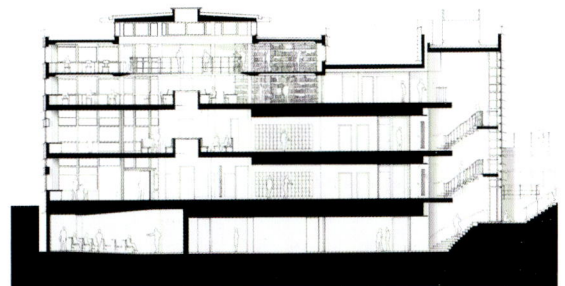

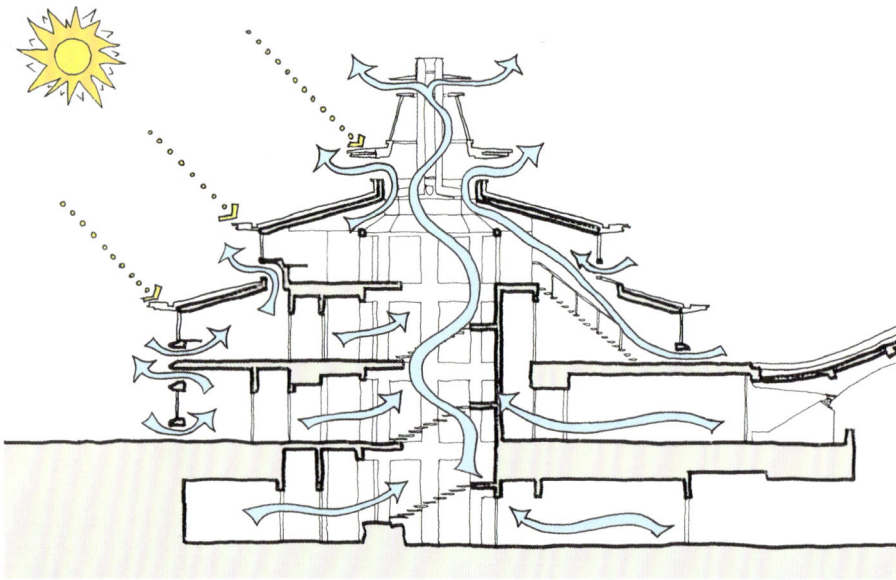

Centre for Mathematical Sciences, Cambridge

A comprehensive low-energy, natural-ventilation strategy was adopted at a large scale in the series of interlinked pavilions.

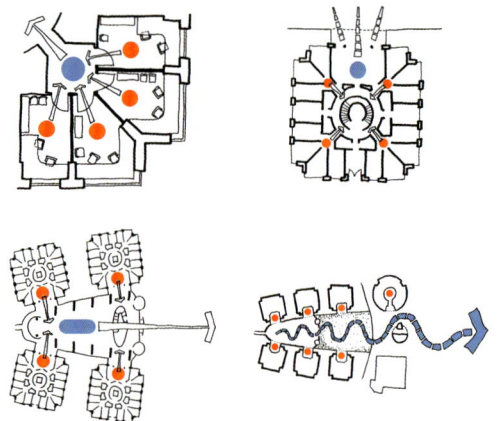

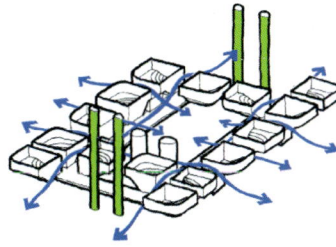

radial bookstacks, is filled with light from perimeter glazing and a central rooflight from which daylight passes through two round glazed apertures to the ground floor entrance hall.

The holistic environmental approach takes its clearest and most radical form in the Centre for Mathematical Sciences (2003). Seven pavilions, each housing a discrete discipline, surround a central reception, cafeteria and administration building, with separate drum-shaped library and gatehouse buildings. The client was averse to sealed, air-conditioned interiors, preferring den-like spaces with openable windows. The design team (with environmental engineer Roger Preston & Partners and structural engineer Buro Happold) considered passive and mixed-mode options, but decided to pursue natural ventilation for almost all the spaces. The resulting strategy combined a set of familiar measures: well-distributed daylighting, solar control, exposed thermal mass, buoyancy-assisted single-sided natural ventilation, and the facility for automatic night cooling; and a high level of occupant satisfaction with the environment was established by independent post-occupancy surveys.[5]

The international competition for Singapore Management University (SMU), won by Cullinan Studio in 2000, called for the masterplanning of a new city centre campus of seven departmental buildings, so the relationship with the existing urban form, landscape and climate was crucial.[6] The design team (which included myself) developed a strategy to promote thermal comfort in the external spaces, utilising shade and air movement, as well as inside the buildings, to help minimise the demand for air-conditioning. 'Breezeways' and shaded courts are used as informal gathering spaces, planted facades face into the gardens, 'raintrees' shade

passageways and reduce the impact of re-radiated heat, and transitional spaces are naturally ventilated, reducing energy use as well as the thermal shock of moving from outside to inside and back again.

Concern that environmental aspects should be integral to the design process was of course only part of Ted Cullinan's holistic approach. From the outset he immersed himself in the physical realisation and experience of building as a process through a series of self-build projects which in turn informed his whole ethos. In openly involving and sharing his ideas with colleagues and consultants he would also encourage others to put forward ideas, though only occasionally, very gently, he would have to remind them who was in charge.

Above, left The masterplan for Singapore Management University placed particular emphasis on thermal comfort both within and between campus buildings.

Footnotes
1 'Edward Cullinan Architects' (RIBA Publications 1984).
2 Colin Davies, 'School Refurbishment, Fleet, Hampshire' (Architectural Review, Feb 1985).
3 Brian Ford, 'Daylighting Solar Heat Gain and the Design of Fenestration for Schools' (1986 Proc PLEA Conference, Hungary).
4 Jonathan Hale, 'Ends, Middles, Beginings' (Black Dog 2005).
5 Chris Parkin and Rod Bunn, The Centre for Mathematical Sciences (BSRIA Delta T 2006).
6 See Ford, Schiano-Phan & Vallejo 'The Architecture of Natural Cooling' (Routledge 2020).

119

Principles of collaborative design, user consultation, inclusiveness and equality have been part of the Cullinan practice ethos from the outset, for both pragmatic and moral purpose

Practicing Architecture
Peter Inglis

The Cullinan cooperative model, which dates back to the founding of the office in the mid-1960s, still retains an air of the dangerously exotic. Whenever I talk about how we do things in our practice it is clear from the ensuing conversations that the model is regarded as fascinating, but maybe best observed from a distance. The idea of employee-ownership has flourished in the UK in the last decade, however, guided by the Employee Ownership Trust that talks to government about propagating the 'John Lewis' idea. But even in that world, some of the fundamental ways that Ted and his original collaborators set things up more than 60 years ago – and how we continue to operate today – still mark the company out as a radical outlier.

Ted was certainly aware of this. In the speech he gave to welcome new members into the cooperative, he would often remark how none of the previous members, who had so believed in the model, had copied it when setting up their own practices. These were fortifying words for a young partner, and they certainly conveyed the idea that we were custodians of something precious. But Ted's remark has always made me wonder what our predecessors saw and baulked at when things got serious.

Before I joined the practice in the mid-1990s I was aware of Cullinan's through its published work. Seeing the joyful images of the RMC headquarters in the Sunday Times convinced me that I had to study architecture.

The Cullinan cooperative ethos seemed to be intrinsically linked to how the work of the practice was portrayed in the late 1980s and early 90s. I had begun to understand how architecture was an inclusive process, and one in which I could imagine playing a part, even though I didn't fully understand it at the time. There was something about the way all the project team members were credited that was quite unusual, and made me think how one might fit into the office. Therein, however, lies the apparent contradiction that I came across very quickly in my early days in the studio. How could a genuinely open sharing of thoughts and ideas co-exist with Ted's self-acknowledged raging design ego that in the end

had to triumph? I had often heard it remarked that 'I know about Cullinan's cooperative – you cooperate with Ted', but the reality was much more subtle than that.

The heated discussions, the metaphorical arm-wrestles in the studio, were actually rigorous examinations of the whole team's ideas. The need to test ideas to destruction was a way of anticipating strengths and weaknesses so that defences could be prepared and fall-back plans gathered. Ted needed to be sure of his ground, and to do that he needed to 'own' the design. But that ownership was always generously acknowledged to clients and the public alike as being shared.

For the business itself, the cooperative principles are elegantly simple, although their execution has always been somewhat elastic. The Cullinan Studio was never technically a cooperative nor a partnership, although we refer to the cooperative principles and call ourselves partners. At its heart is an open and equitable income share, and a barrier-free model to partnership. But as we adapt to continually changing business and environmental contexts, we constantly check back to the founding principles as a kind of moral compass.

In the early days of the practice (I'm reliably informed), when a fee cheque arrived it would be fairly shared among the members. One presumes that when a bill arrived, there would be similar whip round. We don't quite do it like that anymore, although the same principle remains. Everyone agrees each others' proportion of the overall salary pot, based on value and experience. There is a maximum pay differential of 1:3 – which has been in place since the beginning. This negotiation of the division happens in an open meeting once a year. It can be emotionally challenging, but it is vital to the whole ethos of fairness that underpins the company. If you feel undervalued, you can make a case for a larger slice, but that gets cut from everyone else. In that way the equilibrium of an equitable settlement for the following year is found. The salary pot is then re-assessed each quarter, based on predicted fee income and other outgoings, so pay rises and falls according to the performance of the

business. It means everyone understands the worth of what they do, and takes collective responsibility for the effect of their decisions on the overall wellbeing of the office.

It is a fundamental principle that no one has to buy in and no one builds up capital. The shares are held in a trust, and the assets will go to charity, should the company ever be dissolved. This means that there is no financial barrier to becoming a partner, and no one is hanging around for a pay out. The idea is to build a committed team, with members investing in each other and in making a success of the business. It's also a model in which no one is ever likely to become wealthy, but the pain of hard times is also shared, and that can indeed be painful.

Everyone needs to accept the model for it to work – and it has to be said that the model wouldn't work for everyone – it can be draining, especially in tough times. The easy-go aspect means that when people have decided it's time to leave, it can be done without the difficult transactions of dissolving a partnership or selling back shares. There's now a large network of former partners, spanning six decades, who nevertheless still feel a bond.

Setting up as a cooperative at the outset could be seen as an act of egalitarian magnanimity by Ted, in that it rejected the idea of an owner building up capital at the expense of the workers. It's also clear from the early manifesto that he and his first partners were motivated by the idea that how you did something would manifest itself in what was created. If you wanted to shape an architecture for an egalitarian society, you had to start with the practice itself. But it also proved to be an extremely pragmatic way of arranging a system that allowed him to concentrate on the architecture. At the same time he could put trust in others to worry about all the other stuff. Perhaps to protect him from his own worst instincts when it came to money?

Despite being the founder of a far-sighted and radical practice model, Ted wasn't commercially minded. He gave the impression of being generally hopeless with money and I'm not certain that, for all his considerable architectural talents, even if he had wanted to, he would have made a financial success of a traditional sole principal type practice. It's certainly true he was openly disdainful of that type of set-up, but mostly for how its exploitation of the workforce eventually led to cynicism and devalued the architecture produced.

There is an enigma somewhere here about true motivations, but the structure was clearly developed over the years around his very particular personality, to liberate him to do architecture and work with others as he wanted to do it.

Ted was adamant that the cooperative was only ever supposed to be a means to achieving great architecture, and not as an end in itself. 'If it stops serving that aim, we'll do it another way.' That's still true: the details of its operation will evolve with the balance of skills and personalities of the current custodians of the cooperative, but at its most fundamental level, it still serves its purpose well.

> Cullinan drew on history and tradition not as an academic exercise but as a way to demonstrate a meaningful connection between the making of a building and the art of architecture

Purposeful Architecture
Meredith Bowles

Like many others, my introduction to Ted Cullinan was at a lecture – telling stories through his inimitable drawings – when he came to the University of Sheffield in 1982. As students we had been taught that the city's Park Hill housing estate was a heroic failure of modernism, and we were navigating our way between the lure of Charles Jencks' 'postmodernism' and the much more exciting 'high-tech' architecture of Rogers and Foster. Prince Charles' 'carbuncle' intervention was yet to come, but there was certainly a polarised debate, with ideas about the city and our western classical heritage contrasting with the modernist ethos of a 'machine-à-habiter'.

Against this bewildering backdrop, with impish delight Ted delivered a talk about making buildings, drawing a step-by-step account of how they are put together. I later understood Ted's great wealth of architectural references, but on that day he didn't choose to dress up the buildings in theory, preferring to give us the facts of the matter, and convey the delight to be had in practical problem solving. He described in detail the amazingly complex geometrical construction of St Mary's church at Barnes, which was yet to be completed. I didn't know then where to place Cullinan in relation to architecture, although his was the first talk I'd heard that connected the physical making of buildings with the art of architecture.

A few years later I was given a book as a gift. Edited by Denys Lasdun, 'Architecture in an Age of Sceptism' was a collection of essays, including one by Ted, among other more established voices. Illustrated with black and white photos, it had a slightly old-fashioned quality and a lack of showiness. What brought the architects together was a seriousness of purpose, a resolve to make an architecture 'that can play its part in creating and maintaining the well-being of society'. These essays allowed me to hear directly from architects whose work seemed less concerned with fashion, and was freighted with a sense of the continuity of time, and of social purpose. It was an antidote to the prevailing debates about 'style', and urged me as a young architect to look again at recent architecture, rather than seeking

Above, right St Mary's church, Barnes, was radically remodelled after a fire in 1978 that had left only its walls standing.

Left Greene & Greene's 1908 Gamble House, Pasadena.

novelty for its own sake, or looking backward to a classical past. It was an attempt to place modernism within the evolution of architectural history, rather than as a break from the past in the way that we'd been taught.

Ted's essay in Lasdun's book outlines the genesis of his thinking through a series of single houses, which he describes in terms of the process of construction, before he moves on to larger commissions. The essay is infused with context; of time and place, and an acute awareness of past architecture and how it retains its relevance. He enthused about California, the 'on-the-spot invention' and his excitement at seeing buildings by Neutra, Schindler and Maybeck. His experience of this optimistic culture framed the work that followed. He described the arts and crafts buildings of Greene & Greene in a way that could equally apply to his own work: 'wood (Californian redwood) has finally emerged to construct a house and the great canopy over it, logically and without unnecessary effort but with supreme care and grace in the joints and in the ends; where abstracted space is created from the parts, from sticks and planes and openings and voids, where the whole is the parts and the parts are the whole'. His study of architecture was a personal, visceral adventure.

Visiting St Mary's Barnes years after Ted's lecture and well after the building had been completed, I was struck by the balance between preservation and new interventions. The space created is far removed from a traditional linear hierarchy, and allows for communal worship, with a single space belonging to the whole congregation. A stage had been set for music concerts, and within the space everyone is close to the stage or altar. The great roof, with its complicated geometry of 'sticks', tumbles down at the sides, coming almost to the ground like a great enveloping cloak – it feels like an embrace. Externally, it's hard to understand how this unorthodox interior remains hidden. The retained medieval church and remnants of the Edwardian additions are extended and absorbed by a new architecture that is both contemporary and familiar. The brick and stone detailing of

the walls allows the ancient and the new to knit together as a whole, and the red plain tile roof is continuous. Between the two is a break of dark stained timber and clerestorey glazing, a clue to the exposed construction within; and a curious stunted tower signals the unorthodox plan.

The Barnes church is an amazingly complex work, where the power of the newly created space is contingent on the circumstances that constrain it. An appreciation of history, the arts and crafts' love of detail, on-the-spot invention, and the social act of architecture are all present at once. The structural and geometric invention of the roof, the play of materials in the solid base and lightweight top, and the qualities of light and space came back to me once I'd been introduced to what Sandy Wilson called the 'Other Tradition' of Scandinavian modernism. I visited Sverre Fehn's buildings, and later Johannes Exner's Islev Church, and saw the work in a new light. I wondered what Barnes would have been like without the constraints.

St Mary's, Barnes
Exterior and interior views, and hosting a music recital.

Above, right The Cartesian node, in which components intersect and by-pass in three orthogonal directions, was employed by Gerrit Rietveld in furniture designs as well as buildings, hence the 'Rietveld Joint'. The reading of components and planes as distinct elements extends to layers and planes in Cullinan's work. Inger and Johannes Exner's Islev Church, Copenhagen (1969).

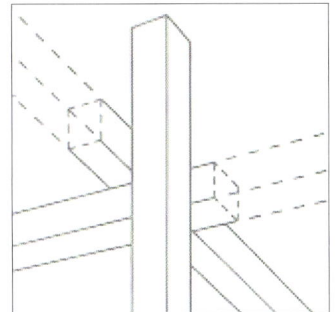

125

Cullinan was in his early 30s when he embarked on 'two years of weekends' building his house in Camden Mews – a brilliant exploration of his architectural ideas, simple and direct. His well-rehearsed explanation of the building, using animated additive drawings, derived from the construction sequence, with one layer adding to the last: one step enclosing the space of the site, the next framing the space of the building in concrete, then spanning the roof in timber, and the brilliance of hanging the front wall from the roof. It's as if he was urging us to all build for ourselves: try it yourself, it's not so hard!

Cullinan had a gift for imparting his enthusiasm and making people believe they could achieve great things. As if we too – through hard work and friendship – could take architectural history, concentrate it into a personal statement, and force it into being.

There's an intensity in the little Camden Mews house, with so much packed into such a tight site. Cleverly using half the plot, he created a long south-facing elevation, with a single 'gallery' room on the upper floor, glazed on three sides and closed to the north. This room overlooks the garden – in fact more a landscaped construction raised on the garage roof. The route to the house takes one up steep brick steps to the 'garden', and from there, a leap across a bridge to the suspended timber upper floor – it's an adventure in arriving home. The brick and concrete ground-floor 'hull', entered down a tiny winding stair, houses a series of bunk rooms with clerestorey lights set deep within its earthy base.

The details at Camden Mews are both simple and allusive. They hold something in common with contemporaneous buildings such as David Levitt's

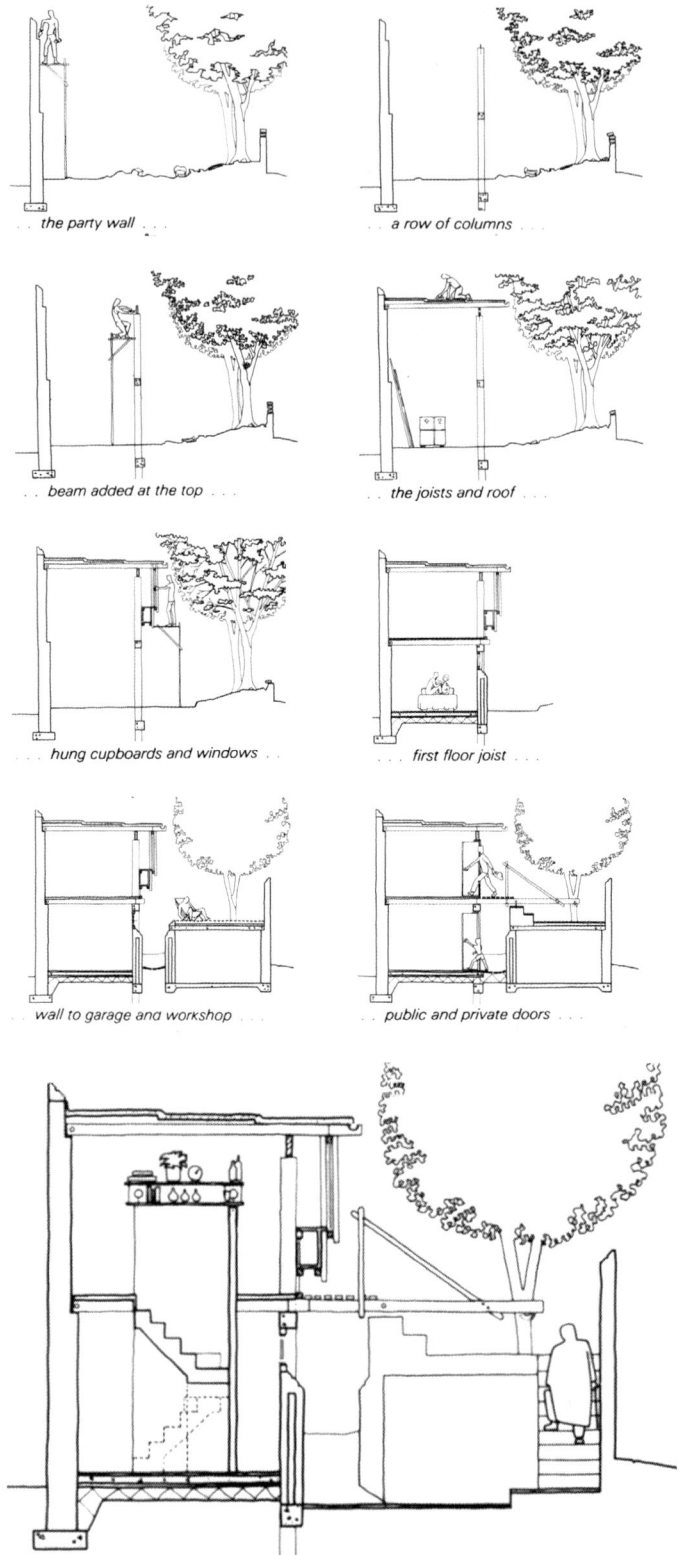

... the party wall

... a row of columns

... beam added at the top ...

... the joists and roof ...

... hung cupboards and windows ...

... first floor joist ...

... wall to garage and workshop ...

... public and private doors ...

Camden Mews
Cullinan's celebrated
sequence of drawings, much
repeated in lectures, reveals
the logic of its sequential
construction and the
sectional arrangement.
On the upper level a linear
storage box is set between
the in situ concrete columns
and the large windows that
hang from the roof joists.

Right Cullinan worked with
Denys Lasdun on the design
of the Norfolk and Suffolk
Terraces – the 'Ziggurat'
student residences – at the
University of East Anglia.
The stepped section of the
student rooms, whereby the
window cills are level with
the roof of the room below,
became a recurring theme in
Cullinan's work.

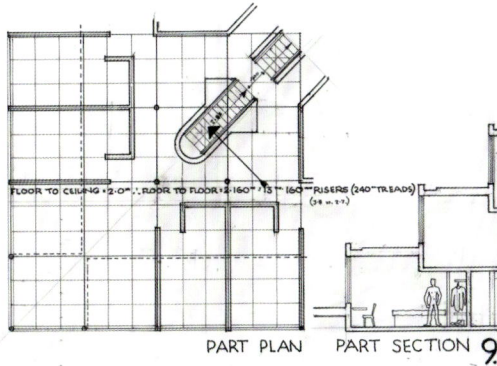

PART PLAN   PART SECTION 9.

house at Ansty Plum and Peter Aldington's
Turn End. But the dark stained timber and the
mannerist jointing could come from Greene &
Greene's Gamble House, or Rudolph Schindler's
own house, with its expressed roofs and
clerestorey glass slotted between the joists,
coupled with its concrete tilt-up wall construction.
Through Schindler there is an allusion to Japan,
via Frank Lloyd Wright, but all of this leads back
somehow to the elemental nature of vernacular
timber building, of building houses raised out of
the earth, whether in Japan or medieval England.

My son, who was just born when I built my own
house, later lived in one of the 1960s Ziggurat
student residences at the University of East
Anglia, Cullinan's project when he was working
at Denys Lasdun's office. It's a stunning building,
heroic in scale with grand staircases threading
through to a high-level connecting walkway,
and with refined, beautifully judged elevations.
Each student room has the requisite storage,
desk, bed and sink, a perfect cell for study.
As in Le Corbusier's La Tourette monastery,
the wash basin is separated from the sleeping
and study area by a timber screen, here
containing a bookshelf. Constructed from a series
of paired timbers, it is bolted through the frame,
reminiscent of Rietveld's Highback armchair and
an obvious antecedent of much of Ted's detailing,
including the hanging windows at Camden Mews.

The room has huge south-facing windows, which
for a few months of the year are perfect, but in
summer it can overheat, partly because the
retrofitted safety locks limit the window opening.
My son found a tool to remove the restrictor, so
he could open the room fully to the park. He
would sit out on roof, contemplating his future
in the sunshine, in an act of defiance that I'm
sure Ted would have endorsed.

127

Storytelling was how Cullinan
made sense of the world,
both to himself and to others,
and many of his buildings –
not least the RMC headquarters –
were conceived and developed
around an invented narrative

Building Stories
Richard Gooden

Although Cullinan hesitated at being included in the stable of 'Romantic Pragmatists', an epithet invented in the mid-1980s by Architectural Review editor Peter Davey, much of his work bore clear signs of romantic or individual expression. Every building displays invention in how materials are brought together, a fascination with craft and also an interest in storytelling.

As well as a considerable architect, Cullinan was an accomplished and much sought-after stand-up. His absorbing routines, accompanied by hand-drawn acetates on an overhead projector, had a beginning, middle and end, a plot and often a great deal of humour. They were stories in quite a traditional way. During one of many car journeys to the RMC site in Thorpe, Surrey, Ted told me that one of his favourite books was 'The Good Soldier' by Ford Madox Ford. Written at the start of the first world war, Ford's book is anything but traditional – it plays with time, uncertainty, truth and half-revealed facts. On reading the book that summer, I found myself intrigued that Ted should rate it so highly – it seemed that he enjoyed ambiguity more than I'd ever thought.

Where Ted was presented with a project that included buildings that had to be retained, one way he sought to make sense of the situation was by creating new reality, through fiction. From the early project at Minster Lovell Mill, using the vernacular language of Cotswold stone to stitch together a group of disparate buildings, to St Mary's in Barnes, where burnt-out fragments of the original church were threaded onto a new armature of steel and timber trusses – including the bold move of turning the nave through 90 degrees – it is possible to see a really inventive storyteller at work.

This approach reached an apotheosis with the RMC Group headquarters (1986-90). Ready Mixed Concrete (now part of Cemex) was then one of Europe's largest construction supply companies and its chairman, John Camden – as no-nonsense as the name of the company itself – wanted to build a new headquarters to replace its nondescript offices in Surrey. RMC owned considerable areas of gravel pits in the Green

RMC headquarters
Located in Surrey near Thorpe Park amusement park, itself built around former gravel pits owned by Ready Mix Concrete, the RMC headquarters (1986-90), incorporates a listed eighteenth-century classical house and stable block, a late nineteenth-century arts and crafts villa, also listed, brick garden walls and protected trees. New accommodation set into this historic framework included offices for 200, a foyer, restaurant, dining rooms, squash courts, gym, pool, teaching rooms, bedrooms, laboratories, meeting and board rooms. The walled perimeter, penetrated by key entry points, enclosed a world of grass roofs and landscaped courts. The RMC was a pioneering low-energy project, with all the buildings naturally-lit and -ventilated and highly insulated.

'Cemex, which acquired RMC and its headquarters in 2005, applied in 2013 to demolish the building and redevelop the site for luxury housing. Its site assessment characterised the Cullinan work as "a modern office block" and asserted that the only buildings worth retaining were the three original houses. We were galvanised into action, and fortunately English Heritage came to a different conclusion, and in 2014 the site became one of a very few late twentieth-century buildings to be listed as grade II*. Recently, new designs to convert the complex into a "retirement community" were given consent. I always imagined that a collegiate use for the site was waiting in the wings and embedded in its story.'
RG

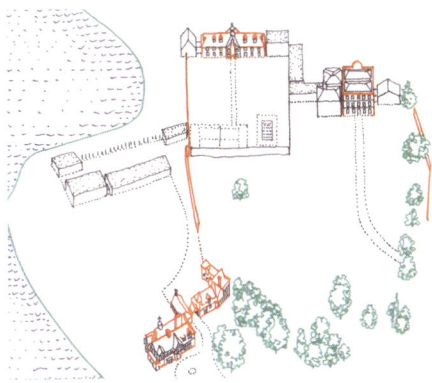

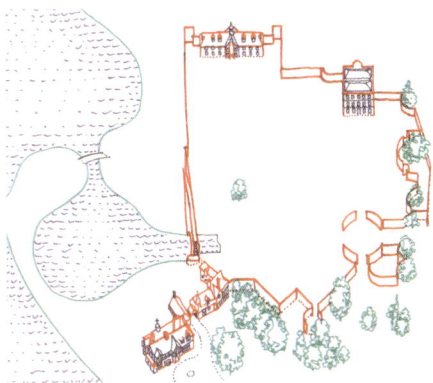

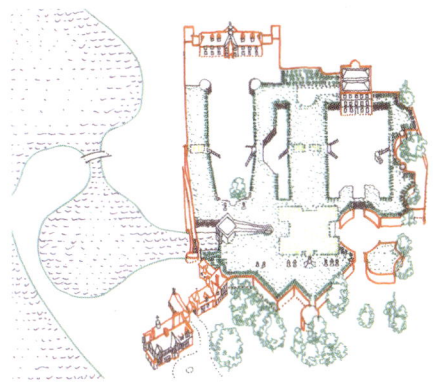

Belt, many where the M25 and M3 motorways meet, some of which were turned over to leisure use and became Thorpe Park. The headquarters was to be based around a group of three converted houses and gardens which the company already used as a training base. One of the buildings – Eastley End House – was listed, as were the garden walls encircling the three. Partly because the move to the new building was away from the bright lights of Staines, the brief included leisure, restaurant and other facilities intended to keep the executives fit, fed and entertained. A training centre was also to be provided, including short-stay residential accommodation.

Early designs by other architects had looked likely to be refused planning consent and Cullinan's was approached to bring new eyes to the matter. Ted harnessed his charm and persuasive powers again and again throughout the design period, planning refusal and subsequent successful public inquiry to elaborate the story of how the three historic houses could be extended – firstly and close to – in their own styles and then beyond as inhabited gardens. This approach won over the tough client and the Planning Inspectorate, and latterly, English Heritage.

As Ted often conceded, this was a deliberately romanticised story, based on the clear-eyed observation that the way to an English person's heart is through their garden.

In reality, however, there was something much more subtle and less straightforward at play. The generally axial composition of the RMC building brings clarity to the site, but the experience is also discursive and sometimes even unsettling. There are moments where it is not clear what is ground level and what was newly constructed. Hanging yew hedges enclose seats for rooftop meetings, necessary elements such as rooftop ventilators are recast as chess pieces, and there is a paved chess board from which they might have escaped. And there's a pavilion based (loosely) on one of Cullinan's favourite houses – Joldwynds – built just a few miles away by Philip Webb in 1874, but demolished in 1930.

130

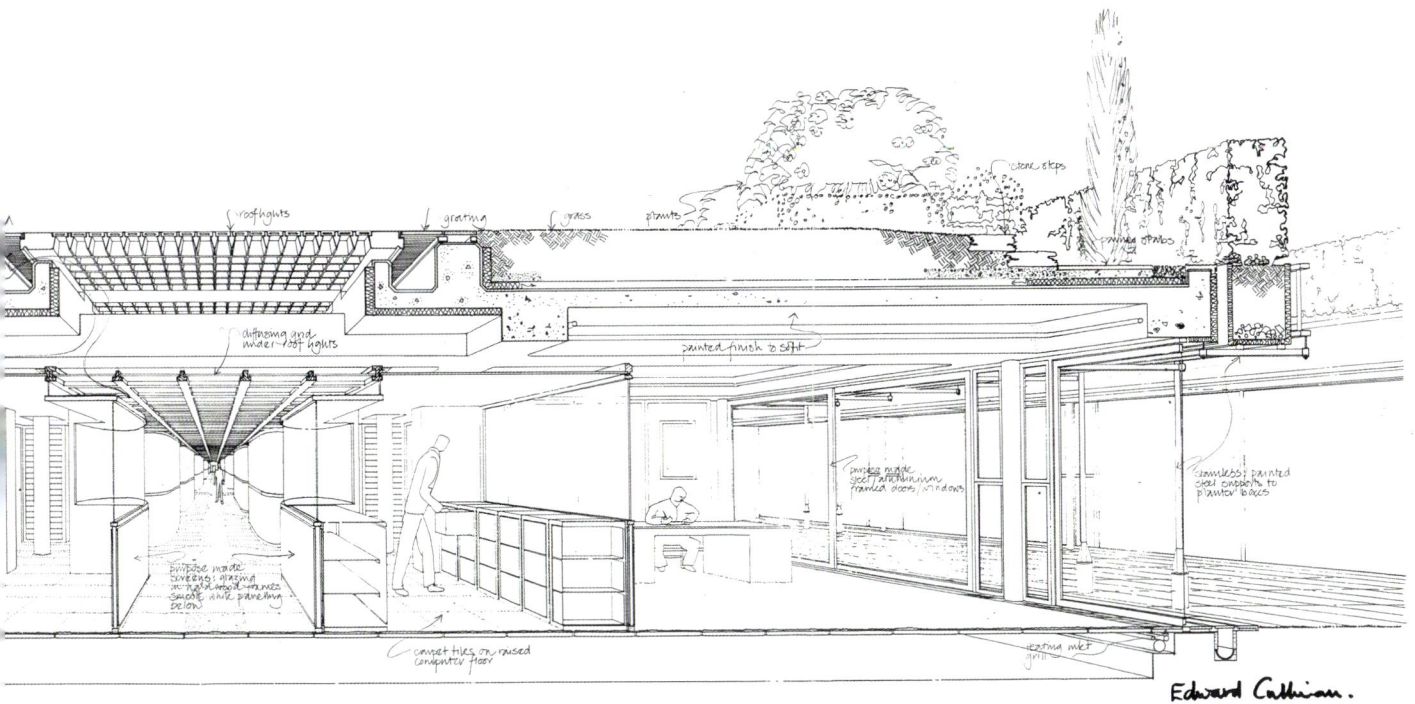

Edward Cullinan.

Below RMC aerial view; rooftop 'chess piece' ventilation extracts over the pool and dining areas; linking staircase to the grassed roofs.

The RMC entrance foyer (horribly mangled in an early-2000s makeover) terminated in an open-sided swimming pool, with views of the lake beyond, and entry to the offices was gained only by passing the restaurant and squash courts, a move intended to enhance social interaction. Defied expectations and surprises were present throughout.

Time and space are played with in a thoroughly modern manner. The building creates a place that – because it embraces the original houses – feels like it has always been there. But it also provides an episodic narrative of old and new where each maintains its own strength and qualities. In retrospect, I shouldn't have been a bit surprised about Ted's liking for 'The Good Soldier'.

Besides his engaging humility, it was Cullinan's dogged determination to get things done that motivated his colleagues – even with protracted and frustrated projects such as Stonehenge, Shahhat and a kitchen extension in Suffolk

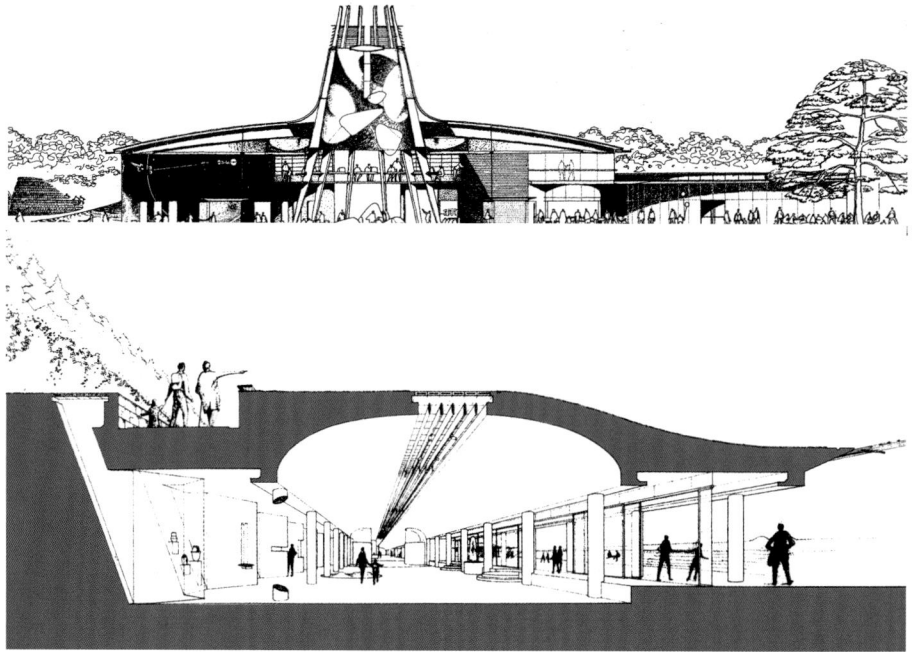

Circular Tours
Mark Whitby

In presenting his vision for a theatre in Telford, Ted's performance was worthy of a great thespian, drawing live with coloured pens on an overhead projector. The city officials probably didn't notice the series of dots that guided his unfolding perspective in the thoroughly rehearsed performance. What appeared informal and genial was underpinned with a determined rigour – how could they not choose us?

Disappointingly they didn't, but the 'us' was relevant, as Ted fully embraced his team and for him the engineer played Iago to his Othello. The process of making buildings was a performance where each played off the other. There was no sense of other members of the team being silent partners. Ted enjoyed his engineers and I was secretly jealous of his relationship with Ted Happold and Mike Dickson at Hooke Park, and particularly for the Centre for Mathematical Sciences in Cambridge.

Cullinan was a gentle architect, whose architecture reflected his humanity. As with a number of other architects with whom I have been fortunate to work – such as Bob Maguire – we felt our way while he encouraged and cajoled. In the event we actually built little with Cullinan's – the Faculty of Divinity in Cambridge and the University of East London on the dockside opposite the city airport – both involving round buildings. But what defined our relationship were the projects we didn't build.

In 1992 we worked with Cullinan's on the winning scheme for a new visitor centre at Stonehenge. Little did we realise what was involved and how it would shape a decade of work. The competition came about as a result of Jocelyn Stevens' appointment as chairman of English Heritage, who regarded the old visitor facilities as a national disgrace. The Ministry of Defence objected to the siting of the proposed visitor centre at Larkhill and we were sucked into a battle with the Department of Transport, which was pushing through plans to widen the A303 road past the stones. It was a monumental exercise as we schemed up tunnels and alternative routes only to be shot down on cost, thwarted by archaeologists or blocked by secret military establishments (mostly protecting ammunition dumps too fragile to move). It was a

SITE PLAN

Above Edward Cullinan Architects' first competition-winning proposal for Stonehenge visitor centre was for a site at Larkhill, one kilometre north of the monument (plan drawing by landscape architect Georgina Livingston).

Right Cullinan's sketch plan highlighting the ecological and archaeological sites threatened by the planned coast road from Apollonia to Ptolemais in Libya (the plan was accidentally mirrored). Perpective of the practice's proposed residential district at Shahhat.

Opposite Sections of successive proposals for Stonehenge visitor centre on different sites, and Ted Cullinan's sketch of visitors approaching the monument.

tragedy on the scale of Hamlet, with Stevens furiously facing down the Department of Transport, while amidst it all Ted primed the encounters with his beautifully engineered sketches. Oddly he took me aside after one meeting to tell me to 'keep on talking'. I am still not quite sure if I understood what he meant. The competition was rerun a number of times but eventually we lost out.

Our relationship was reversed ten years later when I led a major study of the Jabal al Akhdar, the 'Green Mountain' region in Libya. Again a road became a focus of attention and Ted, whose team was drawing up plans for a new town in Shahhat, joined us in formulating a response. Contractors had already started constructing a 70-kilometre coast road, ploughing through a virgin wilderness and threatening some extraordinary archaeological sites. We needed an alternative and had to demonstrate its value. From a wonderful office high in the mountains overlooking the ancient city of Cyrene we drew up the plans together, and I was entrusted to take them the 600 miles back to Tripoli. Arriving late in the afternoon I briefed our client who then took me to meet a series of nameless officials, each of whom made calls and sent us on to meet others. Was this the 'cabinet'? It was best not to ask. Rather embarrassingly, the map we had drawn was mirrored, with south at the top, but it mattered little as three days later construction was halted. Ted, as always, was optimistic and encouraging – just as he was later in a quixotic tryst with Network Rail in Manchester and, in a more lighthearted manner (but for an equally lost cause) in preparing a wonderful sustainable vision for Letchworth.

More recently Ted and Roz visited our house in Suffolk, and the conversation inevitably turned to how we might exploit the view. The felt tips came out and a design for a circular kitchen extension ensued. We didn't build the extension but we did salvage a safari hut that had floated away on a recent flood, sliced it in half with a chain saw and transported it on the forks of a tractor to a new location high up in the garden where, re-clad, it has lost its former connotations. I'm sure Ted would have appreciated the whole process, though I suspect he'd rather it had a copper roof.

Drawing on his experience in the
1970s – parallel with Cullinan –
in developing new solutions
for low-rise high-density housing,
Edward Jones revisits Highgrove
in Hillingdon and Netherfield
in Milton Keynes

50 Years On
Edward Jones

The view from the rear window of my study looks north to a loose assemblage of warehouses. Here, approached from Jamestown Road, is where Ted Cullinan's studio was based in the early 1970s, with engineer Max Fordham upstairs. It is difficult to think about this part of Camden Town without being reminded of Ted, his spirit, his friendship and passionate commitment to his practice. As opposed to the sense of philanthropy normally associated with those involved with the production of public housing, Ted brought something different. Possibly encouraged by his time as a student at Berkeley on America's west coast, whereby working for London councils had a democratic rather than charitable imperative. His use of the overhead projector in lectures also allowed him to intimately draw and discuss design thoughts to a broad popular audience.

As a young architect one was aware, not without a touch of envy, of Ted's appropriation of this urban territory, of his design of Dingwalls dance hall at Camden Lock and his occupation of the Jamestown Road warehouse. All this by way of contrast to weekends spent at his rural retreat at Gib Tor, with the voluntary physical exertion of manual labour and the marvellous bleakness of the Derbyshire moors. Despite all this admiration, working with Ted somehow never happened. Was it something to do with Cambridge versus the Architectural Association, Dutch structuralism versus Alan Colquhoun, or the 'arts and crafts' opposed to the 'heroic period' of modern architecture? But then, possibly more as a result our own competitiveness, we (Cross, Dixon, Gold and Jones) drove daily up and down the M1 to participate in Derek Walker's initiative to design and build early housing for the emerging city of Milton Keynes.

This was a period of considerable social change and, dare one say, moral purpose under Harold Wilson's Labour government; firstly, for declining assistance to American imperialism in south-east Asia, and then giving encouragement to a huge public housing programme. Sydney Cook's Camden was the most visible, characterised by Neave Brown's expanding scale of projects, from a modest terrace at Winscombe Street to the urban

Highgrove housing, Hillingdon
Site plan/section and gardens at Highgrove; the interstitial alleys have been softened by the mature landscape (right, on completion; left, now).

Below In the 1970s the Cullinan office was off Jamestown Road in the backlands of Camden Town.

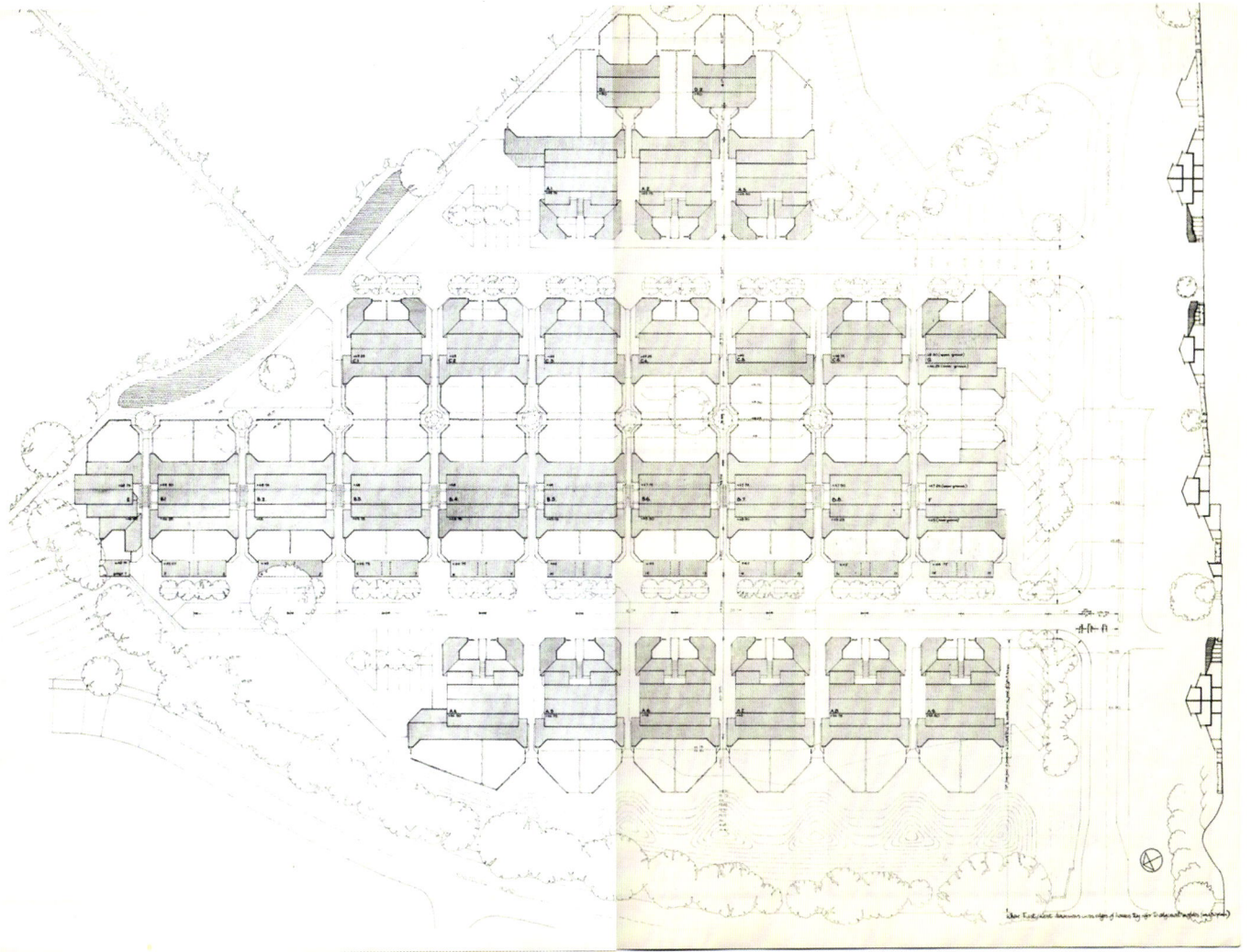

block at Fleet Road and concluding with the monumental stepped terrace of 500 dwellings at Alexandra Road. During this period, the Cullinan studio was designing the Highgrove houses for the London Borough of Hillingdon (1972-77) and our journey up the M1 resulted in the Netherfield estate (1971-77). While not of a similar scale (113 houses at Highgrove and 1068 at Netherfield) or similar context (a leafy London suburb compared to the brave new world of an entire Milton Keynes grid square), a comparison seems not uninteresting. But the question might inevitably be asked, what has a patch of London suburbia got to do with a New Town dominated by the inspiration of Los Angeles? Although it hasn't gone unnoticed that the arterial roads of Clapham, Streatham and Tooting bear some likeness to the American strip, and LA in particular – and so, two contrasting takes on the suburb.

The comparison between Highgrove and Netherfield is not entirely arbitrary. Both projects exhibit an enthusiasm for straight lines set against a gentle and undulating ground plane; both projects emphasise the importance of the roof, at Highgrove blue metal, at Netherfield a single datum of a near-kilometre in length; and both adopt a single house idea for the site as a whole. In the case of Highgrove the semi-detached pavilion, with four houses back-to-back, had its origins in Ted's own house in Camden Mews, and the narrow lanes between the buildings reflected the dense occupation of the interior of the Jamestown Road block. However, despite both being designed according to Parker Morris space standards and coming under not dissimilar influences, the results could not have been more different – as Brendan Woods has observed, Frank Lloyd Wright's Broadacre City versus Mies van der Rohe's Lafayette Park in Detroit.

The concept of low-rise high-density housing was emerging at this time, in opposition to 'mixed development' – the combination of stubby towers and three-to-four storey maisonette blocks which had disfigured much of post-war British housing (from its Swedish origin, the only country building during the second world war). An early unbuilt investigation into 'carpet' housing was made by Le Corbusier at Cap Martin in 1948, but it was not until 1962, with Atelier 5's Siedlung Halen in Bern, that a convincing low-rise high-density paradigm finally emerged. Later, in Cambridge in the early 1970s, Lionel March and Leslie Martin published 'Urban Space and Structures', further demonstrating that the densities of mixed development could be matched by three- to four-storey terraces in squares typical of the nineteenth-century city.

Right The original blue steel roofs, angled at the eaves and since replaced, lent a striking unity to Highgrove. Section and plans of type B houses on the southerly side of the site.

Below left Cross Dixon Gold Jones' Netherfield housing at Milton Keynes. 'Our arrival in MK in 1971 aroused mixed feelings of the national service we never did (producing architecture along military lines) and the start of Evelyn Waugh's 'Brideshead Revisited'. This is not to suggest that the development corporation's Wavendon Towers hq had anything to do with Hawksmoor (Castle Howard being the setting for a 1981 television adaptation), or that chief architect Derek Walker might have been mistaken for Lord Marchmain. But, not unlike Waugh's Captain Ryder, we arrived rather apprehensively with a job to do of supposed national importance. Site visits were characterised by a landscape of barbed wire, rotting sheep, stinging nettles and polluted air from the Bedfordshire brickworks. Netherfield, Coffee Hall and Canal Side were truly utopian in scale, superimposed abstractly on Llewelyn-Davies' masterplan. When Jim Stirling visited the 'Advanced Factory Unit' where we were working on the long terraces he commented that "it was a bit much". I wasn't sure whether he meant the length of the terraces or the windowless yellow box in which we were condemned to work, or possibly both.'
EJ

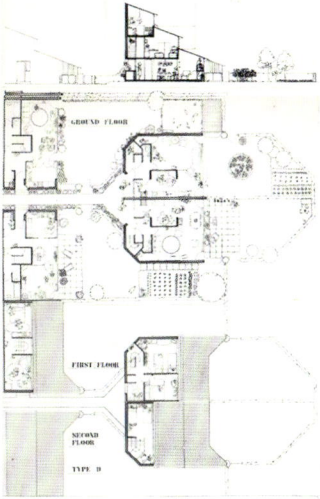

Whereas such investigations might have significant implications for the inner city – as characterised by Neave Brown's Fleet Road – for the New Towns and the suburbs the benefits were to be found in the generous provision of public and private space. At Highgrove, with its nine-metre frontages, there is the celebration of the individual family and the importance of the private garden offering a generous and desirable life in the suburb. The frontages are twice the dimension of Netherfield's and the normal convention of terraced housing. At Netherfield the inspiration was instead public space, immediately accessible to all dwellings and providing a clear landscaped park and public front to the houses, and a back devoted to private gardens.

Left Netherfield today. The use of metal for the roofing and cladding represented the 'idea of mass production in response to the urgent need for housing. Netherfield's mixed earlier reception has softened, and when recently demolition was suggested, the residents came out in vociferous support of the project. The initial concept of an interplay between the historic field boundaries and the orthogonal grid of buildings has given a sense of authenticity to these public spaces which are now valued by the majority of residents.' EJ

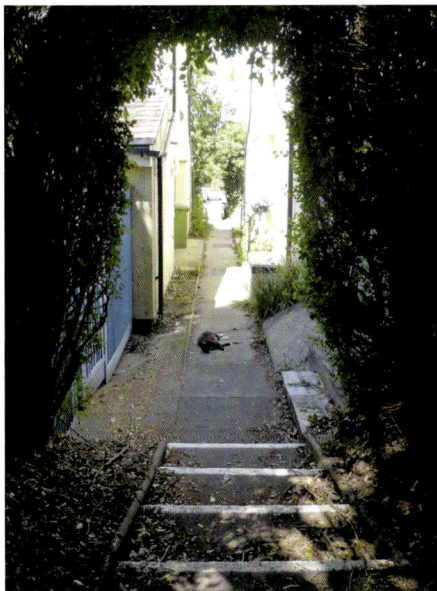

Left, right, below The site plan of Cullinan's Highgrove project was based around two roads with intersecting alleyways, and generous landscaped areas. Since their completion (left) the houses have been subsumed by hedges, their blue metal roofs replaced by tiles that have acquired a patina of age, and their windows, as at Netherfield, replaced by standard plastic units with a profusion of mullions. The interstitial alleyways, from which the houses are laterally entered, are defined as much by greenery as built form.

A recent visit to both projects 50 years on was a revelation – normally the unforgiving hand of the forced occupation in public housing has a debilitating effect over time on the physical fabric and the place. But in Hillingdon and Milton Keynes the intervening decades have allowed the growth of nature to settle both buildings. In the case of Highgrove the maturity of the hedgerows has rendered the houses almost invisible and bestowed on the public lanes separating them the vitality of the original Cullinan diagram. At Netherfield the patina of use and the matter-of-factness of the everyday have removed the awkwardness of the new. In both cases the conventions of standard roof tiles and facing brick were subsequently introduced. At Highgrove the blue metal roofs have been replaced by tiles, whereas at Netherfield the grey metal cladding and red doors have been randomly replaced by an accumulation of different materials and colours.

Whether the Highgrove roofs are metal or tile in no way modifies Cullinan's achievement as to the scale and general liveability, however, although the blue of the original roofs set against the new abundance of green would have retained a characterful ingredient. At Netherfield it might be said that the plan was sufficiently stable that a certain variety in the elevations is permissible which can be seen to enrich the whole.

Highgrove's hedges now give an emphasis to the lanes as opposed to the buildings, resulting in a magical sense of Arcadia. At Milton Keynes the previously barren landscape is now ordered by regular lines of mature trees which impart a definite European and civic character. As with Highgrove the singular emphasis is no longer on the buildings but on a complementary relationship with landscape. One is reminded of the barren and very unpopular squares of Bloomsbury when first occupied in the eighteenth century, which today are the pride of London. All the more apposite perhaps, given how these domestic projects were achieved from oblique observations on the mews and backlands of Camden Town and by way of contrast the open spaces of local parks like Primrose Hill, which both continue to provide a positive inspiration for urban life.

what
Ted
taught

'I never had a theory of architecture, I just did things.' Everything Cullinan built, drew and taught was founded on a rigorous set of principles, but he eschewed the 'fancy jargon' of theoretical discourse

Did Ted have a Theory?
Nicholas Ray

In 1967-68 Ted Cullinan taught our second year studio. We'd been through a first year with John Meunier, firmly within the formal tradition established by Leslie Martin in Cambridge some ten or so years before. Martin had appointed Colin Rowe, whose amanuensis Peter Eisenman had been teaching while he completed his thesis 'The Formal Basis of Modern Architecture'. As Meunier reveals in the recently published 'On Intricacy': 'I went to Cambridge and found myself teaching first year studio [and] argued that architectural form had three origins: use, technology, and the examination of form itself, beginning with the square/cube, and the circle/sphere/cylinder (good old Plato). I guess I never got beyond the rewards implicit in the square and its sense of resolution.'[1]

Meunier's tripartite 'use, technology and form' echo the famous Vitruvian aside, translated by Henry Wotton as 'commodity, firmness and delight'. Christian Norberg-Schulz's 'Intentions in Architecture', which we studied assiduously, similarly defined these three 'pole-objects which may enter the architectural totality' as 'Building Task, Technics and Form'.[2] At any rate, we had learned a respect for the manipulation of form, primarily as an exercise in geometry.

But when we encountered Ted, we met with a rather different approach. He was gently amused at our search for formal clarity, and didn't try to suggest an alternative set of principles, but spoke about and drew buildings in a different way. There tended to be a narrative when he talked to you, and so when you presented your designs to him you naturally found yourself describing the sequence of events that you yourself intended to choreograph: arrival and greeting, moving towards the light and the sunshine, finding a place to sit – or a journey to the great outdoors which beckoned beyond. Forms came along to help that process – they were not 'givens', which you were required to subject to analysis. Many years later, Jeremy Stacey [ECA 1987-91] told me that Ted had explained that there were only two types of building: either you went through a thick back wall to encounter a forest of columns, or you approached a forest

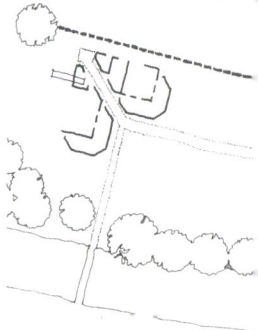

Minster Lovell Mill (1967-76)
Anthony Ambrose, a developmental psychologist who had inherited the riverside site with its range of run-down Cotswold stone mill buildings in Minster Lovell, Oxfordshire, commissioned Cullinan to reconfigure the setting as a 'Centre for Advanced Study in the Developmental Sciences'. The conference centre was adapted in recent years for use as a luxury hotel.

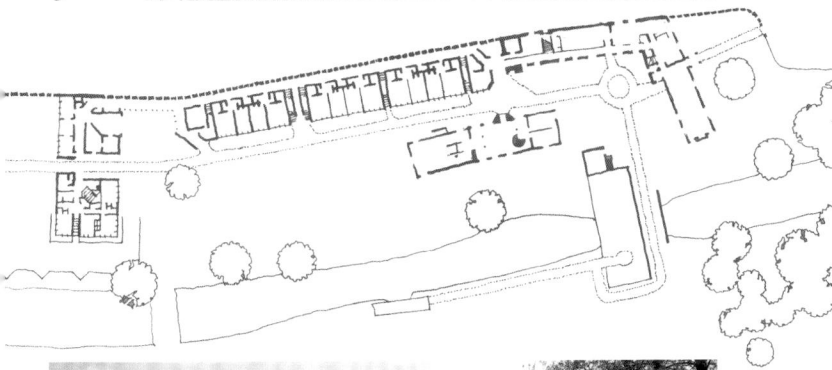

of columns and came to a thick back wall. That was apparently as close to theory that Ted got. But was it?

Our major project in that second year was the design for a Centre of Developmental Sciences. The brief was based on that for Ted's building at Minster Lovell, and during the year we met his charismatic client. What we had missed in school as we struggled with our studio designs was engagement with the actual materials that make a work of architecture. For us (as for most students without any experience of building) the lines we drew of window details at 1:5 meant little. It was not until my third year when I visited Minster Lovell, then under construction, with Julian Bicknell [ECA 1966-67, 69-71] that I discovered that Ted had completely rethought what a window could be: frameless sheets of glass slid between paired timbers which energetically clasped the walls beneath to provide support for the great pitched roofs. When I began designing back extensions in my 'year out', I tried out various versions of that idea, which promised to liberate the whole wall and make the roof float in a Wrightian way.

In 1984 the Heinz Gallery mounted an exhibition of work by Edward Cullinan Architects, which I reviewed for the Architects' Journal.[3] I found that Brendan Woods, writing in the Architectural Review a year before, had encapsulated a truth about Cullinan's designs when he suggested that Ted's own house provided the precedent for most of his subsequent architecture, combining 'a fascination for the cave dwelling and the birds' nest'.[4] In my own article I mostly applied this perception to the various projects on display. At the larger scale, the drawings and sketches revealed 'two kinds of space – routes and places' and few were attractive in themselves, indeed several were 'violent and messy'. 'Rectangular spaces on plan are not defined by thin lines crossed at the corners but by big fat blobs. Yet the drawings are not 'blob diagrams' in the sense that they try to identify activities and analyse connections, because they always suggest the nature of the route as well as the fact of the connection.'

143

A decade later, in discussing Cullinan's work in the Macedonian magazine Archin following the publication of Kenneth Powell's monograph in 1995, I suggested that Ted was very English but consciously distanced himself from 'Englishness', which he associated with compromise and a weak neo-Georgian stylistic inheritance. 'I am put off by certain, rather frumpy, parochial and nostalgic aspects of Englishness', he wrote.[5] His heroes were William Morris, for his social idealism, Shaw, Webb and Mackintosh, Frank Lloyd Wright and Greene and Greene in America, Rietveld (for his understanding of 'sticks and planes and of interpenetrating space') and Le Corbusier. In an essay ('Where does my baggage come from?') in the 1995 book, Ted had analysed buildings by these and other architects. But this was not a formal analysis in the manner of Rowe or Eisenman; it concentrated on the celebratory nature of architecture, enjoying the route or promenade, revelling in the texture of the materials employed and the joints that both display the making of the fabric and act as its embellishments.

The 'do-it-yourself' quality of Cullinan's detailing and the formal expression of his buildings were bound up with the way in which they were made. I described Minster Lovell's Wrightian ribbon windows – running between the walls ('dry-built, calculated elemental twentieth century construction... loosely clothed with Cotswold stone') and the steep roofs – and suggested that, before the fashion for neo-vernacular, Cullinan had shown how traditional forms could be reinterpreted and reinvigorated in a contemporary manner. Twenty years later, the visitor centre at Fountains Abbey was an exercise in this vein, embedded in a landscape containing the medieval Cistercian monastery, set within an eighteenth-century landscape garden to which in the nineteenth century a church had been added by William Burges. But I questioned whether the accommodation Cullinan's architecture made between heroic modernism and traditional materials would not be seen by some as too easy an option. Where was the anxious deconstruction we might expect in the mid-1990s, or the calculated opposition of the artificial with the

Fountains Abbey visitor centre (1987-92)
Set around a welcoming courtyard that frames an intriguing view of the top of the abbey tower, the visitor centre combines traditional materials and landscaped embankments to anchor the building in its context. Planar slate roofs are juxtaposed with curving lead roofs, dry stone walls and cedar screens and windows. The initial proposal (opposite), for a different site, envisaged facilities flanking a linear route that emerged on axis with the abbey tower. In the built scheme, which adopted a courtyard form (below), the axis is less explicit.

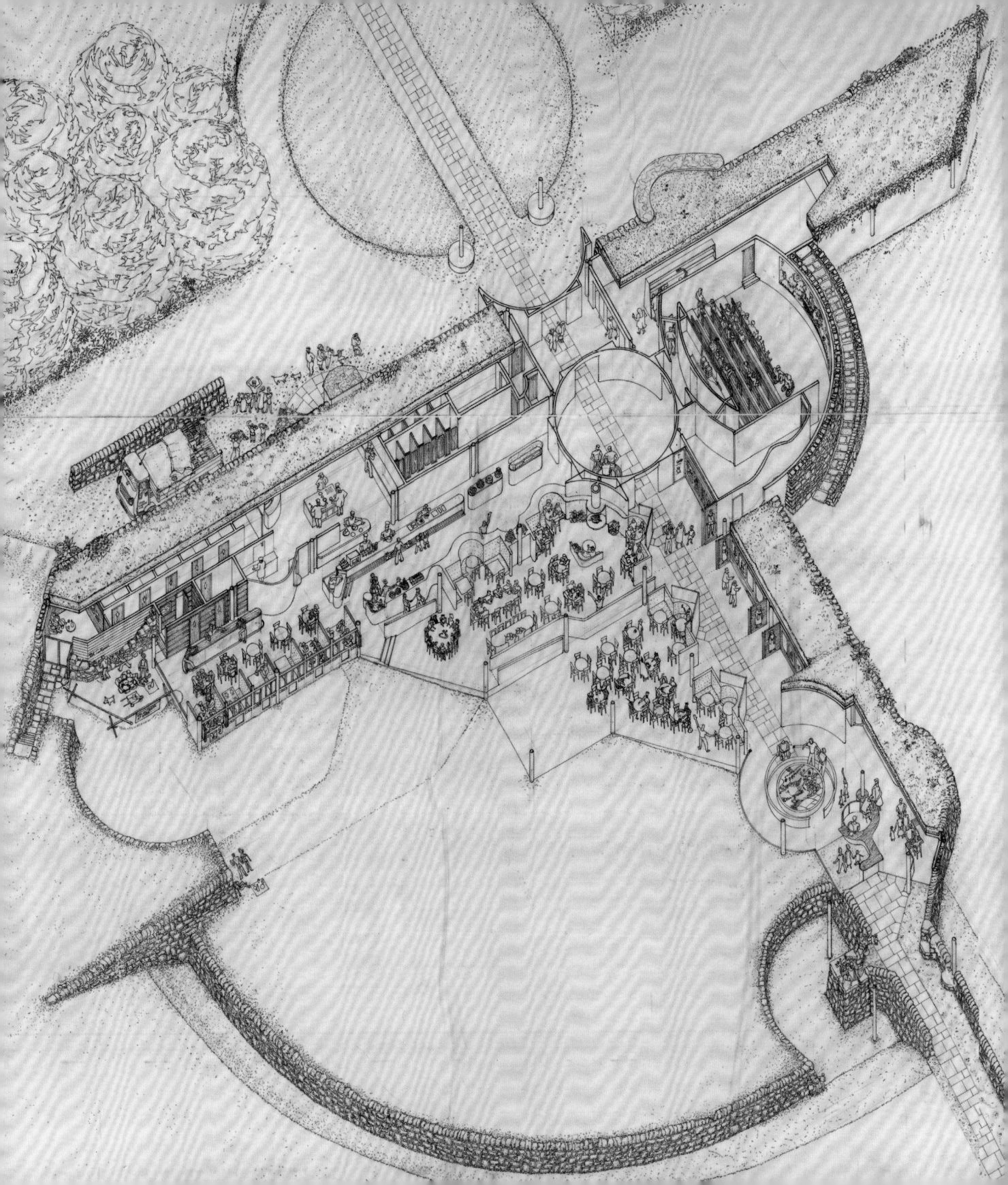

natural? I thought his concern with context and organic Wrightian connection with nature might look decidedly old-fashioned to some readers.

Although Cullinan made a pretence of unsophistication ('I never had a theory of architecture, I just did things'), his essays in the book revealed him to be a thinker and a reader. In opposition to OMA's 'pleasure of eating oysters with boxing gloves', he expressed a 'predilection for building dry stone walls while having cocktails'[6]. He explained that the cocktail stands for 'those aspects of twentieth-century architecture that celebrate the luxury of choice, deliberate self-expression and the pleasures of artificiality: the Duesenberg, Scott Fitzgerald, and the foyer, ramps and terraces of the Villa Savoye', while he used the dry stone wall 'to characterise those aspects of twentieth-century architecture that enjoy limited means and hope for honesty, truth to materials, creating architecture as a democratic experience: the lightweight bike, the Chaplin film, the hedges, paths and houses of the garden suburb'.[7]

Architecture, for Cullinan, was practice: 'the daily, hourly and minute-by-minute practising of the process of composing suitable, responsive, comfortable and expressive buildings, places and things'. This approach could be compared with the more 'sophisticated' and certainly more fashionable position of someone like Bernard Tschumi, an architect who had recently started to engage in practice after many years of teaching and writing. Unlike Cullinan, whose passion for

Philip Webb or Le Corbusier was so evident, he seemed not to be moved by buildings: 'my own pleasure has never surfaced in looking at buildings, at the great works of the history or the present of architecture, but, rather, in dismantling them'.[8] Inspired by the writing of Jacques Derrida, Tschumi had suggested that a way of distancing architecture from the dilemma of either pure formalism or reductive functionalism was for the architect to concentrate on shocking those who engage with it by de-familiarising form. A cornerstone of Tschumi's argument was that architecture cannot any longer be about either function or form, since these are now quite arbitrarily combined – 'railway stations become museums and churches become nightclubs'.

But this position was not Cullinan's. Between 1970 and 1972 he had designed a series of branch offices for Olivetti on unpromising fringe-of-town sites. The building in Carlisle later became a Chinese restaurant, then a night club. 'Such are the vicissitudes of commerce and the demands of flexibility', Ted had commented. As a practitioner he was committed to the idea of celebration. He acknowledged that this is more difficult in speculative office buildings, for example, than in those for identifiable patrons. For building types such as these, it 'becomes important to search for usefulness, logic and grace in the general parts of a building against which the heightened quality of particular parts can be placed: and to discover

Olivetti branches (1970-72)
Following Edward Cullinan Architects' refurbishment of Olivetti's Haslemere headquarters, where James Stirling built a training wing (project architect Robin Nicholson later joined Cullinan's), the practice was asked to build new branches in Belfast, Carlisle, Derby and Dundee (right). The U-shaped concept featured 'tails' 'painted the colour of dried blood like a dismembered limb... to remind Olivetti to allow the building future growth'. Belfast was later reclad and Carlisle became a restaurant (below).

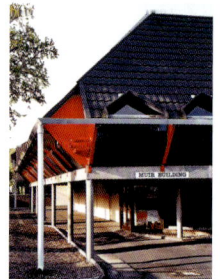

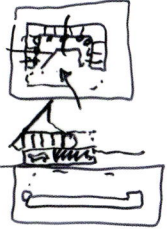

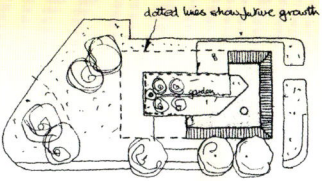

dotted lines show future growth

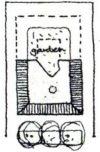

garden

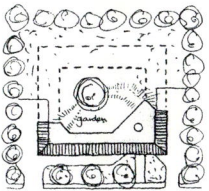

garden

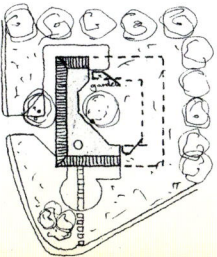

which parts can usefully be particular'. Rather than despair at the possibility of improving man's lot in a system that is far from perfect (as late-twentieth-century capitalism self-evidently was) the architect should embrace the philosophy of William Morris. Cullinan cited Morris's 1879 lecture 'The Arts of the People', comparing it to what he saw as Marx's 'desperate theory that a revolutionary socialist should not try to make a better present because that might delay the revolution – as if better things needed no practising for – oh dismal theory!' His suggestion of how much fashionable aesthetic positions may owe to the residue of vulgar Marxism is thought-provoking.

I had somewhat artificially set the 'practitioner' Cullinan against the sophisticated Tschumi.

But there was a genuine difference: Cullinan claimed that human needs were central to the architect's concern whereas Tschumi argued that 'to make buildings that work and make people happy is not the goal of architecture but, of course, a welcome side effect'.

Thinking through Ted's 'theory' again, I find the frequently quoted paper that John Summerson gave at the RIBA in 1956 is still relevant. 'The Case for a Theory of Modern Architecture'[9] outlined the problem in the twentieth century of finding such a theory: he did not believe any kind could be 'abstracted out of prevailing practice and ideas', because the enterprise would be 'hopelessly gimcrack'. 'Only imagine for a moment the horror of stirring around in the

Above
Fountains Abbey visitor centre is sited north of the largest Cistercian abbey ruin in Europe, since 1768 part of the Studley Royal estate. The building is approached along a series of alternately directed and denied views to existing landmarks on the site. Arrival across the gravelled courtyard reveals a framed view of the upper part of the abbey tower.

rag-bag of aphorisms, platitudes and fancy jargon and trying to determine their common trend and resulting meaning. The imagination boggles...'

Summerson is mostly dismissive of the attempts by architects to build a modernist theory, but he detects two strands, represented on the one hand by Le Corbusier's 'Vers une Architecture' and on the other by Moholy-Nagy's 'The New Vision: from Material to Architecture', based on lectures given at the Bauhaus in 1923-28. Le Corbusier's propagandist statements reflect his French rationalist heritage, whereas the Hungarian Moholy-Nagy represents a different tradition (and personal psychology) in that he 'postulates a new theory which would fit the biological (let us say psycho-physical) needs of man'. This suggested that it was the architect's programme, rather than any interpretation of the past or rationalisations based on geometry, that was the 'source of unity' in the twentieth century. Summerson traced the history of how such a notion came about: 'First the rationalist attack on the authority of the antique; then the displacement of the classical antique by the medieval; then the introduction into medievalist authority of purely social factors (Ruskin); then the evaluation of purely vernacular architectures because of their social realism (Morris); and finally the concentration of interest on the social factors themselves and the conception of the architect's programme as the source of unity – the source not precisely of forms but of adumbrations of forms of undeniable validity. The programme as the source of unity is, so far as I can see, the one new principle involved in modern architecture.'

Architectural forms in themselves, Summerson is careful to point out (and Peter Smithson, incidentally Ted's teacher at the AA, emphasised

in discussion), are something else. Le Corbusier's formal vocabulary may have arisen from 'the school of Picasso, Braque and Léger', but 'where forms come from, as any art historian knows, is a very great mystery indeed. They come from the artist's personality, his totality of experience'.

If we agree with Summerson's distinction, the education of the 1966-69 cohort of students went from a first year within the (confessedly Platonic) rationalist tradition, where form is ordered by geometry, to encounter Ted, who represented an alternative (arguably Aristotelian) approach. Unlike Sandy Wilson, who was on a similar journey, and for whom Alvar Aalto and the 'Other Tradition' represented a route out[10], Ted apparently knew just where he stood and found no need to theorise in print. Occasionally he would mention a book he had read with pleasure, as I recall: Ford Madox Ford's 'The Good Soldier – A Tale of Passion', which famously begins 'This is the saddest story I have ever heard', or Ernest Hemingway's 'Across the River and into the Trees', which he possibly liked especially because of its resonant title, so reminiscent of a route that Ted himself might trace on a drawing and describe. But in general he just got on with it: building, drawing, teaching.

Summerson remarked in his lecture that theory 'has a life of its own', and not all great architects could be said to hold a theory: 'Who has ever had a more powerful effect on architecture than Michelangelo? Yet his effect on the theory of architecture was nil.' Surely Cullinan, through his many pupils and collaborators, and the buildings they made together, had an extraordinary effect on British architecture, representing a sufficiently powerful response to those fashionable and dangerous theories couched in 'fancy jargon' that have a life of their own.

Footnotes
1 Patrick Lynch, ed, On Intricacy – The Work of John Meunier Architect (Canalside Press, 2020).
2 Christian Norberg-Schulz, Intentions in Architecture (Allen & Unwin, 1963). His later books, such as Genius Loci, take a very different position, although when I met him some years later and suggested that, he denied it.
3 'Reflections on Cullinan' (Architects Journal, 26 Sept 1984).
4 Brendan Woods, 'The Cullinan Phenomenon: The Act and Art of Building' (Architectural Review, Sept 1983). We may be reminded of Cyril Connolly's frequently quoted definition of architecture, parodying Virginia Woolf, as 'a Womb with a View'.
5 Edward Cullinan Architects, Kenneth Powell (Academy Editions, 1995).
6 Ibid p86. The reference was to an article in Architectural Design (May 1977).
7 'House, Architecture, the Cocktail and the Dry-Stone Wall', in Edward Cullinan Architects; first published in Toshi-Jutaku (Oct 1980).
8 This and subsequent quotes are from Bernard Tschumi, Architecture and Disjunction (MIT Press, 1996).
9 'The Case for a Theory of Modern Architecture' (RIBA Journal, June 1957). The lecture is reprinted in John Summerson, The Unromantic Castle and Other Essays (Thames & Hudson, 1990).
10 Colin St John Wilson, The Other Tradition of Modern Architecture (Academy Editions, 1995).

Ted Cullinan's talks were
not to be missed, not just for
their captivating stories
and clarity of thinking,
but also for demonstrating
how buildings can be authentic,
appropriate and poetic

Grounding
in Reality
Graham Morrison

Ted began his lectures and preceded many of his sentences with a long 'uuuhh'. The resonant baritone of the utterance was a perfected elaboration of the way many of us would use the shorter 'um'. But in his case it wasn't because he needed to give himself thinking time, it was more as a fanfare, a call to attention and a way of emphasising a sentence at the beginning rather than at the end. Such spoken sounds, bounded by silence, exist not in our notes but only in the memory of those of us who were privileged to hear him talk. Ted's talks were not to be missed.

He was a regular contributor to the small but enthusiastic band of Cambridge architecture students in the early 1970s. An all-day 'crit' in which we presented our work in the hope of a mark of his approval would be followed by an evening lecture which, if you were late, would have only standing room. To us, he was undoubtedly 'cool' and, with his striking looks and always dressed in a black crew-neck sweater and jeans, he presented an image to be imitated and I suspect many of us included that infectious 'uuuhh' into our own sentences. If we could talk like him, maybe we could think like him.

Though we were captivated by his stories of California and enthralled by the houses he had not only designed but built, it was the clarity of his thinking and the simplicity of his explanations that made him so compelling. Ted never used notes and we sat spellbound when he drew (with chinagraph crayons on acetate sheets projected by epidiascope onto the lecture room screen) an animated sequence of sketches to explain an idea or how something was made. His talks were compositions in themselves with each sentence dependent on the last and flowing with conviction into the next. Ideas simply unfolded.

He would talk of the site, of a plan and a cross section and of a way of making a building. It would be economical, appropriate to the task and distinctive. The thought process was important and there was always a reason for a decision. How you got 'there' was as carefully considered as the 'there' and the getting 'there' – the designing and the making – was as poetic as it was rational, just as the outcome was as inventive as it was inevitable.

He described an architecture that became beautiful because of the way a problem was solved. It was architecture devoid of gesture that came from an organised mind, curious about the possibilities in which a project could be made and alive to the compositional potential of how it might be assembled. We could see architecture happening and that was why it was so very engaging.

Though he had worked for Denys Lasdun, he had left behind the relative brutality of Corbusian influence and had sought instead a gentle but direct authenticity. It seems appropriate that on my bookshelf Cullinan should follow Corbusier. To us in Cambridge at that time, Ted was the antidote to architectural arrogance and the opposite of the showmanship of Archigram, whose members visited occasionally, but only for lectures, and who would bombard us with slides in fast-moving and highly energetic performances that were ultimately more romantic than real. Their imagery was speculative and forecast a future that seemed then and still seems overwhelming. Ted's teaching was grounded in reality.

Perhaps a school under the tutelage of Leslie Martin was always going to be less receptive to such bombastic presentations. I remember when one of Archigram's lectures ended there were no questions – only a comment from one of our tutors that they thought the graphics were nice. Ted's lectures, by contrast, were followed by more questions than there was time to answer. He was,

however, always generous with his time, and when I once had the temerity to ask a question about what I felt was an unnecessary elaboration of the cross section of the 1971 project for Olivetti's new branches, looking back, his answer about being direct and cutting an exact amount from a standard sheet of plywood mattered less than the memory of an architect I admired who had kind eyes and from whom I had learned so much.

It was the details and how they affected the sensibility of a building that stuck with me. In the extraordinarily tight planning (both in space and budget) of those early houses, there were ideas that, at the time, were breathtakingly straightforward. In the 1964 Kawecki house, a tiny plot at the end of a terrace, the windows were fixed but opaque panels were openable. And when they opened, they transformed the light in the room. It was a detail that was simple and direct, economic and easy to make, but which brought surprise and joy. It was an architecture we loved and I can still see the glint in Ted's eye as he described it, because he loved it too.

Kawecki house

Built in 1965 on Bartholomew Villas, north London, the house provides living and sleeping accommodation on a middle floor with a music gallery above and a flat and garages below. The south-sloping 'lean-to' completes the bombed-off half of a nineteenth-century villa. The split section allows a low clerestorey window with a full-length bookshelf under the cill.

Left Olivetti branch under construction and sketch section.

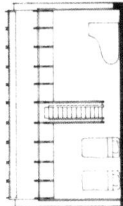

half a villa in Kentish Town, the other half bombed off in the war

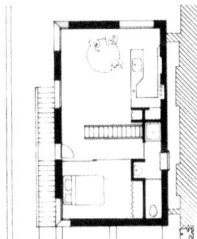

extend the stucco base to contain garages

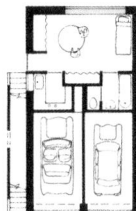

and build a living floor and a studio floor on top.

Cullinan set out to make buildings robust enough to embrace the clutter and messiness of life, and this radical reassessment of what architecture can be has resonated across generations of architects

Life as Lived
Cany Ash

Every generation of architects has an equivocal relationship with the preceding generation. On the one hand you've just started the immensely difficult craft of architecture, and older practitioners seem effortlessly to compose works which you can only dream of matching; and on the other you have a slightly superior disdain for what seem to be the preoccupations and limitations of their cultural outlook. We didn't have much time for the high-tech set; or the ever-so-'umble aesthetics embraced by Rod Hackney and his ilk under the banner of community architecture; or the lumpen pontifications of the Smithsons; or the displacement activities imagined by Cedric Price. But there were one or two singular presences who stood outside such (obviously we now realise, facile) categorisation: Jim Stirling of course, perhaps also Ralph Erskine, and in our case, Ted Cullinan. What we appreciated was their sheer ability as plastic artists to make resonant and memorable form.

I visited the outside of Cullinan's house in Camden Mews with my mother Clare when I started at secondary school, a stone's throw away. She loved the house which looked like a little stage set, a Japanese palace transported to London, especially so when the mews had a more industrial feel. My parents' house, converted by Camden architect Anne Swain in a most dramatic fashion in 1962, served as a nursery school by day – a playful, noisy, mix-it-all-up adventure in a house of two immigrants who didn't recognise the British decorum of place, nor the separation of work and home. New ideas in architecture about how to rid ourselves of stuffy front rooms and let in some life took on a wider significance.

My mother was drawn to modern architecture because it promised to help fix a lot of what was broken, of which she'd seen plenty when working in teacher training and visiting some of London's toughest schools. She loved to hear architect friends talk about their projects and, in working on a series of television programmes, wrote that 'to be on the stage at the beginning of a building's life is exciting… a building can claim to be modern if it suggests that something

Camden Mews
The self-built Cullinan house comprises a timber and concrete base and timber superstructure.

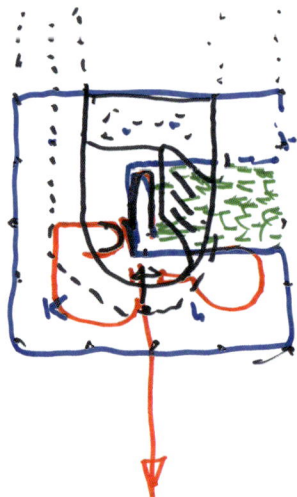

new could happen in it – if people might be tempted to experiment in living'.

The practice of creating functional shells within which people could get on with everything they might want to do was for her an abdication of responsibility. 'Perhaps the simplest way to describe the architecture that would be featured in these programmes is that it not only works but it has atmosphere. It accommodates mess, clutter, a dozen things happening simultaneously. It looks best when it is being used. In fact, people are aesthetically essential to the scene – part of the design.' There's certainly a parallel in Ted Cullinan's determination to make buildings robust enough to embrace life as it is really lived.

Revisiting the Cullinan house today, there is still much to admire – not least the way Ted eschewed building over the whole of the tiny mews plot so as to preserve two venerable trees – counter-intuitively, the plan runs front to back across just half the site. The entrance sequence is logical, mad and brilliant. The in situ concrete frame, pockmarked with areas of rough aggregate, has a hand-built quality just this side of adequate. The walls of second-hand London yellow stocks seem to dematerialise at the cills and parapets with a nuanced stepping-in detail. The infill timber framing is chunky in some places and delicate in others, and cantilevers out from the structural frame in a way that is straightforwardly logical in itself but also reminiscent of Japanese and Chinese eaves details – it must allow a wonderful play of filtered light in the first-floor living space. In describing his design approach, Ted would often start with his reading of the empty site, and then locate the building within it. The approach was in contrast to many of his contemporaries, and aligned him with an alternative modern tradition – that of say David

Lea who, like Cullinan, was deeply appreciative of Japanese traditional domestic architecture.

My first visit to the Cullinan office was to get my RIBA Part-III logbook checked by Sunand Prasad. My log was largely about the ups and downs of self-building a pair of mews houses which had a layered history and many structural mysteries. Sunand was very upbeat. The friendliness and creativity of the studio was palpable, and I remember thinking that here is where I'd want to work, had Robert Sakula and I not rashly just struck out on our own. Recently I asked Frances Holliss what it was like working for Ted. 'Terrifying', she said. 'On my second day he invited me to have a sketch design session with him, which actually meant a competition between just the two of us… it wasn't quite the collaborative design process I had expected!'

The culture of curiosity and openness that Cullinan and his partners instilled in their practice is very much a touchstone for what we try to do at Ash Sakula. We loved Ted's live drawing, confidently building up an analytical three-dimensional, semi-transparent sketch using the unpromising medium of felt tip on an overhead projector. Re-watching a recording of his analysis of Le Corbusier's Ronchamp chapel, what is most impressive is his communication of the 'whatness' of the building, how you come to it, enter it, move through it, and experience its light and its acoustic. This experiential 'promenade architecturale' is inherent to his intimate understanding of structure, construction and geometry. Ted's personal fondness for the building doesn't cloud his analysis, nor does the analysis bury his emotional response – heightened perhaps by his long bike ride across France – and his greatness lay in his extraordinary ability to harness both.

155

His crits were unmissable
and his lectures were legendary –
Ted Cullinan was among
the most positive, engaging
and inspirational teachers
of his generation,
and a father figure to many
followers and admirers

Inheritance
Tracks
Richard Murphy

Serendipity can play a role in one's life and I now realise that, while my own formal architectural training in the 1970s was with a few exceptions uneventful, luck brought me into contact in the 1980s with three architects who became formative influences and great friends. Richard MacCormac, for whom I worked in the mid-1980s; Isi Metzstein, my professor when I returned from London to teach at Edinburgh; and Ted Cullinan, who Isi appointed as visiting professor in the same year. Indeed it was Richard who came in to the office one morning and told us about his dinner the previous evening at Camden Mews, where Ted had introduced everyone to Denys Lasdun as his architectural 'dad'. I now realise that those three giants – Richard, Isi and Ted – were my dads, if one is allowed three. They were joined perhaps by a posthumous dad in Carlo Scarpa (who sadly died four years before I discovered his work), who I feel I got to know through intensive study of the Castelvecchio museum in Verona and interviewing his clients, collaborators and artisans.

In his role as visiting professor, Ted came up to Edinburgh on a Monday and went back to London on a Friday, staying in my little 'colony house' which inevitably became party central when he was in residence. He would arrive with a bottle of malt whisky as his 'rent' and on the Friday, having himself consumed most of the contents through the week, would present me with a second identical bottle.

Ted was undoubtedly the most positive, engaging and inspirational teacher I have ever witnessed. I went to as many of his crits as possible and he passed on a very useful teaching tip: no matter how talentless or disinterested a student, always say something positive about their work to start with. In that way they will be more receptive to criticism. If you do the reverse, the shutters will come down and nothing will be learned. It sounds simple but I'm always amazed at how many of my occasional fellow critics have never tumbled to this ploy.

His lectures were legendary. When describing work from the Cullinan studio his technique was to draw the story of the evolution of a design

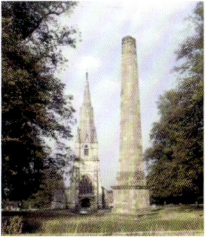

Fountains Abbey
The new visitor centre
(1986-92) was sited after
extensive landscape studies.
The Studley Royal estate was
laid out in the eighteenth
century by John Aislabie, and
it came to include an avenue
(C), on axis with Ripon
Cathedral. Cullinan's new
entrance road (A) is aligned
with William Burges' St
Mary's Church (B), before
diverting to the visitor centre
(D) from where the abbey
tower is seen (E); to the east
is a walk to Anne Boleyn's
seat (F). Cullinan's sketch
shows the tower gradually
coming into view.

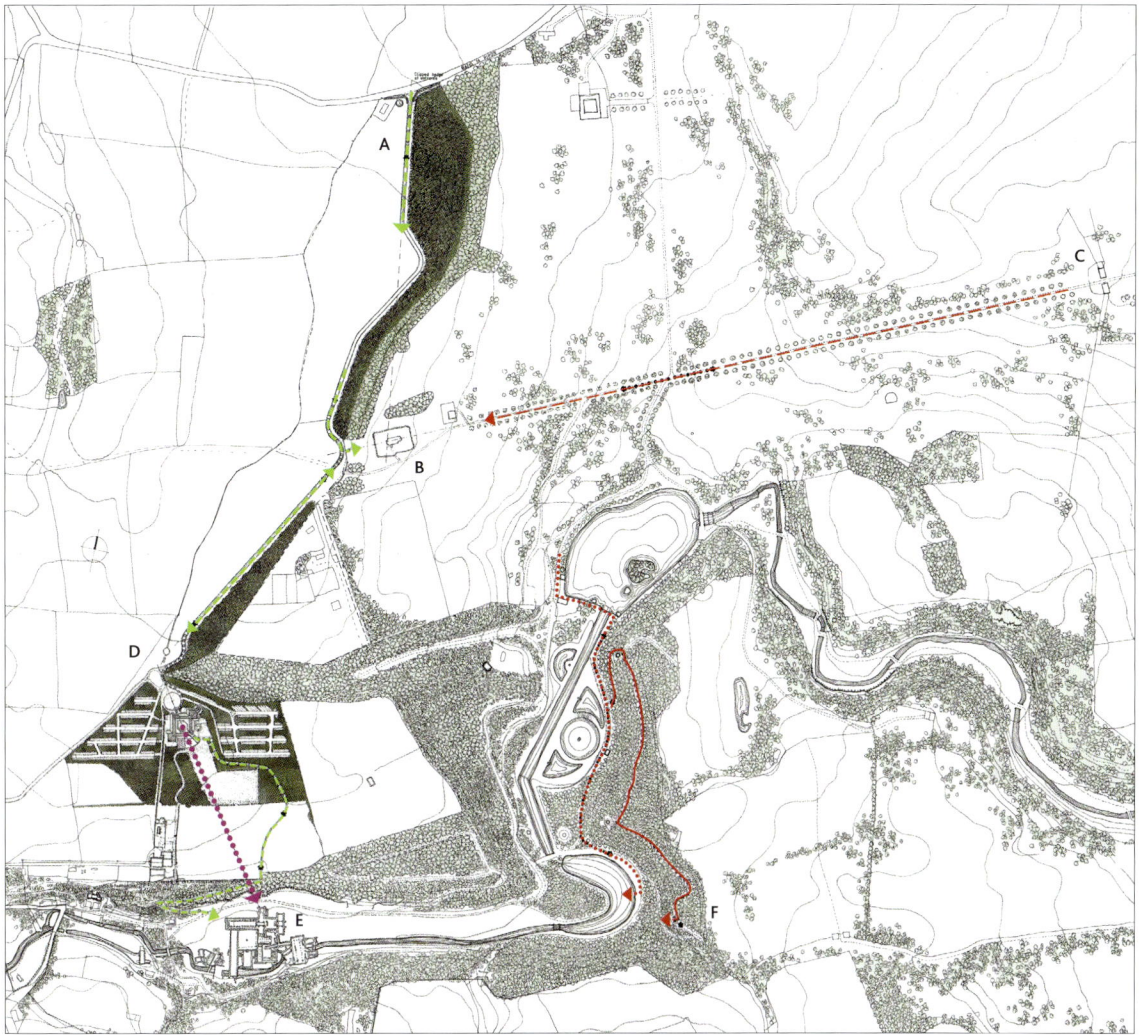

using coloured felt tip pens on an overhead
projector. His audiences were always enchanted
and absorbed, and I confess it's a method I have
shamelessly appropriated. Critically he never
started with the final building but with an
introduction to the site, acknowledging the way in
which the reading of context can lead directly to
the inspiration behind the design. For example,
in a lecture about the visitor centre at Fountains
Abbey, I recall an enormously long introduction
taking the audience through the historical
phases of the landscape of the entire estate,
from medieval abbey, through the picturesque
eighteenth-century landscape of Studley Royal,
through various Victorian developments and
seamlessly into his own proposals. The

introduction invariably took far longer than the
description of the final design. This approach
demonstrated how Cullinan saw his work as
fundamentally connected with both place and
time; connections which 'modernism', as defined
by some, stood accused of neglecting. Indeed,
the 'modern movement', erroneously, had been
portrayed by some as a revolutionary break with
history. And Henry-Russell Hitchcock's title
'The International Style', coined to describe the
movement in general, similarly suggested that
place and architecture were also effectively
divorced from each other.

That idea of the continuity of history was the
theme of 'Where does my baggage come from?',

Ted's famous lecture delivered at the Royal Society of Arts in 1986 and repeated many times since. We were privileged to hear it at the 25th anniversary of my own practice, the 'Murphfest' in Edinburgh in 2016. In one of his legendary lecturer introductions Isi Metzstein, in mock puzzlement at Ted's title joked 'usually I'd like to know where my baggage has gone!'. Sometimes subtitled 'From Red House to Ronchamp', the lecture was a typically engaging story of the connections (which many initially found surprising) from Philip Webb through to Le Corbusier. Ted would describe a building not in the way a historian might in terms of styles or the dry language of the architectural glossary but using felt tip pens to draw how a facade might be composed of the interpenetration of wall planes and windows, how scales would juxtapose, how balanced asymmetries might be concocted, how a building would 'meet the ground' and 'meet the sky', and how elements might be functional and at the same time expressive. His descriptions of Norman Shaw's New Zealand Chambers and Mackintosh's Hill House were particularly memorable in this respect. Much later, when I was researching Carlo Scarpa, his former assistant Arrigo Rudi told me that Scarpa used to say the same thing: 'is this solution expressive enough?'.

Denys Lasdun may have been Ted's 'dad' but the true family patriarch was his ideological hero, William Morris. A man of impeccable socialist credentials, a maker of objects and buildings, and a tireless campaigner, Ted once went so far as to set his students in the United States a project to design Morris wallpaper using American flora. He introduced me to a thrilling passage from Morris's address to the Society for the Protection of Ancient Buildings annual meeting in 1889: 'It cannot be, it has gone! They believe that we can do the same sort of work in the same spirit as our forefathers, whereas for good and for evil we are completely changed and we cannot do the work they did. All continuity of history means is after all perpetual change, and it is not hard to see that we have changed with a vengeance, and thereby established our claim to be the continuers of history.' If ever there was an appropriate riposte to conservation officers and 'nimbys' in general, that is it. I have used the quote in writing about Scarpa, as I think he too, consciously or subliminally, subscribed to Morris's view of history as a continuum.

The project by the Cullinan studio that best exemplifies this concept of history is St Mary's church in Barnes, the radical reworking of the ruins that survived a devastating fire in 1978. The collapse of architectural confidence in the future that was engendered by Prince Charles in the 1980s ensured that such bold interventions in historic buildings were unlikely to happen again for at least a generation; witness the spineless restoration of the Great Hall at Windsor Castle after the 1992 fire.

Above Cullinan's oft-delivered lecture 'Where does my baggage come from?' featured analytical drawings of his favourite buildings, from Charles Rennie Mackintosh's Hill House in Helensburgh to Norman Shaw's New Zealand Chambers.

Opposite Drawings of Antoni Gaudi's Casa Batlló in Barcelona and Le Corbusier's Villa Savoye in Poissy, about which Cullinan once wrote: 'What a powerful idea of interpenetrating space and movement, requiring through its formal power only the smallest amount of embellishment and highlight'. St Mary's church in Barnes represented a progressive approach to renovation rather than pedantic restoration.

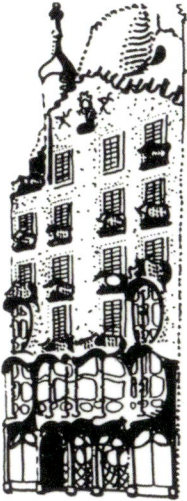

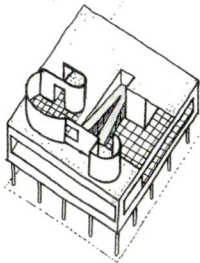

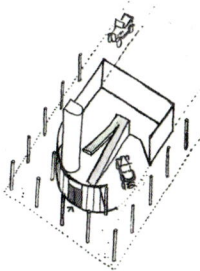

The notion of the architect as maker was central to Cullinan's work, and he himself was a great builder and gardener. His exquisite self-built mews house in Camden – lucidly described in sectional drawings in which one element is piled on top of another – or the playful interventions in the family retreat of Gib Tor, the Derbyshire farmhouse high up in the High Peak, both show an indivisibility between design and making. Ted coined the maxim 'architecture is the celebration of necessity' or as I put it the expression, indeed over-expression, of how a building is made.

Ted related how Peter Smithson, his teacher at the AA, would tell his first-year students that 'they would be very lucky if they ever had an original idea', a sentiment that has certainly kept me going for 30 years. Ted, however, was very honest about tracing his ideas back. He derived the 'stick-on-stick' assembly of the corner of the Camden Mews house from Greene & Greene, who in turn drew on Japanese traditions, which were probably inherited from

the Chinese, and so on back into pre-history. Cullinan shared this fascination with making with both MacCormac and Scarpa, and it's something I hope I have inherited from all three.

The scope of Ted's thinking – from the tiniest detail to ideas about city planning – can be glimpsed in a talk he gave to the Association of Consultant Architects' conference in 1978, where he suggested that 'we should make buildings in the city declare their individual weight through the character of their faces or facades, through the nature of their entrances and approaches to them... we must decide how to start our buildings at the ground, terminate them at the skyline, turn corners, make enclosure, relate small to large, declare the value of various openings, have a plan and a section that are parts of the same organism, and have a language and style that is sufficient and expressive enough to encompass the whole range of relationships, from major public places, loud with massed activity, to the private cell of a single bed or bathroom.'

As thrilling as it is all-encompassing, this passage also appeared in the catalogue to 'A Question of Style', a student symposium organised by Wilfried Wang at the RIBA in 1978. The very title was a provocation since the word 'style' was an anathema to 'modern movement' architects. In fact storm clouds had been gathering against the modernist consensus as early as 1966 with the publication of Robert Venturi's 'Complexity and Contradiction in Architecture'. But it was still another six years before Prince Charles sent a hurricane though the architectural establishment with his infamous Hampton Court speech of 1984, which sought to cast the profession – at least in the eyes of the public – into a branch of the criminal classes.

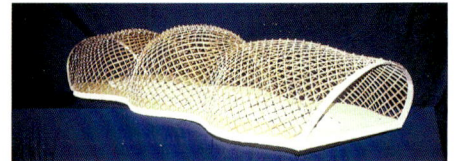

Weald & Downland Gridshell (1998-2002)
The workshop building, based on research modelling by Buro Happold, provides the museum with space for teaching, conferences and other gatherings. The double-curved form of jointed green oak battens was achieved by lifting the horizontal assembly, bolting the edges to the floor deck (which sits on a masonry base) and cross-bracing with horizontal laths which were then clad in bands of local Western Red Cedar and polycarbonate glazing in two continuous rooflights.

Right, below Minster Lovell Mill (1967-74) – Cullinan's largest project at the time – helped established an approach to building in historic contexts. Richard Murphy's Edinburgh house reflects the priority Cullinan attached to the sectional design.

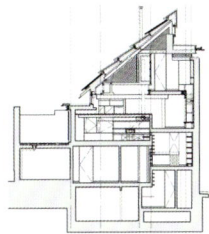

The 1978 symposium was a curate's egg in terms of speakers, ranging from Richard Rogers to Quinlan Terry, but Cullinan's contribution was about how the public sector – in the vanguard of architectural patronage since the war – had become ossified into a bureaucratic jungle with which the architect had to battle. Cullinan described his buildings – all too briefly – through the cross section. This was the first time I became aware of his work, and the idea that Ted was above all an 'architect of the section' has always stayed with me. The cover of the little book on the practice published by the RIBA in 1984 (my favourite to date) has a diagrammatic section through the brilliant Lambeth Community Care Centre, a stunning reworking of the cottage hospital idea – when asked about the project's pitched roofs, Ted rephrased the question, saying that they were 'floating inclined planes'!

In a discussion at an examiners' meeting in Edinburgh, Ted was asked about his greatest influence. 'Cubism', he responded with typical candour – he loved the period of artistic ferment before and after the first world war, and he certainly saw himself as a 'modern' architect. It's my guess that he bristled at being labelled a 'Romantic Pragmatist' in September 1985's Architectural Review, which also featured MacCormac, Peter Aldington and Maguire & Murray. Editor Peter Davey described them as having 'a pragmatic approach to building organisation and construction, and a romantic sensibility'. While appealing to a particular English perspective, this was probably a fairly superficial idea that there was a place for a gentle modernism, an 'in-keeping' architecture of local materials, pitched roofs, impeccable manners and deference to neighbours. To see Cullinan as 'romantic' was surely a misinterpretation of his enthusiasm for the arts and crafts period. Rather,

I believe, he identified with that era not for some sort of cosy nostalgia but for what it led to.

In later years Cullinan's architecture could still contemplate the shock of the new, and one of my favourites is the Downland Gridshell, about as radical an object you can find anywhere in the English countryside. In fact, if you place it at the opposite end of a timeline from Minister Lovell Mill you can see how his work became more, not less, radical.

When Ted and Roz travelled to Edinburgh in 2016 for the 'Murphfest' they stayed in my little house in the New Town – their home in Camden Mews and Peter Aldington's Turn End had long been my inspiration to design my own. They had the full tour before we sat down for tea on the roof terrace, and I was beside myself with nerves as to what Ted would think. Suddenly Ted said in his characteristic slow drawl 'Richard... this is so beautiful'. All kids crave their parents' approval – even architectural ones – and words can't describe how happy I felt at that moment.

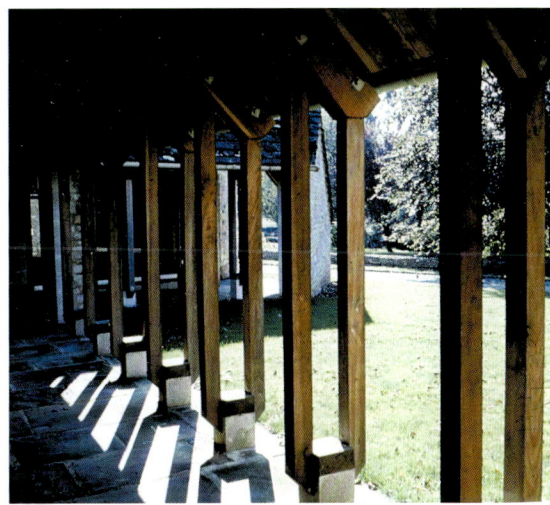

Cullinan's lifelong devotion to teaching young architects has reverberated across several generations, not least that of latter-day Cullinan Studio partner Hannah Durham, 57 years Ted's junior

A Human Architect
Hannah Durham

My first encounter with architects was as a 14-year-old, when I keenly observed their habitat and rituals on my work experience at Edward Cullinan Architects. Ted was positioned at his desk like a spaceship commander, centre stage in the open-plan office, drawing tools at hand and his team sitting around. Occasionally he would bellow out to them but mostly there were long periods of silence while he concentrated intensely on drawing.

Ted oozed energy with a passion and focus for his architecture. To help bring it to fruition he surrounded himself with individuals who brought different skills to the team, which he then nurtured, encouraged and united behind the shared vision of the cooperative's longstanding manifesto that declares 'architecture is a social act'. The office has a family atmosphere in which duties are shared, with rituals such as taking turns to make the Friday lunch for the team and guests, the four o'clock tea break and the start-of-the-week group huddle. The Friday lunches celebrate the end of the week with a team member preparing a small feast; the aroma drifts through the building ahead of the one o'clock descent to eat and share stories. It's an occasion to bring other people in to the office, so there are often family members and industry guests sharing tales, and later spilling out onto the canalside guerrilla garden for some weeding and watering while the day's nominated pair of clearers wash up and pack away the tables. The whole office culture is permeated by this unconventional ethos, which in

Below Communal Friday lunches are a longstanding tradition in the Cullinan studio.

Left Cullinan's drawing of the proposed Hooke Park campus, as if from a balloon.

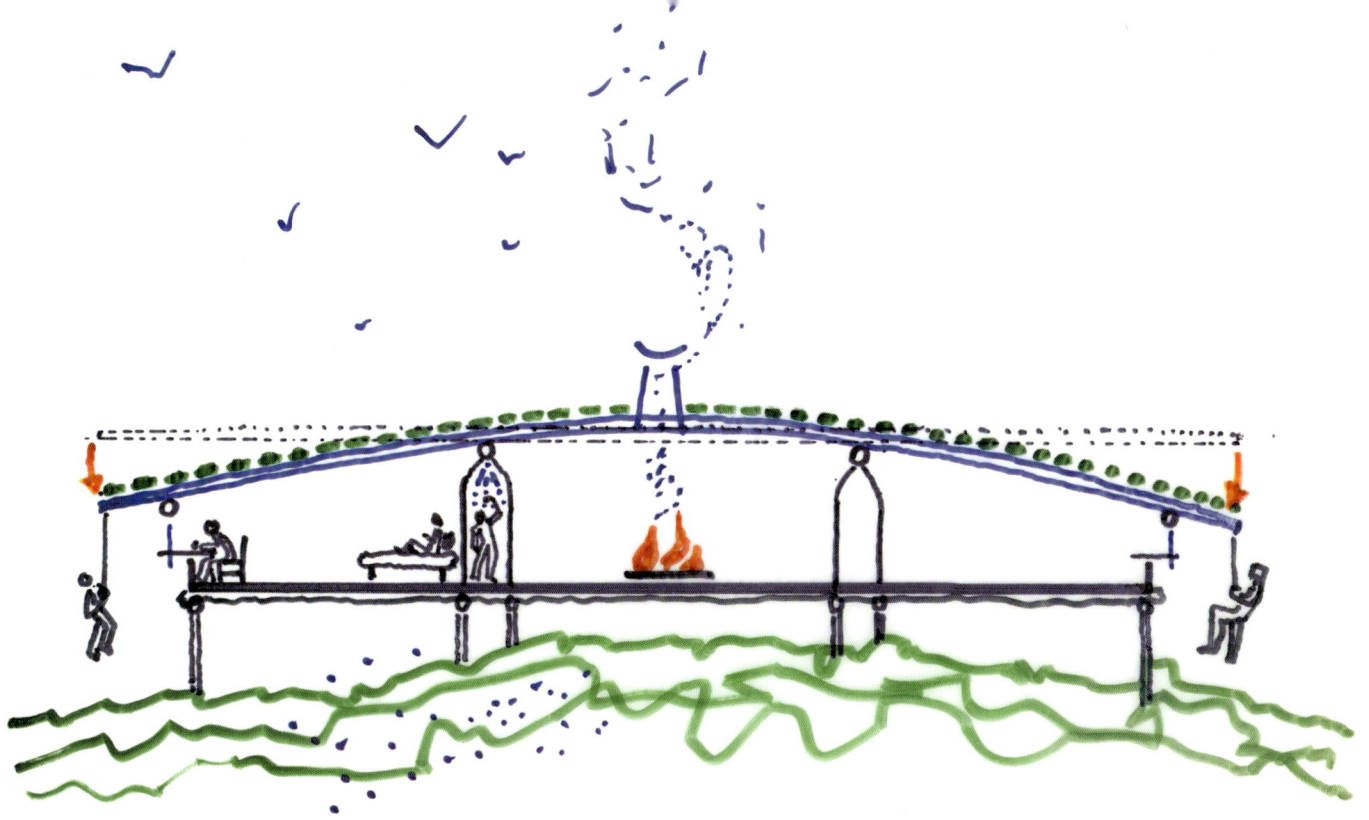

Above *Sketch section of Westminster Lodge at Hooke Park.*

recent years often meant that Ted could be found snoozing on a chaise longue in the afternoons.

A few years ago Cullinan gave a series of 12 'Ted Talks' in the office, taking us through his life story from his childhood and education to his key buildings. His witty storytelling, which wove together the various characters he met along the way, was accessible to everyone, whether a client, an engineer or a child. Everyday life is celebrated in Ted's drawings too, which reveal his understanding of life's playful messiness and his vision of an informal, friendly, relaxed world. As a student searching for the kind of architect I wanted to become, discovering Ted's drawings, stories and buildings convinced me, like many others, that the design of buildings can be a 'social act' enjoyed by everyone.

I was particularly fortunate as a young architect in being able to experience and begin to understand Ted's architecture first hand when I lived for three months in Westminster Lodge, a building completed in 1997 at the Architectural Association's Hooke Park woodland campus in Dorset. A tranquil and inspirational place to stay and study, this experiment in greenwood construction, designed with engineer Buro Happold, uses waste young woodland thinnings in the round from the surrounding wood. A specially developed technology of jointing and assembly was used to create a cross-shaped lattice roof that was laid over a supporting structure of timber posts and rammed earth walls. The lattice is pulled down by the columns and pushed up by the walls, so as to form a shallow section within the roof, with the highest point in the central communal space and the lowest height at the perimeter of the building within each student room. The process of roof construction included using buckets of water to encourage the roof lattice to bend, a pragmatic replacement for the muscle men that Ted showed in his drawings.

The building provides eight twin student rooms around a large, central communal space with a wood-burning stove, lounge and kitchenette. Each student room has a full-width window desk with a view out to the dense woodland, and its own private door with a ladder down to the woodland floor. Two prefabricated fibreglass cylinder pods, each with a curved door, contain a toilet and a shower, with a sink and mirror sitting between them.

The hairy grass roof is punctured by a circular skylight above the centre of the communal space. The timber roof lattice is exposed throughout, as are the columns. Three corners of the square communal space have a corner window so the

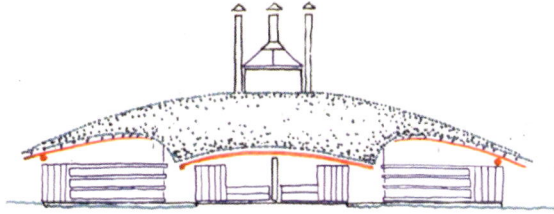

Westminster Lodge, Hooke Park
Designed by Edward Cullinan Architects with engineer Buro Happold for the Architectural Association's woodland campus in Dorset, the lodge was built using green wood from Hooke's forest. It provides eight en-suite rooms arranged around a communal space with an open fireplace. The bent lattice structure of spruce thinnings supports a planted turf roof. The building was conceived as the first in a series of five, each serving a different social purpose.

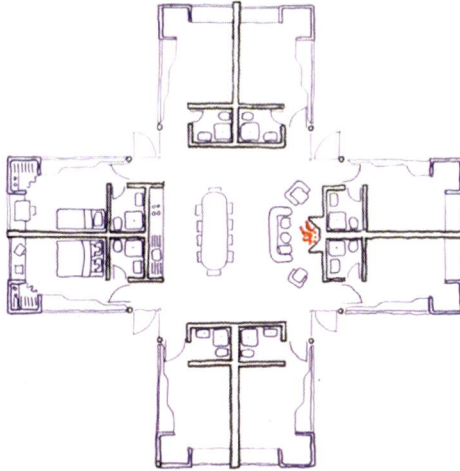

corners can be opened, as if unpeeling the building to the woodlands. In the fourth corner is the entrance door. Within the building you see the exposed thinnings of the roof above laid horizontally, then outside through the windows the trees growing vertically. Some of the trees outside are the same diameter as the roof thinnings above. Perched above the ground among the trees and sheltered by its woven lattice roof, Westminster Lodge is like a huge bird's nest. Sited away from the workshop and working yard, it is entered via a timber bridge into a lobby where you leave your muddy site boots. The ground level slopes away, leaving the building seemingly hovering among the trees. Windows frame the views out, like a hide, from where you can spot deer, birds and other wildlife.

Living in Westminster Lodge, and helping to construct buildings using timber felled from the Hooke Park estate, was a profound experience that has stayed with me. Keen that others should share in this, I have led student trips to Hooke Park for the last four years and co-led groups at Studio in the Woods supporting teams in making full-size timber structures.

Reflecting on Cullinan Studio's unusual cooperative structure, I see the practice as a living experiment which, by placing its people at the core of decision-making, suggests a much more human way of running a business. When considering Ted's impact on my generation, it could be summed up as demonstrating that when the connections with people and nature are placed at the heart of practice, architecture has the capacity to deliver a happy outcome for our collective future. With all this in mind, it was appropriate that Ted left us with the message: 'Stay progressive, inventive, imaginative, energetic and don't get conservative'.

Cullinan was an extraordinary
critic who would fill students
with self-belief by drawing out
their ideas and elevating
them into 'layered and nuanced
works of architectural complexity'

Seeing the Wood

Piers Taylor

I first met Ted Cullinan when I asked him to speak at the University of Bath in the early 2000s. Collecting him from the station, I was struck by the lightness with which he moved through the world – he arrived off the train from London dressed in jeans and a tee-shirt, carrying nothing. On the way uphill to the university campus, we reminisced about Alison and Peter Smithson and their time in Bath, arriving at their '6 East' school of architecture and engineering building where Ted stopped for a few moments before professing: 'It's wonderfully batty'. It was a critique that stayed with me – both for his succinct summary of the Smithsons' output, but more for how it exposed a slightly skewed world view of architecture and the things he enjoyed.

Ted's lecture was – as were all of his lectures – a delight. He spoke as he always did, with the aid of an overhead projector and coloured pens, telling the stories of how his buildings were made. To describe a house he had worked on in California in the 1950s he drew the huge redwoods, drew the huge lorry that transported them to site, drew the freewheeling self-built nature of the way the house was constructed and then drew the life that was lived in it once it was completed.

Cullinan spoke in a manner that was different from most other architects. His descriptions were always generous, rooted in people and circumstances, and always highly specific in terms of how his buildings were made, and how the process of construction informed the reading and experience of them. I still have his drawings of the house that he made for himself and his family in Camden, and remember how vivid his experiences remained. As he drew the house, explaining the ideas around the sequence of building it, he described many architects' experience of getting the house watertight and then, of course, moving in before it was finished to spend many years tinkering with details.

He described Jim Stirling visiting when it was finally finished, and how he was thrilled when Stirling declared it as 'not bad'. As he told the story of the house, he drew Big Jim's ample form climbing the steps to the front door. The weaving

Right Sketch of the California redwood delivery destined for constructing the Marvin house. Cullinan's characteristic lecture technique, with felt pens, acetate and an epidiascope at Studio in the Woods, and appreciating the students' self-built structures.

Left 'Walking through a glade, full of interest and discovery'.

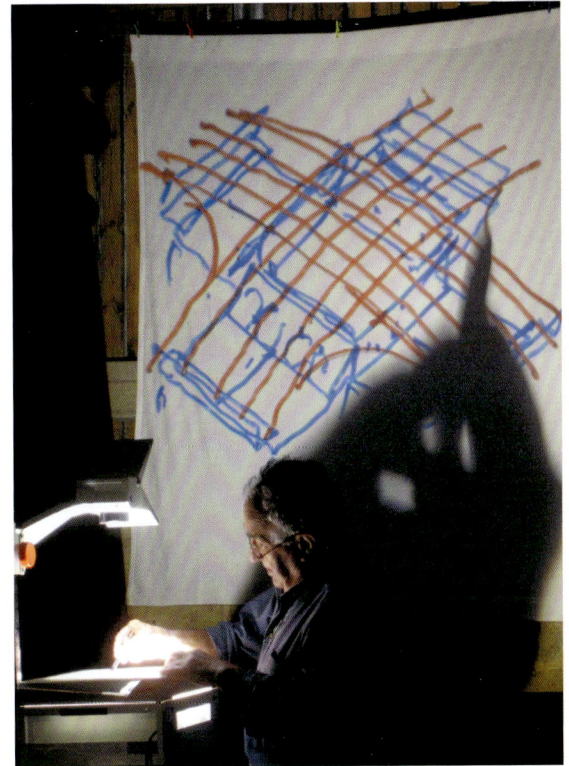

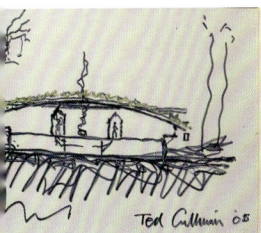

in of the 'before' and 'after' with the people involved was how Ted described everything. After the lecture we had dinner at my recently completed self-built house, 'Moonshine', and I had my own Jim Stirling moment when Ted, needing a pee, proclaimed 'can't I just piss off the deck?' Naturally, I took it as the highest compliment.

Soon after Ted's lecture at Bath, a group of us hatched a plan for a summer 'making' workshop – Studio in the Woods – where students would come to the woodland around Moonshine to build full-size structures over a long weekend in groups led by my architect friends. We asked Ted to be the roving critic at the end of the weekend, and this established an annual tradition whereby he came to Studio in the Woods, talked about his own work to the 70-strong group on Sunday night and then walked around the dispersed projects proffering advice, wisdom, support and encouragement.

Most architectural 'crits' are combative and overt displays of power, but Ted's approach was

different. In summing up our first tentative fumblings in Studio in the Woods year 1, Ted proved an extraordinary critic. He managed to elevate even the most clumsy structure into a layered and nuanced work of architectural complexity, making sense of it and re-presenting it back to the students. From our bodgings, Ted drew out universal ideas that were wide-ranging. He could see a cathedral in the most primitive structure and see tectonic sophistication in a few sticks. The point was not merely to make a student feel good, but to make them believe in themselves and persevere, and also make them see how architecture is everywhere – how it is a language with which we can see the world, and how we can make architecture with the most limited of means if our intent is intact.

Ted would also sketch each student's project for them, making sense of it and describing it with enormous clarity. Instead of seeming a master to the apprentice, Ted made it seem as if the student had imagined the project in that way all along. Most importantly, it gave students encouragement that what they were doing was worthwhile, and that the making of architecture was a messy, human process that was part of life, rather than separate from it.

Over the next 15 years, Ted came to Studio in the Woods every summer. He would arrive on Saturday afternoon and wander around the student projects over the next few hours before taking to the overhead projector to describe his own work in the context of how it was made, and how the process of making informed the architecture. In his drawings and descriptions, there were often people hanging off beams, testing and bending timbers. I am still unable to look at Westminster Lodge at Hooke Park without seeing Ted's description of how the roundwood larch was tensioned down over the prefabricated bathroom pods next to his sketch of a Citroën 2CV's rippled bonnet – drawn to show how curvature adds stiffness.

In an era of sanitised and strict health and safety regulation, his projects and constructions always seemed incredibly human, full of a freewheeling experimentation, with people, families and children centre stage. He once drew for us the difference between construction sites in the 2000s and the 1970s, with people dressed in hard hats, steel toed boots and regulatory high viz contrasted with people stripped to the waist, bare feet, joint in hand, and flowers in their hair. We still have this drawing on the stairs in Moonshine. Ted's world seemed very much infused with the spirit of this hippy era, and even in more recent projects, this spirit was retained: the sense of buildings being bound up in the people that conceived, made and lived in them as one large overlapping family.

My own practice – Invisible Studio – also grew from Cullinan-infused making and the desire for

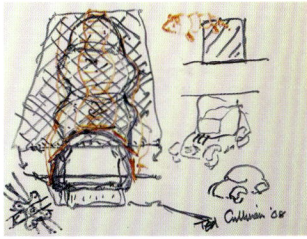

a life where work and play were intertwined. Ted's enthusiasm for a more homespun mode of practice was at odds with the predominant corporate culture of many offices, and his encouragement of intellectual enquiry born out of practical making was against the prevailing ethos. When we started Studio in the Woods, it seemed as if no one else in UK architecture was talking about 'making', and the sense from the architectural establishment was that it was a bit strange, and a bit fringe. But Ted gave us the confidence that not only was making interesting, it was also an essential part of the process of conceiving of architecture. He made me rethink the whole relationship between how buildings are imagined and how they are made. Studio in the Woods would have been impossible without Ted's mentoring and support, as would many of the things that subsequently spun off from it, like the Design & Make masters course at the Architectural Association's Hooke Park campus.

In 2012, even though he had recently suffered a very serious illness, Ted still came to Studio in the Woods. The event coincided with his 80th birthday and again he seemed in his element, surrounded by activity, young students and the creative chaos of making-related idealism, as he pitched in with a saw and hammer where needed and climbed in and out of precarious structures, drawing parallels between them and Buster Keatonesque train wrecks, Henri Lefebvre and Jackson Pollock.

The last time Ted came to Studio in the Woods – then in the Wyre Forest – he was frailer but still a vital presence. In touring the projects, drawing and describing them for participants, he also helped make students see that not only was there a different path that could be travelled, but in travelling that path they could be happier, more creatively fulfilled, and with this, live and work with an integrity that defied the system.

> The humanist, collaborative and ecological values that Cullinan espoused were prescient in the 1960s but they should become mainstream in the twenty-first century

A Cullinan Education
Nathan Breeze

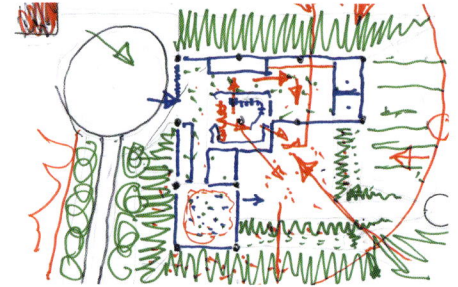

The culture of openness and collaboration that informed the blueprint for Edward Cullinan Architects in the mid-1960s is still at odds with much of architectural education. Most schools of architecture tend to favour individual student competition, reinforcing an understanding of architecture centred on individual architects and their buildings.

I first became aware of Cullinan's work during my part-one studies at Bath University (2006-10). Ted was admired by many of the department's teachers for his practice's holistic approach to architecture as well as its environmentally conscious, highly crafted buildings with their strong relationship to landscape. He was a regular guest at final crits and several of my peers worked in the office after graduating.

Encouraged by their stories of the office's design-led, friendly atmosphere, I applied and joined the renamed Cullinan Studio in 2015. The initial steep learning curve felt like a new university course, albeit one focussed on collective learning and mutual support. Being a young 'partner' in the cooperative allowed me to understand how an office's design culture, manifested in its architectural projects, can be enabled and sustained by its business structure. And the challenging but rewarding process of collective problem solving, harnessing the skills and experiences of a diverse team, was the ideal preparation for progressing as a project architect. Nevertheless, a culture of openness and collaboration often requires strong leadership to elevate, inspire and guide the collective endeavour. Not surprisingly, Ted's significance in this respect was confirmed in the numerous stories told by colleagues who had spent their entire careers at the practice.

I was very fortunate to work with Ted as project architect for the extension to the Maggie's Cancer Care Centre in Newcastle between 2018 and 2019. Although less active at the age of 87, he always made time for Maggies, travelling up to the centre on many occasions to present the proposals to users, staff and benefactors. His famous live sketching presentations on the overhead projector encapsulated the practice's culture of generosity, openness and good humour, enabling all

stakeholders to engage with the design process: 'architecture as a social act' was an oft-heard mantra. These presentations, together with numerous conversations with Ted, taught me much about his design method, carefully establishing principles of geometry and scale (between domestic and public at the Maggie's Centre) as well as the relationship to the sun and the landscape. These principles acted as a constant reference when designing the extension to the centre, guiding the project from concept through to technical detailing.

This rigorous process of establishing design principles, learned from Ted and others in the practice, is something I try to pass on through teaching. It's a sad irony that so many students haven't heard of Ted Cullinan, especially in light of the ever-increasing relevance – and popularity – of many of the practice's early ideas and priorities, from low-energy buildings that positively impact health and well-being to the growth of employee ownership and the prioritisation of social value. However – as Ted would readily acknowledge – assigning credit for the early adoption of these ideas is beside the point. Rather his legacy might be that the next generation of architects is judged on its ability to work holistically, collaboratively and bravely to mitigate pressing and complex global issues. Architectural education, both within universities and in practice, needs to reflect this collective challenge.

Maggie's Newcastle
Built in the grounds of Freeman Hospital in 2013, Maggie's Newcastle is one of a series of cancer care centres, each designed by an eminent architect. In 2018 Cullinan was asked to extend the original building to the south (indicated by the red arrow below).

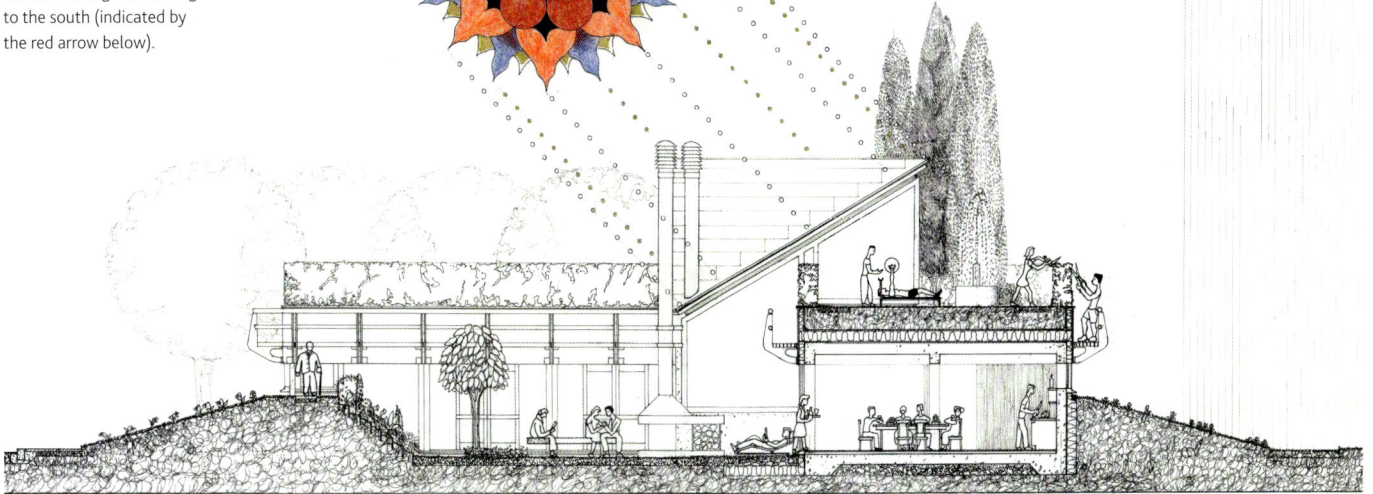

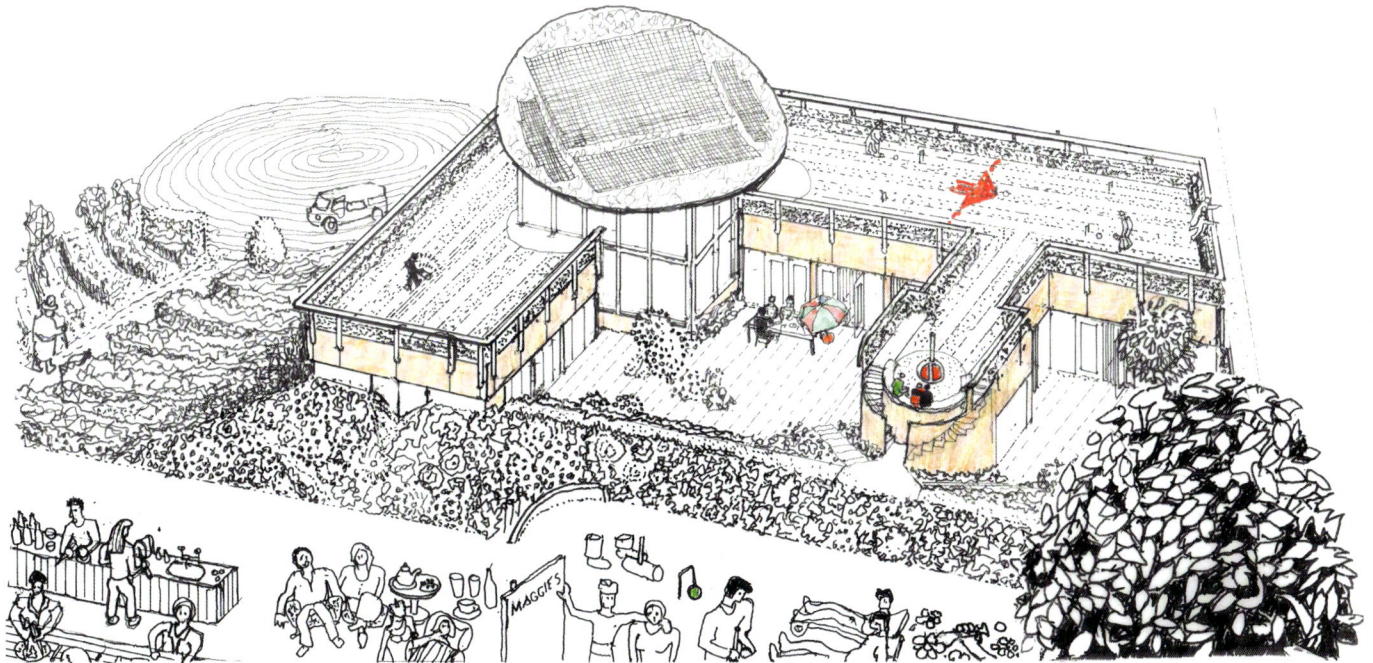

Writers

Bob Allies founded Allies and Morrison with Graham Morrison in 1984, after his studies at the University of Edinburgh, and a Rome Scholarship in 1981. An architect, teacher and writer, he co-edited The Fabric of Place, which forms the foundation of the practice's urban masterplans that include Kings Cross, Olympic Games and Legacy, Greenwich Peninsula and Brent Cross Town. He has been a visiting professor at the universities of Reading, Edinburgh, Maryland and Bath, and taught at Cambridge, the Bartlett and North-East London Polytechnic. He was an Architectural Association council member, served on the Mayor of London's Design Advisory Group, is chair of the South East Design Review Panel and is on the Council of the British School at Rome. He was awarded an OBE in 2016.

Mary-Lou Arscott is studio professor and associate head of the architecture school at Carnegie Mellon University in Pittsburgh. After finishing at the Architectural Association she studied carpentry and worked for ten years as a joiner, cabinet maker and educator. Mary-Lou returned to architecture in 1986, first at Casson Conder and later Edward Cullinan Architects (1987-94), where she worked on a series of arts and educational buildings. In 1996 she was a founding member of Knox Bhavan where she worked for ten years on a range of historic buildings and residential projects.

Cany Ash began working with fellow architect Robert Sakula as designer builders in the early 1980s. They founded Ash Sakula Architects in 1994, a studio of architects, urbanists, story-tellers and filmmakers. Cany's early experiences include working in New York with architect Barry Benepe on a proof of concept for the first modern farmers' market, saving farmland and bringing together growers and consumers; with urbanist Nicholas Falk and DEGW on Kirkaldy's Testing & Experimenting Works in Southwark; with Nick Wates on alternative incremental development for London's Limehouse Basin; and with puppeteer Cath March and the Bubble Theatre, constructing waterborne structures and setting them alight against the futuristic townscape of Thamesmead.

Mark Beedle is an architect in private practice, lecturer, teacher, examiner and critic. He trained at Cambridge University and gained his diploma from the Architectural Association. He was a member of Edward Cullinan Architects from 1970 to 1995, and was closely involved in many of the projects for which the practice is well known, including Highgrove housing, Leighton Crescent, St Mary's Barnes, Uplands Conference Centre and St John's College Library. Mark moved on to establish his own studio and carry out a wide range of projects, encompassing urban design, special works, furniture, interiors and landscape. Throughout his career he has taught, lectured and been a visiting critic in schools of architecture across the UK; he was also a visiting professor at the graduate school at MIT and, for a decade, a visiting critic at UCD Dublin.

Alan Berman studied at Cambridge and UCL, worked with Maguire & Murray, and in 1981 set up in practice with Pedro Guedes. In 1996 this became Berman Guedes Stretton, whose work included award-winning educational projects. Author of several books on design and sustainability, Alan edited Jim Stirling and the Red Trilogy and Stirling and Wilford American Buildings, and set up the AJ/BGS Writing Prize. He is an associate fellow of Green Templeton College and an honorary fellow of Wolfson College in Oxford, where he is currently an adviser to five colleges and schools.

Sasha Bhavan co-founded Knox Bhavan Architects with Simon Knox in 1996, having worked at Edward Cullinan Architects (1985-95) since studying at the University of Portsmouth. In addition to practice, she is a part-time teaching fellow at the University of Bath, and an external examiner at Falmouth University, the University of Portsmouth and the City School of Architecture in Sri Lanka; she has also been a visiting critic at Carnegie Mellon in Pittsburgh. A jury chair for RIBA Awards and an assessor for Civic Trust Awards, Sasha is currently an RIBA competitions advisor, sits on TRADA's advisory board and is a design review panel member for Hertfordshire and The Royal Borough of Kensington & Chelsea. She was trustee for Art in the Park at Burgess Park, Southwark, and for the Creative Education Trust.

Meredith Bowles studied at Sheffield University, the Royal College of Art and the Architectural Association. After working in New York, Taiwan and London, he established Cambridge-based Mole Architects in 1997. He was a member of RIBA Awards from 2012-16, and chair of RIBA's House of the Year Award in 2016. He is a vice-chair of the Cambridge Quality Panel, co-chair of the Suffolk Design Review Panel, and chair of the Cambridge Forum for the Construction Industry. Meredith has taught at the universities of Cambridge and Sheffield, and is an external examiner at Nottingham University and visiting professor at the University of Suffolk. He is a regular writer and conference speaker, and has featured on BBC and Channel 4 broadcasts.

Nathan Breeze studied at the University of Bath and the Bartlett, with an Erasmus year at the Technische Universität in Munich. He is a director of Studio Sutton, an associate lecturer at Oxford Brookes University and a visiting design critic at the University of Bath. Nathan was a partner at Cullinan Studio from 2015-20, where he was project architect for the extension to Maggie's Newcastle and a residential development in London's Borough Market. He has mentored students at the University of Cardiff and as part of Open City's Accelerate into University programme, which aims to increase diversity in the architectural profession.

Peter Clegg set up in practice with Richard Feilden in Bath in 1978, after studying with Ted Cullinan at Cambridge, later taking a masters in environmental design at Yale. The Architecture Shop evolved into Feilden Clegg Bradley, now FCB Studios, whose Accordia housing project in Cambridge won the 2008 Stirling Prize. A pioneer in low-energy design, research and education, Peter has led projects at Yorkshire Sculpture Park, London's Southbank, Brighton Dome and the Leventis Gallery in Cyprus; his education projects include an engineering school in Toronto and an academy in Bangladesh. He was chair of the RIBA Awards Panel and the South West Design Review Panel. A professor at Bath University since 2005, Peter has held visiting professorships at Cambridge and Oregon, and was appointed as a Royal Designer for Industry in 2010.

Gillian Darley is a writer and broadcaster. She studied history of art at the Courtauld and politics at Birkbeck and has written and lectured widely. Her many books include Villages of Vision, biographies of John Soane, Octavia Hill and John Evelyn, and subjects ranging from factories to Vesuvius and Essex. A former chair and trustee of The Society for the Protection of Ancient Buildings, Gillian has been president of the Twentieth Century Society since 2014, and dissertation supervisor at The Bartlett and New York University since 2017 and 2011 respectively.

Hannah Durham is an architect, lecturer and researcher. She studied at Oxford Brookes University, Royal Melbourne Institute of Technology and the Architectural Association and worked at Cullinan Studio from 2015-20. Hannah was the oral history interviewer and researcher for the AA XX 100 project, collecting life stories of women alumni for the AA Archive. She is currently a lecturer at Oxford Brookes where she leads a design studio exploring storytelling and architecture. She is also a co-leader of timber workshops at Studio in the Woods, an education and research project designing and making at 1:1 scale.

Brian Ford is emeritus professor of architecture at the University of Nottingham. He practiced as an architect with partners who had worked with Cullinan (Peake Short & Partners, Short Ford & Associates) and later as an environmental design consultant (Brian Ford & Associates, WSP Environmental). He worked as a consultant to Edward Cullinan Architects on Hampshire Schools (1984-85) and Singapore Management University (2002-03). His books include, as co-author, The Architecture of Natural Cooling.

Richard Gooden, director of 4orm since 2012, studied at Cambridge and the Polytechnic of Central London. He worked at Edward Cullinan Architects from 1986-1992, and subsequently at Anshen Dyer and Penoyre & Prasad, working on health, housing and arts projects, and as senior lecturer at De Montfort University (1995-96). He was assistant head of architecture at Hampshire County Council (2005-11), and in practice as Richard Gooden Architects before setting up 4orm with Stephen Coleman, also from Penoyre & Prasad. He served as vice-chair of CABE's school design panel and as chair of examiners in professional practice at Cambridge.

Simon Henley is a principal of London-based architecture studio Henley Halebrown which was shortlisted for the Stirling Prize in 2018. Simon studied at the University of Liverpool and the University of Oregon. He combines practice with teaching, writing and research, and is the author of The Architecture of Parking (2007) and Redefining Brutalism (2017). Simon is a postgraduate unit master at the Kingston School of Art. He is a fellow of the Royal Society of Arts and brother of the Art Workers Guild. A monograph on Henley Halebrown was published in 2018 by Quart Verlag in its De Aedibus International series.

Peter Inglis studied at Strathclyde and joined Cullinan Studio in 1995, where he is a practice leader with a focus on business planning, project processes and design. His work in fostering an integrated, collaborative approach between designers, clients and constructors, from project inception through to occupation, has led to his involvement as a board member on the UK's largest Integrated Project Insurance project, for the Institute of Technology at Dudley College. As a model of enlightened procurement, he believes the project has the potential to radically transform the way buildings are designed and constructed. Peter also teaches, and was a visiting tutor at Cardiff University in 2015-17.

Edward Jones studied at the Architectural Association and has been a principal in private practice since 1973. In 1983 he won the competition for Mississauga City Hall in Canada and in 1989 co-founded Dixon Jones, whose projects include the Royal Opera House, the National Portrait Gallery and National Gallery in London, and Saïd Business School in Oxford. Edward has served on many competition juries, including the Laban Dance Centre and Hepworth Gallery, and on the Royal Gold Medal jury. He has taught at the RCA (1975-82), Harvard, Yale, Princeton, Cornell, Philadelphia, Rice, Toronto, Waterloo and Kent State University, Florence and UCD Dublin. Co-author of the Guide to the Architecture of London, his honorary awards include a doctorate at Portsmouth, a professorship at Cardiff, and a fellowship of the Royal Institute of the Architects of Ireland; he was awarded a CBE in 2011.

Roddy Langmuir is practice leader at Cullinan Studio, which he joined in 1987 after studying at the University of Edinburgh and working in Canada and with Wickham Associates. An empathy with landscape and place is rooted in his upbringing in the Cairngorms; he competed as an alpine skier in the 1980 Winter Olympics and was head coach of the British junior ski team in 1985-87. He chairs design forums for Architecture & Design Scotland. His projects at Cullinan's include Stonebridge Hub, Archaeolink, John Hope Gateway at Edinburgh botanic garden, the Centre for Mathematical Sciences in Cambridge, and the National Automotive Innovation Centre at Warwick University.

Ian Latham is a writer, editor and publisher. He studied architecture at Oxford Brookes and worked for Peter Moro, joining Architectural Design magazine in 1979 and Building Design in 1983. In 1989, with Mark Swenarton, he conceived and launched Architecture Today. After three decades as AT's publishing editor, Ian now runs Rightangle Architectural Publishing, whose books include monographs on Dixon Jones and Allies & Morrison (both two vols), Richard MacCormac and MJP, Feilden Clegg Bradley, Eric Parry Architects and Peter Ahrends. He has served on the Royal Gold Medal jury, chaired RIBA's dissertation awards panel for ten years and was made an RIBA honorary fellow in 2015.

Graham Morrison is a founding partner of Allies and Morrison. He first met Ted Cullinan in the early 1970s when he was a student at Cambridge University and later he and Ted worked together as Royal Fine Art Commissioners. He was awarded an OBE for services to architecture in 2016 and continues to work as an architect and is now also a co-owner of Fisher Morrison, a furniture making and joinery workshop, the existence of which he attributes to the influence of Ted's teaching.

Richard Murphy studied at Newcastle and Edinburgh universities, founding his practice in 1991. His buildings range across education, arts, healthcare and housing, and include two British embassies and his own house within Edinburgh's New Town World Heritage Site. Richard is a fellow of the RIAS, an academician of the Royal Scottish Academy, a fellow of the Royal Society of Arts, a fellow of the Royal Society of Edinburgh, and an honorary fellow of Napier University. He is an authority on the work of Carlo Scarpa, lecturing widely, broadcasting and writing three books, including Carlo Scarpa and Castelvecchio Revisited.

Robin Nicholson is a fellow of Cullinan Studio, having joined the office in 1979 after working with James Stirling. He is convenor of The Edge, chair of Cambridgeshire Quality Panel, a design review chair for Cabe and a member of the NHBC Foundation Expert Panel. He has been vice president of RIBA, chair of CIC and was a founder member of the Movement for Innovation board. Robin was awarded a CBE in 1999, an honorary fellowship of the Institution of Structural Engineers in 2002 and an honorary fellowship of the Chartered Institution of Building Services Engineers in 2013. He is an honorary professor of the University of Nottingham.

Anthony Peake studied at the University of Cambridge from 1961-67, incorporating a year at Princeton. At Evans & Shalev he worked on Newport High School, before joining Edward Cullinan Architects in 1972. He left in 1986 with ECA colleague Alan Short to set up Peake Short & Partners, where his projects included John Lewis at High Wycombe. From 1991, as Anthony Peake Associates, his buildings include One Brindleyplace in Birmingham. In 1998 he moved to rural Herefordshire 'to renovate a large Regency house, do some light farming and restore some old cars'.

Ian Pickering trained at the Architectural Association and worked in a local authority architect's department before joining Ted Cullinan's practice at the outset. He worked on the drawings for the Marvin House that Cullinan built in California, and helped with the construction of the Cullinans' Camden Mews house. Ian also worked on the Garrett House in south London, and on a project for a printworks and warehouse in Witham, Essex. He taught at the Polytechnic of the South Bank, the Royal College of Art and the Architectural Association in London, and later at the Mackintosh in Glasgow; he currently lives in France.

Greg Penoyre worked at Edward Cullinan Architects from 1982-87. He is a consultant to Penoyre & Prasad, which he co-founded in 1988, and was involved in the design, procurement and delivery of most of the practice's projects, and developed specialisms in senior living, healthcare, education and procurement. He has served on design review panels, the RIBA Awards Group and many awards and competition juries. Greg has been involved in teaching, course validation and external examining at a number of universities, and is visiting professor at the University of Sheffield. He draws, paints and sails as much as he can.

Sunand Prasad worked at Edward Cullinan Architects from 1977-85 and co-founded Penoyre & Prasad with Greg Penoyre in 1988, since when the practice has completed more than 300 projects, notably in healthcare and education. Brought up in India, Sunand studied at Cambridge and the Architectural Association and took a PhD at the Royal College of Art. He was RIBA president in 2007-09, taking a robust stand on environmental issues. He has chaired many design review panels, and is a London Mayor's Design Advocate, chairs the UKGBC board of trustees, the Journal of Architecture advisory board and the board of trustees of humanitarian charity Article 25. He is author of many books and articles, broadcasts regularly and cycles everywhere.

Nicholas Ray was an undergraduate at Cambridge from 1966-69, where he was taught by Ted Cullinan in his second year. He attended the Bartlett for his diploma and worked in London with Shankland Cox and later Colin St John Wilson on the British Library. He returned to Cambridge to practice, initially with Hughes & Bicknell before setting up Nicholas Ray Associates (later NRAP) in 1989, and to teach. Nicholas is author of books on Alvar Aalto and Rafael Moneo, as well as theoretical studies, and is currently a consultant to NRAP, reader emeritus at Jesus College, Cambridge and a visiting professor at the University of Liverpool.

Mark Swenarton is emeritus professor of architecture at Liverpool University and editor of Architectural History, the journal of the Society of Architectural Historians of Great Britain. An architectural historian, critic and educator, his books include Homes fit for Heroes (1981, 2018) and Cook's Camden (2017). As co-editor of Architecture Today (1989-2005) he published many Cullinan projects and in 2012 chaired Ted Cullinan's last talk at the Royal Academy.

Philip Tabor was writing his PhD on computer-aided design at Cambridge when he first met Ted Cullinan, whose Camden Mews house and the ideas behind it he hugely admired. He worked at Edward Cullinan Architects from 1970-78, and later entered full-time teaching and became director of the Bartlett School of Architecture. In 2001 he moved to Italy to teach at Interaction Design Institute Ivrea, and later co-founded the Interaction Design masters course at IUAV University of Venice.

Piers Taylor is an architect, teacher and broadcaster. He studied at the University of Technology in Sydney and the Architectural Association, and in 2012 founded Invisible Studio as a model of collaborative-based practice. He was an inaugural studio master on the AA's Design & Make programme at Hooke Park, a design fellow at Cambridge University, and is convenor of Studio in the Woods. He is taking a doctorate at Reading University on the relationship between design and making. As a television presenter his shows include The House that £100k Built and The World's Most Extraordinary Homes. He has recently upgraded his off-grid, self-built home and studio, Moonshine, near Bath.

Mark Whitby is director of engineer Whitby Wood and a former Olympic sprint canoeist. His projects include the Tate Modern extension, the BBC hq, the British Antarctic Survey base, Hepworth Wakefield, Mossbourne Academy and Bracken House in London, and British embassies in Dublin, Sana'a and Berlin. In 1984 Mark co-founded Whitby & Bird, which merged with Ramboll in 2007. He is a fellow and past president of the Institution of Civil Engineers, fellow of the Royal Academy of Engineering, and a RIBA honorary fellow. He founded the Engineering Club and co-founded built environment think tank, The Edge. Mark has taught widely, holding posts at Oxford Brookes, Cambridge and the Architectural Association, and visiting professorships at Nottingham and the Bartlett.

Brendan Woods studied architecture at Edinburgh University and worked for Gillespie Kidd & Coia before moving to London and the Architectural Association. While sharing a flat with Tchaik Chassay in the late 1960s he first met Ted Cullinan. He later worked for David Roberts and taught in Cambridge, and from 1973-78 at Edward Cullinan Architects. A regular writer and critic, he has taught at many architecture schools, and as an architect also worked with Solon (1983-86), Julyan & Tess Wickham (1986-91), and in his own right. He has recently designed a Passivhaus on an island in the Thames.

Thanks

This book is a collaboration of ideas and effort, creatively conceived, constructively critiqued and carefully crafted – and so, we hope, it reflects the spirit of its subject. While Ted Cullinan may not have craved attention for its own sake, he enjoyed the limelight, especially if it allowed him to spread his 'passion' for architecture. By bringing together many different views of his life and work, this book aims to explore that passion as well as the legacy of his ideas.

Following Ted Cullinan's death in November 2019, Alan Berman, who was then teaching, became concerned that Cullinan's particular way of being an architect should endure as an example to young architects. He was encouraged – not least because he was a relative 'outsider' – by Ted's colleagues at Cullinan Studio, particularly Robin Nicholson, Roddy Langmuir and Peter Inglis, as well as by Sunand Prasad and Peter Clegg. Alan first approached Ian Latham as publisher, whose role extended to co-editor as the book became a substantial collaborative effort.

Ted's daughter Kate Cullinan generously made available the tributes and messages of condolence received by the family, that are worthy of a volume in their own right. His sister Susan Cullinan checked and commented on Alan's introduction, while background on Ted's brother Anthony was supplied by Hilary Wilson. Invaluable insights into the early work were offered by former members of the Cullinan office, notably Brendan Woods, Sunand Prasad and Mark Beedle, while Roddy, Robin, Amy Glover as well as many others in the Cullinan Studio were generous in making time to assist, check draft essays and gather illustrations.

From its inception the book grew in scope and ambition, drawing together the perspectives of colleagues, other architects and historians. They each responded readily and enthusiastically at an extraordinary time when lives were anything but normal, and we are deeply grateful to them all.

Alan Berman and Ian Latham

174

The majority of drawings and photographs featured in this book are drawn from Cullinan Studio's archive, and are reproduced with its generous permission. Others were kindly supplied by Edward Cullinan's family and friends, the contributing writers, and a number of other sources. While every effort has been made to seek permission to reproduce and properly credit images, we apologise for any inadvertent omissions; this list will be updated in subsequent editions.

Front cover: Piers Taylor
Back cover: Ted Cullinan's sketch of the RMC headquarters (CS)
2 Patrick Morreau (t), Monica Pidgeon (m), Piers Taylor (b)
4 Bradwell Common (CS)
6 Cullinan Studio (l), Kate Cullinan (m, r)
7 CS
8 CS (t, m), Henry Taunt (br)
9-10 CS
11 CS/Martin Charles
12 CS
13 CS, Brian Housden (m, b)
14 Brian Housden (t, m), Caroline Ainscough (bl), CS (plan)
16 CS/RIBA
17 Sunand Prasad (tl), CS (tr, bl/r)
18-22 CS
24 CS, Staatsgalerie Stuttgart (r)
25-29 CS
30 CS, Peter Durant (mr)
31 CS, Sunand Prasad (b)
34-45 CS
46 CS, University of California – Berkeley – Sigma Phi Soc (tr, mr)
47 University of California/ Berkeley/Sigma Phi Soc (tl), CS/Richard Learoyd (r)
48 GNU/Creative Commons
49 CS
50 CS
51 CS/Martin Charles (b)
52 CS, Sasha Bhavan (rb)
53-58 CS
59 CS, Martin Gledhill (t)
60-66 CS
67 CS/Brian Housden
68 CS/Martin Gledhill
69 Piers Taylor
70 CS
71 CS, Martin Charles (t)
72 CS, Brian Housden (t)

73-74 CS
75 CS, Tadao Ando (b)
76 CS
77 CS/Mark Wickham
78-79 CS
80 CS, Martin Charles (l, tr), JJ Photoservices (br)
81 CS
82 CS/Martin Charles
83-86 CS
87 CS/David Wild (t), RM Leonard (tl)
88 CS
89 CS/RM Leonard (t), David Wild (m), Ian Latham (b)
90-92 CS
93 CS, Ian Latham (b)
94 CS
95 CS/Mark Wickham
96-102 CS
103 (l-r, t-b) Brian Housden, Mark Wickham, CS, Mark Wickham, David Wild, CS, Martin Charles, Martin Charles, CS
104 CS, Mark Beedle archive (sk)
105 CS/Martin Charles, Mark Beedle archive (sk)
106 Mark Beedle archive
107 CS/Nils Obee, Mark Beedle archive (sk, drg)
108 CS, Mark Beedle (b)
109 CS/Tim Rawle (tl, m), Martin Charles (b,l), Mark Beedle (b)
110-113 CS
114 CS, Martin Charles (m), Bill Toomey/Architectural Review (b)
115 CS, Martin Charles (r)
116 CS/Martin Charles
117 CS
118 CS, Peter Mackinven (m)
119-120 CS
121 CS/Aditi Saxena
122 CS
123 CS/Martin Charles
124 CS/Martin Charles
125 CS, Inger & Johannes Exner
126 CS
127 CS/Richard Learoyd (t)
128 CS
129 CS/Martin Charles
130 CS
131 CS/Martin Charles
132-133 CS
134 Ian Latham, Edward Jones (r)
135 CS/David Wild
136 Edward Jones/Cross Dixon Gold Jones
137 CS/RM Leonard
138 David Wild (t), Ian Latham

139 Ian Latham, CS (plan)
142 CS/Bill Toomey/AR
143 CS/Bill Toomey/AR
144-146 CS
147 CS/Mark Wickham
148-150 CS
151 CS/Mark Wickham
152 CS
153 CS/Richard Learoyd
154 CS/Richard Learoyd
156-158 CS
159 CS/Martin Charles
160 CS/Green Oak Carpentry (tl), Buro Happold (model)
161-163 CS
164 CS/Mandy Reynolds (b)
165-166 CS
167 CS, Piers Taylor
168 CS, Piers Taylor (b)
169 CS, Piers Taylor
170 CS, Paul Raftery (t)
171 CS

Principal references include:

'Edward Cullinan Architects', RIBA Publications 1984

Powell, Kenneth and Edward Cullinan, 'Edward Cullinan Architects', Academy Editions 1995

Hale, Jonathan, 'Ends, Middles, Beginnings', Black Dog 2005

Pearman, Hugh, 'Cullinan Studio in the 21st Century', Lund Humphries 2020

British Library National Life Story Collection: Architects' Lives, 15 interviews with Edward Cullinan by Niamh Dillon (sounds.bl.uk)

Significant writings by Edward Cullinan include:

Bossom Lecture, Royal Society of Arts Journal, CXXXV, Jan 1987

'Contributing to Historic Settings without Kow-towing', 'New Buildings in Historic Settings', Architectural Press 1998

'A Question of Style', Spazio e Società, Jan 1982

Spens, Michael ed, 'Landscape Transformed', Academy Editions 1996

Walker, Derek and Bill Addis eds, 'Happold: The Confidence to Build', Happold Trust 1997

Index